Democracy's Promise

D1188539

The
Politics of Race
and Ethnicity

Series Editors
Rodney E. Hero, University of Notre Dame
Katherine Tate, University of California, Irvine

Politics of Race and Ethnicity is premised on the view that understanding race and ethnicity is integral to a fuller, more complete understanding of the American political system. The series' thematic emphasis welcomes work employing various theoretical perspectives and methodological approaches. The goal is to provide the scholarly community at all levels with accessible texts that will introduce them to, and stimulate their thinking on, fundamental questions in this field. The editors also invite projects that offer original and informative perspectives for the general public on social issues related to the politics of race and ethnicity. We are interested in books that creatively examine the meaning of American democracy for racial and ethnic groups and, conversely, what racial and ethnic groups mean and have meant for American democracy.

The Urban Voter: Group Conflict and Mayoral Voting Behavior in American Cities   Karen M. Kaufmann

Democracy's Promise: Immigrants and American Civic Institutions   Janelle S. Wong

Democracy's Promise

Immigrants & American Civic Institutions

Janelle S. Wong

The University of Michigan Press
Ann Arbor

Copyright © by the University of Michigan 2006
All rights reserved
Published in the United States of America by
The University of Michigan Press
Manufactured in the United States of America
♾ Printed on acid-free paper

2009   2008   2007   2006   4   3   2   1

No part of this publication may be reproduced, stored in a retrieval system,
or transmitted in any form or by any means, electronic, mechanical, or otherwise,
without the written permission of the publisher.

A CIP catalog record for this book is available from the British Library.

Library of Congress Cataloging-in-Publication Data

Wong, Janelle.
Democracy's promise : immigrants and American civic institutions /
Janelle S. Wong.
p.   cm. — (The politics of race and ethnicity)
Includes bibliographical references and index.
ISBN-13: 978-0-472-09913-9 (cloth : alk. paper)
ISBN-10: 0-472-09913-2 (cloth : alk. paper)
ISBN-13: 978-0-472-06913-2 (pbk. : alk. paper)
ISBN-10: 0-472-06913-6 (pbk. : alk. paper)
1. Immigrants—United States—Political activity.
2. Political participation—United States.   I. Title.   II. Series.

JV6477.W66   2006
325.73—dc22   2005026806

To my parents, Daniel & Brenda Wong,
and to my son, Evan Song

Acknowledgments

This book began as a dissertation I wrote while a graduate student in the Department of Political Science at Yale University. I want to thank my advisers, Donald Green, Rogers Smith, and Cathy Cohen, for their guidance and continuous encouragement. Each provided advice, constructive criticism, and insights on many occasions.

While in graduate school, I was fortunate to meet people who have become lifelong friends and cherished colleagues. Dara Strolovich, Vivian Tseng, Elizabeth Cohen, Maria Eugenia Verdaguer, Andrew Rich, Reuel Rogers, Karthick Ramakrishnan, Lisa Garcia-Bedolla, Dorian Warren, and Sandra Lara-Cinisomo shaped this project with their insightful comments and honest observations.

Paul Frymer, Michael Jones-Correa, Jane Junn, Taeku Lee, Pei-te Lien, John Mollenkopf, and Eric Oliver generously provided feedback during my efforts to turn my dissertation into a book manuscript. Kristi Andersen, Cathy Cohen, Michael Dawson, Mark Sawyer, and Katherine Tate extended great support as well as invitations to present parts of the manuscript at workshops and conferences, where I received valuable comments. Dennis Arguelles took time to share with me his expertise about community mobilization.

I finished the book while teaching at the University of Southern California, where Jeb Barnes, Ann Crigler, Nora Hamilton, Gaspar Rivera-Salgado, and Leland Saito offered many useful suggestions on how to improve the manuscript. Beth Garrett, Howard Gillman, Pierrette Hondagneu-Sotelo, Sheldon Kamienieki, Mark Kann, Michael Preston, Alison Renteln, and George Sanchez helped me to refine my ideas and negotiate the publication process. I am also grateful to my USC colleagues Jane Iwamura, Judith Jackson Fossett, Roberto Lint-Sagarena, Viet

Nguyen, Ricardo Ramirez, Apichai Shipper, Cynthia Young, and Karen Zivi for their friendship and encouragement. Jungmiwha Bullock, Efrain Escobedo, Jinee Lokaneeta, Sangay Mishra, and Linda Veazey provided research assistance in the completion of this book.

I thank Jim Reische, my editor; Katherine Tate; and Rodney Hero for encouraging me to pursue and publish this project. I am grateful beyond words to Patricia Rosas, who read the entire manuscript several times and offered substantive and editorial suggestions that greatly improved the project.

I am deeply indebted to the many community organization members, staff, and leaders who allowed me to conduct research and interviews, especially Rosalind Gold and Erica Bernal of the NALEO Education Fund. Their tireless efforts to improve the social and political lives of others are an inspiration to me. Special thanks also go to the Mexican and Chinese immigrants who opened up their lives to me during the course of this research.

Susan Lai and my aunt and uncle, Laurel and Henry Eu, provided me with food, shelter, and support while I conducted research in Los Angeles. This book would not have been possible without them. Ellen Greenberger, Mike Burton, Martin and Liz Greenberger, Kari Edwards, and Jack Farrell also provided great encouragement and support.

While I was writing, as at all times, I have received wonderful support from my parents, Dan and Brenda Wong, and my brother, Jeff Wong. Their constant love and encouragement were as important to the completion of this book as my academic training. While finishing my dissertation, I met David Silver, who read through the entire manuscript and shared his thoughtful ideas, statistical expertise, and critiques with me. He also made the writing—and more importantly all other aspects of my life—more enjoyable, rewarding, and fun than I could have ever imagined.

My research was supported in part by funding from the Social Science Research Council International Migration Program and the Yale Center for the Study of Race, Inequality, and Politics.

Contents

Tables and Figures

Tables

Figures

1 *Immigrants & American Civic Institutions*

*E*ach week during the fall of 1999, immigrant Chinese garment and restaurant workers in New York City demonstrated outside the New York State Workers' Compensation Board. Although most had few economic resources and most lacked English language skills and citizenship, they went with petitions and signs to demand that the board expedite payments and accept accountability for worker safety. Around the same time in Los Angeles, immigrant Mexican day laborers formed an independent workers' association and began participating in political theater groups as part of an effort to demand fair wages. In late September 2003, nearly a thousand immigrants and their supporters from around the country headed for Washington, D.C., as part of the Immigrant Workers Freedom Ride, modeled after the freedom rides conducted as part of the 1960s civil rights movement. The immigrant freedom riders traveled to the nation's capital to demand legalization for undocumented workers, a more efficient and fair naturalization process, policy reforms to promote the reunification of families separated by migration, and greater civil rights and civil liberties protections for racial, ethnic, and religious minorities. The ride culminated in a rally and festival that drew more than one hundred thousand people and included a national congressional lobbying effort.

These examples of political activism stand in sharp contrast to accounts about the apathy and disengagement of contemporary U.S. immigrants. As a group, these immigrants exhibit low rates of political participation compared to the general population. However, in the late 1990s, I noticed that some immigrants were taking part in political activities, and I began to wonder if the statistics that were frequently reported as evidence of immigrants' reluctance to participate politically really told the whole story. Strikingly, those who were organizing and attending protest events were, according to conventional theories of political participation, among the least likely to be politically active—immigrants lacking citizenship or legal residency, with limited English skills, and living on poverty wages. Why would immigrants stuck in some of the country's lowest-paying jobs and struggling to put food on the table take time out of their busy days to attend a rally, go to a march, or lobby Congress?

That question was further animated by interviews I conducted with Chinese and Mexican immigrants and community leaders in New York City and Los Angeles during 1999 and 2000. When I asked about their communities and why they had or had not become involved in U.S. politics, two types of responses stood out. To the question of whether she felt that she was a part of the American political system, a Chinese immigrant woman replied, "The two big political organizations here, Republican and Democrat, mainly just care about white people. Percent of voters, minority, don't carry weight so [they are the] first group to be sacrificed. If all minorities vote, greater percent of voting power. Otherwise, we will continue to be ignored. If we don't vote, we will remain insignificant." Asked about opportunities for participation in the United States, another Chinese immigrant woman paused for a moment and then said, "I guess I only participate in the church. I'm never interested in politics, only if the church says something."

These statements reflect two common claims among the immigrants I interviewed. On the one hand, they often observed that the two major political parties seem to have no real interest in or involvement with immigrants. On the other hand, interviewees remarked that groups that do community-based work—labor organizations, workers' centers, advocacy and social service organizations, ethnic voluntary associations, and religious institutions—involve immigrants in political activities.

Civic Institutions & Immigrant Political Mobilization

This book focuses on the role that American civic institutions play in mobilizing immigrants. My field research led me to some conclusions that challenge the assumption that immigrants' failure to participate more actively in politics is rooted in their shortcomings or attitudes. I concluded that the low levels of political participation among contemporary minority immigrants do not result from individual apathy, lack of assimilation, or even a preoccupation with the homeland, as some popular and scholarly accounts suggest. Instead, the research indicates that American civic institutions' level of involvement with an immigrant community affects the level of political participation by members of that community. Institutions are not neutral actors in the process of immigrant mobilization, and their historical and political contexts, including incentives and the racial attitudes of the American public and elites, influence who gets to participate in the U.S. political system. The incorporation of immigrants into the political system poses challenges and offers opportunities to American civic institutions—including political parties, labor organizations, workers' centers, advocacy and social service organizations, ethnic voluntary associations, and religious institutions. This book challenges institutions to do more in terms of fulfilling the democratic ideal of full participation and inclusion for all citizens and points to how that could be accomplished.

Shifts in the American institutional landscape have affected immigrant political participation and mobilization in specific ways. In the past, waves of immigrants from Europe were at the heart of U.S. politics: "Nineteenth-century immigrants arrived to find important political groups eager to satisfy their material needs. Political party organizations, especially the many urban political machines, needed immigrants' votes and did their best to get them" (Schier 2002, 16). In contrast to earlier immigrants, those of today, who hail mostly from Asia and Latin America, find themselves on the periphery of the American political system. Fundamental differences in how parties mobilize people to participate in American politics partly account for this change. Local political machines and party organizations formerly exhibited a consistent and committed interest in political mobilization at the neighborhood level but are no longer a vital presence in U.S. communities generally and in immigrant communities in particular. Those efforts have been replaced by the centralization of campaigns in the Republican and Democratic national headquarters, where technicalization, in the form of direct marketing and mass media campaigns, has become the norm. Unless the mainstream political parties modify the mobilization strategies that they perfected at the end of the 1990s, other civic organizations may become the most viable institutions for encouraging immigrant involvement in American politics.

In the absence of strong, local-level party activity, the influence of community organizations may be even greater than had previously been the case.[1] This book examines the role of labor organizations, workers' centers, advocacy and social service organizations, ethnic voluntary associations, and religious institutions in immigrant communities' mobilization and participation. By providing immigrants with opportunities to participate in both electoral and nonelectoral political activities, these organizations form an institutional bridge between immigrant communities and the larger political system.

America's Shifting Demographics

Although the shift in the institutional landscape constitutes a significant factor in the process of political mobilization, it pales in comparison to the shift in the U.S. demographic landscape. America is a nation of immigrants, but today, people from all over the world are entering the country in numbers not seen since the great waves of immigration from Europe of the past century.[2] In 2000, approximately 28 million immigrants resided in the United States, about 10 percent of the total U.S. population—the highest percentage since the 1930s.[3] Today, more than one out of every five people living in the United States is an immigrant or the child of immigrants. Because of their immense demographic force, immigrants profoundly affect the nation's institutions and communities.

Latinos and Asian Americans are the two largest and fastest-growing U.S. immigrant populations.[4] Immigration, not the birthrate among those already living in the United States, is the primary factor driving population growth for both groups.[5] In 2002, Asian American and Latino immigrants accounted for more than 75 percent of the U.S. foreign-born population. Approximately one in every four immigrants is Asian American, and one in every two is Latino. The Asian American population grew from 7 million in 1990 to more than 10 million in 2000, more than 60 percent of them immigrants. Although Asian Americans make up only about 5 percent of the U.S. population, in some regions they represent a much larger proportion.[6] Similarly, the U.S. Latino population grew from 22 million in 1990 to more than 35 million in 2000, and almost 40 percent are immigrants. Latinos make up more than 12 percent of the current U.S. population, and, as is the case for Asian Americans, that proportion is much higher in some regions.[7] In contrast, in 2000, fewer than 4 percent of non-Latino whites and 7 percent of blacks were foreign-born (Schmidley 2001).

Given these massive demographic changes, understanding the place of immigrants in the U.S. civic sphere has never been more critical. Not only is the number of immigrants growing, but they and their children are also becoming a larger segment of the political system. Immigrants constitute about 13 percent of the U.S. voting-age population, and their potential political influence is magnified by their concentration in California, New York, New Jersey, Texas, Florida, and Illinois, all states that command a large number of electoral college votes (Mollenkopf, Olson, and Ross 2001). The political mobilization of this group has the potential to alter the shape of the future American political system.

Despite the tremendous growth in the Latino and Asian American populations, their demographic power is not reflected in their political involvement. These groups are characterized by low rates of voting participation, and recent Latino and Asian American immigrants are even less likely to vote than are their native-born counterparts (Ong and Nakanishi 1996; DeSipio 1996; Cho 1999; Ramakrishnan 2005). Among voting age citizens, only 52 percent of Asian Americans and 58 percent of Latinos reported that they were registered to vote in 2004, compared to 69 percent of blacks and 75 percent of whites (U.S. Census Bureau 2005). Just 45 percent of Asian American and 47 percent of Latino adult citizens report voting in 2004, compared to 60 percent of black and 67 percent of white adult citizens. Thus, even when citizenship status is taken into account, these groups continue to register and vote at lower rates than blacks or whites (Schmidley 2001; Lien 2001; Leighley 2001; Jamieson, Shin, and Day 2002; Ramakrishnan 2005).

Low rates of voting participation partly explain why parties have been slow to turn their attention toward Asian American and Latino immigrants. There are few incentives in the U.S. political system encouraging parties to target low-propensity voters. Parties tend to devote their energies toward mobilizing the most likely voters in order to achieve the most "bang for the buck." Whether because of assumptions about immigrant apathy or because parties rarely focus beyond the next election, Asian Americans and Latinos—and particularly the immigrant members of those groups—receive less attention than the general population. Yet the parties' reluctance to mobilize these groups ignores several key points. Research has shown that with the passage of time, today's immigrants will become tomorrow's citizens and voters (Ong and Nakanishi 1996; Mogelonsky 1997; Myers, Pitkin, and Park 2005). In so doing, America's mainstream political parties are missing an opportunity to win these people over as constituents and as a base. More broadly, the parties are relinquishing a responsibility to shape the political socialization of these groups. Their focus on voting trends also turns a blind eye to nonvoting forms of political activity. Involvement in those sorts of activities can serve as a mechanism for political socialization and engagement, both for noncitizens, who cannot vote, and for newer citizens, who may hesitate to turn out to vote. These activities rarely have direct electoral outcomes, but they can form the bedrock for actions that will have those outcomes. Significantly, nonvoting activities can be organized and led by groups that have only tenuous connections (or no connection whatsoever) to American political parties.

The Nature of Democracy & the Role of Institutions in Immigrant Political Participation

The number of immigrants living in the United States today is not the only reason that we must pay attention to immigrant political participation. Political theorists since Alexis de Tocqueville have claimed that involvement in civic life provides the foundation for a strong democracy. Carole Pateman (1970), among others, asserts that civic engagement fosters the skills and attitudes necessary for the democratic process and facilitates the acceptance of collective decisions. Participation in politics in particular is the mechanism by which citizens influence their government. Through participation, citizens communicate their needs, interests, and preferences; participation can take many forms in addition to voting, including protesting, marching, signing petitions, or working for change in community groups (Verba, Schlozman, and Brady 1995). In addition, even when it is not explicitly political, civic engagement helps people to communicate and organize more effectively, which can further strengthen democracy (Pateman 1970).

Numerous political scientists have recognized the importance of institutions for participatory democracy. Sidney Verba, Kay Lehman Schlozman, and Henry E. Brady note that "social institutions play a major role in stimulating citizens to take part in politics by cultivating psychological engagement in politics and by serving as the locus of recruitment to activity" (1995, 6). In his case study of the Industrial Areas Foundation in Texas, Mark Warren demonstrates that the organization fosters social connections and engagement in existing community institutions—that is, churches—to create an important link between community members living in poor areas and the larger political system. He argues that "the foundation for people's development as members of society and as democratic citizens lies in local communities." In particular, "It is the institutions of local community life, schools, churches, and less formal interactions that integrate people into democratic society" (2001, 22).

Robert Putnam's social-capital perspective on civic engagement also emphasizes the importance of institutions. Social capital consists of "connections among individuals—social networks and the norms of reciprocity and trustworthiness that arise from them" (2000, 19). The forging of these connections can lead to greater economic mobility and even greater health and happiness. In large part, these social networks are fostered in civic institutions, which have many benefits for a democracy. They help individuals to make collective demands on government by providing a place for the generation and exchange of information and ideas. "When people associate in neighborhood groups, PTAs, political parties or even national advocacy groups, their individual and otherwise quiet voices multiple and are amplified" (338). Civic institutions reinforce democratic habits by giving individuals an opportunity to learn to run meetings, speak in public, organize projects, and debate public issues (339). Community organizations constitute places where immigrants can build democratic skills.

Robert Dahl (1998) suggests that democracy rests on the assumption that people are equally represented, and that assumption is also implicit in Putnam's vision of a stable, healthy democracy. No person or group should be treated as intrinsically privileged vis-à-vis other people or groups, and there should be parity in participation and representation (Dahl 1998).[8] In reality, lack of parity in participation rates characterizes the country's various groups. Immigrants, especially those from Asia and Latin America, often find themselves on the periphery of the American political system, especially in terms of political participation (Ramakrishan 2005).

Challenges for Improving Immigrant Political Participation

Understanding what shapes patterns of civic engagement and political mobilization among immigrants is the first step toward addressing the disparity in participation and representation (Schlozman, Verba, and Brady 1999, 429). Over the past two decades, observers and scholars have tried to identify exactly why Latinos and Asian Americans are not more involved in the American political system.[9] Some scholarly and popular press accounts point to political apathy or cultural barriers that discourage political participation among immigrants (Skerry 1993; Fletcher 2000). Others attribute low levels of immigrant political engagement in the United States to plans to "return to the old country" and a focus on the politics of the homeland (Barone 2001, 180–81; Huntington 2004, 269, 276–91). Many studies have shown that lack of citizenship and failure to meet voter-registration requirements generally represent the biggest barriers to participation, at least in terms of voting.[10] Individual-level variables, such as lack of socioeconomic resources, not being of voting age, and a language barrier, also contribute to low levels of political participation for Latinos (Pachon 1998; Cho 1999; Citrin and Highton 2002) and, to a lesser degree, Asian Americans (Cho 1999; Lien, Conway, and Wong 2004).

These researchers, however, have paid less attention to the institutional sources of mobilization, especially for Asian Americans and Latinos (see, however, Leighley 2001; Lien 2001). This book remedies that shortcoming by examining mobilization strategies within the institutional context of civic engagement not only to explain the relative absence of political involvement in those two groups but also to suggest ways for those institutions to take a more active role in bringing them into the political system. Steven J. Rosenstone and John Mark Hansen (1993) observe that people are not mobilized equally across the population. One reason the authors cite is that political-party leaders strategically target those people on whom they can count as allies, those who are socially well positioned and influential, and those who are the most likely to respond to mobilization (31). In the United States, mobilization patterns are also linked to race. Verba, Schlozman, and Brady find that whites are much more likely to report being recruited into politics than either blacks or Latinos (1995, 151). In the most comprehensive study of mobilization and race to date, Jan Leighley (2001) finds wide disparities between whites and minorities (blacks and Latinos) in terms of general levels of mobilization. However, she also finds that the gaps depend on type of mobilization. Gaps are widest for "particularized mobilization," described as requests from candidates, parties, or groups for individuals to become involved in specific political activities such as voting, campaigning, or participating in local politics (102). Gaps in mobilization shrink when one considers more general requests to participate, which occur in the workplace, at church, or through voluntary associations (103).

Mobilization entails an effort by individuals or groups of individuals to bring people into the political system through encouragement, incentives, and the provision of opportunities to participate in politics (see also Rosenstone and Hansen 1993). In this book, I distinguish between three types of mobilization: mass, selective, and limited.

Mass mobilization is the recruitment and organization of a large number of people to participate in political action. A mass mobilization does not necessarily have to be effective, and it can occur to force change or to maintain the status quo, but it must involve assembling and organizing a mass of people for a specific action.

Selective mobilization is the strategic targeting of recruitment efforts to expend the least effort to achieve the greatest effect. Political party leaders often engage in selective recruitment during an election campaign, targeting the individuals who are the most likely voters (such as those with substantial socioeconomic resources) and who are likely to mobilize others (especially those centrally placed in social networks) (Rosenstone and Hansen 1993). Historically, parties have engaged in the mass mobilization of immigrants. Today, however, selective mobilization has left many immigrants on the periphery of the political system.

Community organizations, focused on social service, advocacy, or other missions, generally lack the resources to engage in mass political mobilization. Instead, they rely on *limited mobilization,* which involves the recruitment of limited numbers to take part in political action, often relating to a specific issue or concern. By engaging in limited mobilization, community organizations can lay the foundation for mass mobilization in immigrant communities by recruiting some members of those communities to take part in U.S. politics and by imparting critical organizing and communication skills to those immigrants. Because of their long-standing local presence in immigrant communities, community organizations may eventually serve as the institutions from which mass mobilization efforts can be launched in those communities. For mass mobilization efforts to be effective, they may need to be connected to trusted community institutions. Trust can be built through community organizations' current efforts to engage in limited mobilization.

Meeting the Challenges of Mobilizing Contemporary Immigrants

The research I conducted in 1999 and 2000 indicates that political parties are not giving priority to the political mobilization of Asian American and Latino immigrants. Instead, labor organizations, workers' centers, advocacy and social service organizations, ethnic voluntary associations, and religious institutions are engaging in political organizing efforts. These activities offer a window onto the mechanisms and potential for the future incorporation of immigrants into the American political system. This book will point to how civic institutions could do more in terms of fulfilling the democratic promise of full participation by focusing on the limitations and strengths of those institutions for mobilizing immigrants to participate in the political system.

The growing numbers of immigrants to the United States present challenges to American civic institutions. Many conservatives in particular are concerned that contemporary immigrants are preoccupied with economic advancement to the detriment of their civic and cultural engagement (Geyer 1996). Fears that immigrant political apathy or resistance to assimilation will erode the country's civic culture are one element underlying the calls for stricter limits on immigration.

These fears about immigrant apathy and resistance to assimilation neglect the role that immigrants could play in our democratic society were they to become engaged members of the American polity. This possibility unfolds on four key axes: (1) an intensified role for community organizations as agents of political mobilization; (2) the appearance of unanticipated types of participation and processes of mobilization; (3) the role of time in immigrants' political participation and the imperative for mainstream political parties to embrace long-term mobilization strategies to encourage and accelerate immigrant political participation; and (4) an acknowledgment that immigrant involvement in ethnic-based organizations or in homeland politics does not necessarily preclude—or even diminish—immigrant civic involvement in the United States.

Axis 1: Community Organizations as Mobilizing Agents

Local party organizations—the institutions critical to the mobilization of earlier waves of European immigrants—no longer mobilize newcomers in a consistent or committed fashion. In contrast, as in the past, organizations that engage in community-based work continue to mobilize immigrants despite limitations related to lack of resources and to a focus on providing social services rather than on developing political activities (Skerry 1993; Sterne 2001; A. Lin forthcoming). For example, in Los Angeles, the Chinatown Service Center offers classes in English as a second language and in citizenship, and the Day Laborers Project at the Coalition for Humane Immigrant Rights Los Angeles brings together immigrant workers at soccer games to inform them about their rights as workers and helps them to organize collectively around wage issues.

Like the general population, many immigrants who join community organizations are among the most socioeconomically advantaged within their communities. Surprisingly, however, organizations also mobilize those individuals who traditional theories of political participation, especially socioeconomic theories, contend are the least likely to participate: those who have few resources, who do not speak English, and who are not citizens. The ability of organizations outside the mainstream party system to politically mobilize some of the least privileged segments of the immigrant community—day laborers, garment workers, and undocumented immigrants—indicates the potential generally to mobilize the immigrant community. This compels us to revisit theories of political participation that make assumptions about who is and who is not likely to participate in the American political system.

Which features of community organizations make them successful in mobilizing immigrants? Ethnic voluntary associations, advocacy and social service organizations, and even religious institutions are often led and staffed by individuals with strong familial or other ties to the immigrant community they serve. That background endows these people with expertise and understanding about those groups, thereby facilitating mobilization around shared interests and identities. Community groups organize immigrants by recognizing the complexity and multiple aspects of immigrant identity and by being sensitive to the unique histories, traditions, language, and policy needs of local immigrant communities. Studying these organizations provides a powerful lens through which to observe how institutional strategies and behaviors encourage greater mobilization among immigrants generally and helps us to understand the limits to mobilizing immigrants on a mass scale.

Axis 2: Unanticipated Processes of Political Mobilization

Nonparty community organizations' activities may also lead to the development of unanticipated processes of political mobilization among Asian American and Latino immigrants. Those processes could differ in important ways from what European immigrants in the late nineteenth and early twentieth centuries experienced. For example, whereas political parties are credited with bringing European immigrants into American electoral politics, the contemporary institutional dynamic is likely to provide multiple channels of political socialization in a broad range of electoral and nonelectoral activities. In addition, mobilization by parties is likely to lead to organization around a party platform or comprehensive agenda, but mobilization led by labor organizations, workers' centers, advocacy and social service organizations, ethnic voluntary associations, and religious institutions is likely to be driven by issue-specific and issue-oriented mobilization strategies. In addition, contemporary community organizations, perhaps to an even greater degree than in the past (Skocpol 1999b), allow for the retention of ethnic and racial identity and its strong role in organizing. Thus, developing a fuller understanding of political mobilization requires that more careful attention be paid to all these processes.

Critics argue that ethnic-based organizations can be divisive and lead to ethnic balkanization because they promote ethnic identity to the detriment of a common American identity (Skerry 1993; Huntington 2004). Although certain organizations mobilize immigrants around shared racial and ethnic identities, most do not do so at the expense of recognizing other types of identities. Immigrants possess multiple and intersecting identities, and immigrant community organizations mobilize around this array of identities, including identity as a worker or gender identity rather than just ethnic and racial identity. Given that some ethnic-based community organizations have forged multiethnic or multiracial alliances, the likelihood that political mobilization by these organizations will provoke ethnic divisions is also minimal.

Some authors who have studied immigrants' participation have relied heavily on aggregate demographic data (censuses, exit polls), which are restricted to an important but narrow form of political behavior: voting (Mollenkopf, Olson, and Ross 2001; Fraga and Ramirez 2003). "Because casting a ballot is, by far, the most common act of citizenship in any democracy . . . political scientists appropriately devote a great deal of attention to the vote" (Verba, Schlozman, and Brady 1995, 23). However, like those scholars who claim that political participation encompasses more than just participation in electoral politics (Verba and Nie 1972; J. Scott 1985; Kelley 1994; Verba, Schlozman, and Brady 1995; Marable 1984), I have defined political participation more broadly, as an "activity that is intended to or has the consequence of affecting, either directly or indirectly, government action" (Verba, Schlozman, and Brady 1995, 9).

Thus, it is important to pay attention to those activities that are aimed not directly at the formal government but indirectly at those who are perceived to influence or control the distribution of resources and services. For example, to win wider support, a group might organize a protest to draw media attention to a lack of good neighborhood schools rather than directly petitioning the government for increased school funding. Because many immigrants are not U.S. citizens and are therefore barred legally from voting, it is especially critical to consider their involvement in extraelectoral activities. Unlike voting, which is a quintessentially individual act, many extraelectoral activities are best undertaken through civic institutions, which organize around a sense of group membership or shared group interests (Putnam 2000). Immigrants' political activities encompass both traditional electoral participation and such extraelectoral actions as protests, marches, and demonstrations.[11] Immigrants can and will participate in politics through a wide variety of activities, many of which take place in arenas other than the voting booth. Consequently, it is imperative to consider those institutions that mobilize different types of participation at both the grassroots and mass levels (Tate 1993; Harris 1994; Verba, Schlozman, and Brady 1995; Calhoun-Brown 1996).

Axis 3: Political Acculturation over Time and Long-Term Mobilization Strategies

The passage of time, manifested as duration of residence in the United States, inevitably leads to greater immigrant participation in electoral and nonelectoral politics. Gradual acculturation into American life was as important for earlier European immigrants as it is for today's arrivals. This holds true not only across generations but also within the first (foreign-born) generation.[12] Thus, the political participation of Asian American and Latino immigrants can be expected to increase with duration of stay and at a slow and steady rate over many years.

One reason that parties are ineffective in drawing immigrants into the political system is that they are always preoccupied with the next immediate election and consequently usually employ very short-term strategies. This is significant because if political parties do not mobilize immigrants consistently and if other types of civic organizations face resource limitations that prevent them from mobilizing immigrants on a mass scale, long-term socialization may be the only mechanism that reliably will bring large numbers of immigrants into the American political system. Given that political participation for immigrants is time-dependent, American civic institutions ought to adopt longer-term mobilization strategies.

Axis 4: Involvement in Homeland Politics and Transnational Organizations

Some researchers have suggested that immigrants with strong ties to their countries of origin focus on their homeland politics almost exclusively and are thus less active in American politics (Portes and Rumbaut 1996; Barone 2001). Increasing globalization tends to strengthen bonds to the homeland. Air travel and sophisticated yet increasingly accessible communications systems such as the Internet, e-mail, and cell phones facilitate the development and maintenance of transnational attachments. Contemporary immigrants' linkages to their countries of origin are both strong and varied. Many return home frequently, send money, build crossborder social networks and communities, and invest in projects and property in their former hometowns, all of which helps to construct hybrid or overlapping identities. And some immigrants remain politically active in their homelands. In an age marked by rapid globalization, attention must be paid to the transnational character of migration.

However, the assumption that a strong interest in or concern for the country of origin implies indifference toward U.S. political life should be challenged. The widespread belief that first-generation immigrants' concern with homeland issues precludes the possibility of their participation in U.S. politics is not supported empirically. Analysis of surveys and qualitative interviews suggests that transnational political activity is associated with greater political participation for some U.S. immigrants. Institutional strategies should recognize that in certain groups, those active in their homeland politics also tend to be the most politically active in their U.S. communities. This trend has implications for American civic institutions and their relationship to immigrant communities. In particular, rather than dismissing immigrants involved in politics related to their home countries as being apathetic or disloyal to the American political system, civic institution leaders should consider transnational activists a potential source of participatory leadership in U.S. politics.

Studying Immigrant Mobilization

Many studies of immigrant political participation and mobilization have been based on case studies of a single racial or ethnic group, which makes generalization difficult (Jones-Correa 1998; Karpathakis 1999; Rogers 2000a). This book moves beyond that limitation by focusing on Asian Americans and Latinos, two groups for which political mobilization is a critical issue as a result of both their growing numbers and their historical exclusion from the political system. Chinese and Mexican immigrants, the two largest subgroups within those panethnic categories, receive special comparative attention based on interviews in the metropolitan gateway cities of New York and Los Angeles. Chinese and Mexican immigrants share many similar challenges in terms of language acquisition, naturalization, and minority-group status, but they also differ in the size of their U.S. populations, proximity to countries of origin, and average economic resources. Although no ethnic group is reducible to a single, monolithic identity (Benhabib 2002), the comparative focus on these two major groups has led to observations that may apply not only to immigrants but also to minorities and to voters generally.

Data gathered through both qualitative and quantitative methods helps to shed light on the role of American civic institutions in immigrant political mobilization. The majority of the qualitative data was collected during 1999 and 2000, primarily through in-depth interviews with leaders of immigrant community organizations and with immigrants from Chinese and Mexican communities in New York and Los Angeles. I also collected data through fieldwork that involved participant observation at immigrant community events, cataloging and coding printed materials from community organizations, and extensive note taking. In addition, I analyzed quantitative data from three surveys, including the 2000–2001 Pilot National Asian American Political Survey, the 1989–1990 Latino National Political Survey (see de la Garza et al. 1992), and the 1999 *Washington Post*/Henry J. Kaiser Family Foundation/Harvard University National Survey on Latinos in America. (For details on the study's methodology, see the appendix.)

Conclusion

Immigration, primarily from Asia and Latin America, has fundamentally transformed the American population. Scholars and popular commentators have observed that these immigrants participate in politics at lower rates than the general population and often attribute this phenomenon to political apathy or preoccupation with the homeland. Some individuals have voiced concern that lack of participation among immigrants will undermine American civil society. However, little research has investigated the role that American civic institutions play in mobilizing immigrants toward involvement in U.S. politics. The research on which this book is based supports the premise that the political mobilization of contemporary immigrants poses not a threat to the American polity but an opportunity for democratic revitalization.

How do American civic institutions—parties, labor organizations, workers' centers, advocacy and social service organizations, ethnic voluntary associations, and religious institutions—react to the challenges and opportunities posed by new Americans from around the world? What types of American civic institutions provide pathways toward democratic participation for an increasingly diverse American populace? Which civic institutions are becoming less relevant in the face of massive demographic change? What strategies can civic institutions employ to better support immigrants' civic participation? The chapters that follow examine these questions. Although this book focuses on how American civic institutions respond to Chinese and Mexican immigrants in particular, it will also reveal how civic institutions could enhance their support of democratic participation by the American population as a whole.

2 Mexican & Chinese Immigrants in Two Cities

The 2000 Census revealed that the foreign-born population in the United States numbered more than 28 million people, about 10 percent of the total population. Although this is less than the 15 percent figure registered during the peak waves of European migration in the early twentieth century, it is significant nonetheless. Today, Asian Americans and Latinos constitute the nation's largest immigrant populations. Within those categories, approximately 2.7 million Chinese Americans reside in the United States, more than 20 percent of the almost 12 million people who identified themselves as Asians; Mexican Americans account for more than 65 percent of the country's 33 million Latinos (Barnes and Bennett 2002; Guzman 2001).

Although Asian Americans and Latinos are often described as "new immigrants," these groups have occupied an important place in American history, having had a presence in the United States that matches that of many fourth-, fifth-, or even sixth-generation European Americans. The earliest Asian settlements in the United States can be traced to the mid-1700s, when sailors from the Philippines and China arrived on Spanish ships that were part of the Manila-Acapulco galleon trade. They debarked on Mexico's west coast and eventually settled in Louisiana (Okihiro 2001, 21). In 1870, nearly 9 percent of California's population was of Chinese origin (Takaki 1989). The Japanese also had a significant presence in the United States by the late 1800s (Lien 2001). Mexicans have been living in the West and Southwest since the mid-1700s, when that territory was part of Spain's empire. In short, Asian Americans and Latinos had already had a long-term presence in North America at the time the Irish, German, Italian, and other southern and eastern European immigrants began arriving in great numbers. Yet unlike their European counterparts, Asian Americans and Latinos have remained marked as racialized minority groups. Race has significantly shaped the status of immigrants from Asia, Latin America, Africa, and the Caribbean in a way that it never did for European immigrants.

The Racialization of Asian Americans & Latinos

The conceptualization of Asian Americans and Latinos as groups was socially constructed as a result of processes of "racial formation" in the United States (Omi and Winant 1994).[1] Historically, in contrast to European groups, which gradually came to be widely accepted as white, Asian Americans and Latinos endured discrimination based on their non-European origins, which reinforced their minority status as "people of color." Several historical events—perhaps most importantly the mass migration of African Americans from the South to the North—"conspired in the early and mid–twentieth century to heighten the premium on race as *color* and to erode the once-salient 'differences' among the white races" (Jacobson 1998, 95). White identity became more inclusive as Americans of European decent consolidated their position in society vis-à-vis non-European groups (Jacobson 1998). The racial hierarchy that developed as a result of changing definitions of whiteness is represented by the comments of Lothrop Stoddard in *Reforging of America,* published in the late 1920s: "But what is thus true of European immigrants, most of whom belong to some branch of the white racial group, most emphatically does not apply to nonwhite immigrants, like the Chinese, Japanese, or Mexicans; neither does it apply to the large resident Negro element. . . . Here, ethnic differences are so great that 'assimilation' in the racial sense is impossible" (quoted in Jacobson 1998, 98).

Scholars who have traced European groups as they evolved from marginal to full-fledged members of the white majority argue that contestation over white status and the construction of whiteness are critical elements for understanding the unequal distribution of social, economic, legal, and political power in the United States (Haney-Lopez 1996; Rogers Smith 1997; Jacobson 1998; Lipsitz 1998). To study the political mobilization of ethnic minority immigrants, we must examine the racialization of those groups.

Latinos and Racialization

Colonialism structured the racialization of Latinos generally and Mexicans and Puerto Ricans in particular (Horsman 1981). The U.S.-Mexican War began in 1846 when President James Polk ordered U.S. military leaders into the Mexican territory encompassing California, Arizona, and New Mexico (Acuna 1988). The Americans justified the taking of these lands by claiming their racial superiority to the Mexicans, who were depicted as an impure and morally weak mixture of Caucasians and Native Americans. Just one example of this widespread perception appears in a 1842 statement by Waddy Thompson, a member of the Whig administration, justifying American expansion by describing Mexicans as "lazy, ignorant, and, of course, vicious and dishonest" (Horsman 1981, 212).

Following the signing of the Treaty of Guadalupe Hidalgo, citizenship and voting rights were granted to Mexicans based on their perceived whiteness (Perea et al. 2000, 266). Mexicans with dark complexions were barred from participating in the political system. Juan F. Perea and his coauthors note that "the meaning of the grant of citizenship in the Treaty to Mexicans was largely contingent on the Anglo-American perception of the race of particular Mexicans. Dark-skinned mestizos, the mixed race Mexicans of Spanish and Indian ancestry so despised by white Anglo-Americans, were denied citizenship and meaningful political participation" (2000, 265). Most Mexicans who found themselves on U.S. soil after the U.S.-Mexican War were not allowed to vote because of their race. Similarly, the question of Puerto Rican citizenship and political representation turned on race. In 1917, Congress passed the Jones Act, which granted limited U.S. citizenship to Puerto Ricans. Debate leading up to the vote was contentious, with the opposition arguing that Puerto Ricans, like Mexicans, were of mixed ancestry and thus racially inferior and unfit for self-government (Weston 1972, 194–95).

Even after the U.S. Supreme Court ruled in *Brown v. Board of Education* that racial segregation was unlawful, Mexican American children in the Southwest continued to attend segregated schools that were inferior to Anglo schools in terms of infrastructure and resources. Until the Mexican and Puerto Rican citizens of San Bernardino, California, challenged a segregation provision in 1944, people of Latino descent were barred from using one of the city's public parks. In Texas and other parts of the Southwest into the 1950s, Mexican Americans suffered overt racial discrimination in the form of separate bathroom facilities and restaurants that refused to serve Latinos (Perea 1997).

Anti-Latino sentiment was also expressed in the form of nativism and policies that targeted Latino immigrants or, perhaps more importantly, those perceived as immigrants. Mexicans faced mass deportation during the Great Depression, when hundreds of thousands of people, most U.S. citizens, were forcibly "repatriated" to Mexico (Haney-Lopez 1996, 38).[2] From 1953 to 1955, the U.S. federal government ran a deportation program, Operation Wetback, that "repatriated" more than a million people per year of Mexican origin (Acuna 1996, 113).

The 1965 amendments to the Immigration and Nationality Act liberalized quotas based on nationality, and immigrants from Asia and Latin America began to enter the country in increasing numbers. This growth in non-European migration spawned a wave of anti-immigrant sentiment. Politicians capitalized on the anxiety of the native-born by proposing legislation hostile to migration from Latin America, especially Mexico and Central America. In 1976, a member of Congress from Pennsylvania introduced a bill that would reduce legal Mexican immigration from forty thousand to twenty thousand annually. The measure also permitted the deportation of the U.S.-born children of immigrants who were in the United States without legal documents. The 1980s saw the appearance of English-only laws and anti-bilingual-education efforts sponsored by U.S. nativists (Acuna 1996, 115).

By the early 1990s, anti-immigrant sentiment had reached a fever pitch, with politicians in California spearheading policies to discourage immigration. The state's Republican governor, Pete Wilson, emerged as a key proponent of anti-immigrant legislation, even calling for the issuance of identity cards to distinguish legal and illegal immigrants. In 1994, sponsors of Proposition 187, the Save Our State initiative, collected enough signatures to place it on the California ballot. The initiative restricted the social services and nonemergency health care available to undocumented immigrants and denied their children access to public education. Proposition 187 also opened the doors to racial profiling by obliging public agencies to report suspected illegal immigrants to state and federal authorities. The measure passed by a vote of 59 percent to 41 percent, although opponents immediately challenged its constitutionality and the U.S. district court issued a temporary restraining order. Although the measure was declared unconstitutional in 1998, support for Proposition 187 provided the impetus for the U.S. Congress to pass the 1996 Personal Responsibility and Work Opportunity Reconciliation Act, which limited legal immigrants' ability to qualify for means-tested federal benefit programs.

The politics around Proposition 187 illustrate the racialized nature of the immigration debate. Exit polls showed that 77 percent of Latinos opposed the measure, as did 53 percent each of Asian American and black voters; conversely, 63 percent of white voters supported it (Tolbert and Hero 1996). In his bid for reelection, Wilson reasserted his support for restricting immigration. A Wilson campaign commercial that showed brown-skinned men crossing a border fence at night seemed to suggest that the supposedly race-neutral anti-immigrant legislation actually targeted Latinos. The shifting racial makeup of contemporary migration appears to have been the impetus behind the California voter initiative and other anti-immigrant legislation (Valenzuela 1995).

Asian Americans and Racialization

Nativist sentiment in the United States has also reinforced the racialization of Asian Americans. One of the predominant stereotypes of Asian Americans is their characterization as a "perpetually foreign race" (R. Lee 1999; Perea et al. 2000; Wu 2002). Whether recent immigrant or fifth-generation American, Asian Americans are often assumed to be foreigners in the United States. In many people's minds, Asians are aliens in America (R. Lee 1999, ix).

Prior to 1965, U.S. law barred many Chinese, Japanese, South Asian, and Filipino immigrants from entering the United States. Chinese immigrants had begun to immigrate as laborers in 1849 and 1850 but quickly encountered racial hostility, especially in California, where many had sought work in the gold mines (Takaki 1989). In the 1870s, the anti-Chinese movement gained momentum as organizations formed in California to urge employers not to hire Chinese labor and to encourage boycotts of Chinese merchants (Perea et al. 2000, 375). White labor groups justified the movement's goals by painting Chinese workers as racially unfit for the American workforce, uncivilized, and even animal-like: "he is a slave, reduced to the lowest terms of beggarly economy, and is no fit competitor for an American freeman. . . . [H]e herds in scores, in small dens, where a white man and wife could hardly breathe, and has none of the wants of a civilized white man" (broadside printed in the *Marin Journal,* 1876, quoted in R. Lee 1999, 62). Even Irish immigrants, struggling for acceptance on the East Coast, joined San Francisco's Order of Caucasians for the Extermination of the Chinaman (Jacobson 1998). In 1882, Congress passed the Chinese Exclusion Act, which relied on racial arguments to curtail Chinese immigration (Chan 1991a, b; Takaki 1993; Haney-Lopez

1996; Rogers Smith 1997), and in 1917, Congress further restricted immigration by creating the racialized "Asiatic barred zone," which excluded all immigrants from Asia. Around the same time, some representatives also attempted to pass a bill banning immigration for "all members of the African or black race" (Haney-Lopez 1996, 38).

Asian Americans were also barred from citizenship based on racial status. In 1922, Japanese-born Takao Ozawa sought to become a U.S. citizen. His request was denied when the Supreme Court argued that he was ineligible to become a citizen because naturalization was only permitted for "free white persons and aliens of African nativity and persons of African descent" (Perea et al. 2000, 405). This ruling not only reinforced the notion that Asian Americans were racially unqualified to become full-fledged American citizens but also helped to construct a definition of whiteness (Ngai 1999).

In the wake of the Japanese attack on Pearl Harbor and continuing throughout World War II, the use of negative racial images and stereotypes set Japanese Americans apart, and their portrayal in movies and elsewhere as villains and members of a "perpetually foreign" group was used to justify their mistreatment. The U.S. government initiated the removal of Japanese Americans to internment camps based on the unfounded assumption that they were potential spies and saboteurs. Leslie Hatamiya notes that "throughout the course of the entire war, not one episode of espionage or sabotage is known to have been committed by a Japanese American, citizen or alien. On the other hand, a number of people who were not of Japanese ancestry—many of whom were Germans or of German descent—were charged and convicted of espionage or sabotage for Japan" (1993, 12). Yet among all groups in the United States, only the Japanese Americans were forcibly removed from their homes and sent to internment camps during World War II.

The legacy of past exclusion and stereotyping continues to shape the racialization of Asian Americans today. Robert Lee points out that "well after the legal status of alien has been shed, no matter what their citizenship, how long they may have resided in the United States or how assimilated they are, the 'common understanding' that Asians are an alien presence in America is still the prevailing assumption in American culture" (1999, 164). Thus, in 1996, when the Democratic National Committee was accused of accepting illegal campaign donations from foreigners, the committee's first response was to contact all Asian Pacific American donors with "foreign sounding" surnames to ask them to prove their citizenship or legal status in the United States (Nakanishi 1999a, 34).

In 1999, Asian American community groups, elected officials, and others charged the U.S. government with racial profiling because of American officials' treatment of Dr. Wen Ho Lee, a Taiwanese-born naturalized U.S. citizen accused of sharing nuclear secrets with the Chinese government. During his pretrial imprisonment, Lee's arms and legs were shackled and he was forced to speak only English, even to his family members. Given the lack of evidence that he had mishandled classified information, civil rights and community leaders charged that this treatment was excessive. Echoing the concern expressed by many Asian Americans that Lee had been the target of racial profiling, the American Association for the Advancement of Science (AAAS) issued a statement to Attorney General Janet Reno: "Our purpose is to inquire into the reasons for the extraordinarily restrictive conditions to which Dr. Lee has been subjected. Our disquiet with the government's treatment of Dr. Lee does not extend to the issue of his guilt or innocence, which will be decided by our courts. . . . Our concern stems from the possibility that Dr. Lee is being maltreated and may have been the target of special scrutiny because of his ethnic background" (letter from Irving Leach, Chair, AAAS Committee on Scientific Freedom and Responsibility to Reno February 2000 [American Association for the Advancement of Science 2000]). Lee was ultimately found guilty of only one minor count of illegally retaining national defense information, while fifty-eight other counts, most of which carried life sentences, were dismissed.

Europeans and Racialization

Popular history often glosses over the racialization of European immigrants, especially non-Anglo-Saxons, assuming that after arriving on North American shores, they were immediately accepted as part of the white majority. However, historical attention to the discrimination faced by members of what were widely accepted as distinct white races, including the "Celts," "Hebrews," and "Teutons" as well as other European groups, suggests otherwise (Jacobson 1998).[3] Recent scholarship (Ignatiev 1995; Jacobson 1998) underscores the persecution and rampant stereotyping of certain European immigrant groups, including the Irish, Jews, Germans, and Italians. Thus, one might argue that both earlier waves of European immigrants, especially those from eastern and southern

Europe, and contemporary waves of Latino and Asian American immigrants have entered the United States as members of racial minority groups. However, even though the whiteness of many European immigrants was contested in popular and political discussion, the racial discrimination that those groups faced differed in fundamental ways from that of contemporary, non-European immigrant groups.

Those European immigrants who were confronted with widespread hostility never faced the kind of legal racial restrictions on naturalization—on becoming full-fledged American citizens—experienced by non-European groups. Historically, U.S. immigration laws reinforced a distinction between European immigrants in general and groups from other parts of the world. In 1790, Congress restricted citizenship to "free white persons," and immigrants from non-European countries were barred from naturalization because they were deemed "not white." Throughout the early and mid–twentieth century, while racial distinctions between the Anglo-Saxon whites and Jews, Irish, Germans, Italians, and other European groups were being eradicated, the "nonwhite" status of Japanese, Chinese, Filipinos, and Latinos was being reinforced by U.S. naturalization and immigration laws. Asians suffered the effects of the Chinese Exclusion Acts of the 1880s and 1890s and the Asiatic barred zone. During the 1930s, "racialist dogma" fueled the expulsion of hundreds of thousands of Mexican Americans, including, as mentioned earlier, U.S. citizens (Chinea 1996, 11). European immigrants never faced deportation on such a scale. When racial restrictions on naturalization were finally abolished in 1952, it was a moot issue for Irish, Jewish, Italian, Greek, and other European immigrants because U.S. naturalization laws had never classified them as nonwhite (see Guglielmo 2003).

Asian Americans & Latinos: Shared Experiences & Internal Distinctions

In addition to their historical and contemporary construction as racialized minority groups, Asian Americans and Latinos also share other experiences. Both have been subjected to racial "lumping," whereby many Americans and U.S. public policies fail to acknowledge the distinct ethnic groups within the categories "Asian," "Asian American," "Latino," and "Hispanic" (Espiritu 1992; Omi and Winant 1994; Oboler 1995; Skerry 1997). Size of the immigrant population is one of the most prominent traits the two major groups share. Today, more than half the U.S. foreign-born population comes from Latin America. Mexicans make up the largest subgroup, followed by Cubans, Dominicans, and Salvadorans. More than one-quarter of the foreign-born population comes from Asia, with Chinese, Filipinos, Indians, Vietnamese, and Koreans being the largest subgroups. Thus, 75 percent of today's foreign-born population comes from Latin America or Asia, whereas fewer than 20 percent are from Europe, a vast decrease from the 60 percent figure registered in the 1970s (Schmidley 2001).

Because both the Asian American and Latino groups consist of a large proportion of people born outside the United States, many Asian Americans and Latinos face similar adaptation issues in terms of learning English and acquiring citizenship. A 2002 survey found that 74 percent of foreign-born Latinos were Spanish-language dominant, compared to only 4 percent of U.S.-born Latinos (Pew Hispanic Center/Kaiser Family Foundation 2002). The 2000 Census reported that of Asian Americans five years of age and over, 79 percent spoke a language other than English at home (Lien, Conway, and Wong 2004). Further, both groups exhibit a relatively high level of noncitizenship. In 2000, one out of four foreign-born Latinos (Therrien and Ramirez 2001) and about one out of every two foreign-born Asian Americans had acquired citizenship (U.S. Census Bureau 2002). Shared experiences with immigration and issues of adaptation may provide a basis for coalition building between the two groups (see chap. 5; Erie and Brackman 1998).

A final point of comparison is the geographic concentration of these groups in a few major U.S. cities. Most Latinos reside in the New York, Los Angeles, Chicago, Houston, and San Antonio metropolitan areas. Similarly, New York, Los Angeles, San Francisco, Honolulu, and Chicago are home to most Asian Americans. Although the number of Latinos and Asian Americans in midwestern and southern metropolitan areas is growing rapidly, most are still concentrated in immigrant gateway cities on the West and East Coasts (Jones-Correa 2001).

These two panethnic groups clearly share many traits. However, both are also characterized by tremendous internal diversity along nonethnic dimensions, including class, nationality, religion, language, sexuality, number of generations residing in the United States, citizenship status, region of origin, gender, and political ideology. At times, both Latino and Asian American activists, attempting to construct meaningful communities across internal cleavages, have struggled with issues spawned by this tremendous internal diversity (Espiritu 1992; Trueba 1999; Lien 2001; Suárez-Orozco and Paez 2002). Activists have also had to contend with internal group hierarchies based on ethnicity, racialization, class, immigrant generation, gender, and sexuality (see Glenn 1985; Romero 1992; Shah 1994, 1997; Alarcón 1998; Padilla 1998; Sawyer, Peña, and Sidanius 2004).

In summary, both panethnic groups are racialized minorities that mainstream society subjects to racial lumping. Asian Americans and Latinos are notable for the large and growing size of the groups, which include high proportions of immigrants and in particular large numbers who have yet to naturalize in the United States. However, this set of general similarities is crosscut with extensive internal diversity, which creates a complex weaving that is difficult to disentangle as we try to tease out the processes of political mobilization as they are experienced by the members of these groups.

To further our exploration, it helps to look at two important subsets within the panethnic groups, Chinese and Mexicans—specifically, Chinese and Mexican immigrants in two of the country's largest gateway cities, New York and Los Angeles. Examining two different ethnic groups is critical because without comparing groups, it is difficult to separate those factors relevant to immigrant political mobilization that are unique to a particular group from those factors that are important for immigrants more generally. Because geographic context is likely to affect political mobilization, it is helpful to focus on two cities. This makes it possible to detect how geographic context influences political mobilization within a single ethnic group.

Community Profiles of Chinese Immigrants in New York & Los Angeles

A comparison between the Chinese communities in New York and Los Angeles highlights internal differences within the larger Chinese community that shape their political mobilization in the United States. Although a significant Chinese presence has historically existed in both cities, the communities are distinct and have evolved differently. For example, the traditional urban enclave (Chinatown in Manhattan) is central to Chinese immigrant life in New York City and continues to play a vital role in the community. Even Chinese immigrants who live outside of Manhattan, in newer Chinese American areas of settlement such as Flushing, Queens, and Sunset Park, Brooklyn, remain tied to Chinatown via a quick subway ride or private van services. In contrast, Los Angeles's Chinatown has struggled to retain businesses and foot traffic. The Chinese communities in New York and Los Angeles are characterized by unique class dynamics. Further, longtime Chinese residents in both cities encounter distinct groups of new Chinese immigrants: in New York, many new immigrants are from the province of Fujian, located on China's southeastern coast; in Los Angeles, many new immigrants are from Taiwan.

Chinese Immigrants in New York City

By the mid-1850s, Chinese immigrants began to establish a significant presence in Hawaii and California. In 1852, twenty thousand Chinese arrived in the United States through San Francisco, headed eventually to the Sierra Nevada mountains to mine gold. Between 1867 and 1870, forty thousand more Chinese arrived, intent on working on the country's first transcontinental railroad (Chan 1991a, 28). Growth of the Chinese population in the United States slowed dramatically with the passage of the Chinese Exclusion Act of 1882 and did not begin to grow substantially again until the mid–twentieth century (Chan 1991a; Haney-Lopez 1996; Rogers Smith 1997). Historians attribute the decline in the U.S. Chinese population to the impediments Chinese immigrants faced in developing family relationships and creating sustainable communities as well as to the exclusion laws (Takaki 1989; Chan 1991b; Zhou 1992). Most Chinese laborers who came to the United States before the passage of the Exclusion Act were men (the ratio of Chinese men to women in 1890 was twenty-seven to one), and since most states had instituted miscegenation laws prohibiting Chinese individuals from marrying anyone except other Chinese, many of these immigrants ended up living in bachelor societies in Chinatowns (Kwong 1996, 14).

Chinese immigrants had begun to arrive in significant numbers in New York during the 1880s. In 1870, the city's Chinese population numbered about 300 but twenty years later had risen to more than 2,500 (B. Wong 1982; see also Wang 2001). Largely as a result of illegal migration, the number of Chinese in New York City continued to grow slowly from 1900 until the 1940s (Kwong 1996). The U.S. alliance with China during World War II led to the 1943 repeal of the Chinese Exclusion Act; however, immigration laws passed in 1924 permitted the immigration of only 108 people per year of Chinese origin, and immigration from that country did not increase significantly until the discriminatory quotas were lifted in the mid-1960s (Kwong 1996). Thereafter, the Chinese population rose at a steady rate, and between 1965 and 1990, approximately two hundred thousand Chinese settled in New York City (H. Chen 1992).

Manhattan's Chinatown, a dense urban space with many shops and residences, remains the nation's largest Chinese American settlement (J. Lin 1998) as well as one of the city's most homogenous Chinese neighborhoods. In 1940, its population was 11,000; by 1985, it had exceeded 100,000 (Kwong 1996; New York City Department of Planning 2001a). In 2000, the population in the Lower East Side/Chinatown Community District neared 165,000, with Asian Americans, primarily Chinese, making up the district's largest ethnic group (36 percent) (New York City Department of Planning 2001a).[4]

The socioeconomic status of New York's Chinese population mirrors U.S. immigration policies that favor family reunification and professionally trained individuals. Peter Kwong (1996) describes the effects of the preferences on the post-1965 Chinese American population:

> [Professionals and reunified families] foster two very different types of Chinese immigrants. Those who arrive with professional skills are better able to integrate into the American society and do not settle in Chinatowns. They are the Uptown Chinese. While the 1965 Immigration Act favors professionals, 74 percent of the quota is actually reserved for the relatives of American citizens. Since most citizens of Chinese descent were traditionally of humble origin, mainly from the rural areas of southern China, their relatives are likely to have similar backgrounds. Immigrants in this category tend to settle in Chinatowns with their sponsoring relatives. They comprise the Downtown Chinese. (22)

Kwong's study suggests that many Chinese immigrants settle in Manhattan's Chinatown because they easily find jobs there, even when their occupational or English skills are low. Compared to many other immigrants in New York City, immigrants from China are more likely to come from poor, rural, and working-class origins. Chinatown's unemployment rate is minimal, although a large number of workers are concentrated in industries that pay less than minimum wage. Rent-control provisions mean that Chinatown's rents are generally lower than those in other parts of Manhattan, but about 80 percent of the area's inhabitants live in privately owned tenement housing, which is often deteriorating and not up to code (J. Lin 1998).

Chinatown is dominated by traditional industries, such as garment manufacturing and retail (including restaurants), but there has been a recent and significant trend toward finance, insurance, real estate, and high-wage professional service occupations (J. Lin 1998). Kwong (1996) reports that the community's 450 restaurants employ approximately 15,000 workers and that the approximately 500 garment factories employ about 20,000 workers. Local senior-citizen centers, English-language schools, and hospitals employ Chinese-speaking residents. In addition, some residents in Chinatown are small-business owners who operate gift shops aimed at tourists or businesses related to the restaurant or garment business, such as restaurant supply stores. As Chinatown's immigrant population has grown, businesses that serve immigrants have also appeared.

Before the 1970s, immigrants to Chinatown came from the southeast coast of China, including Guangzhou (Canton), as well as from Kwangtung and Hong Kong (Kwong 1996; Wang 2001). Many of the migrants who came to New York around the early 1900s were from Toishan, a rural area south of Guangzhou (Sung 1967). Until recently, Cantonese-speaking Chinese immigrants, including ethnic Chinese from Vietnam, Laos, and Cambodia as well as mainland China, settled in Manhattan's Chinatown. Since 1990, however, the population has begun to shift as an increasing number of immigrants arrive from Fujian Province, and by the early part of that decade, about fifty thousand people from Fujian lived in New York City, many in Chinatown (Frankel 1993). The exploitation of Fujianese immigrants by unscrupulous members of human smuggling rings received attention in 1993, when a ship, the *Golden Venture,* ran aground in Rockaway Beach, Queens. Many of the three hundred passengers aboard were undocumented Fujianese immigrants who had paid up to thirty thousand dollars for passage. By 2002, Fujianese immigrants reported paying as much as sixty thousand dollars (Guest 2003).

The Chinatown community has become characterized by increasing diversity along class, regional, and linguistic lines (J. Lin 1998). Tensions between Fujianese residents and other Chinese immigrants illustrate how such diversity shapes the neighborhoods. Many Fujianese arrive in New York with few economic resources and are channeled into the lowest-paying sectors of the Chinatown job market. More established Chinese residents in the neighborhood hold negative stereotypes regarding Fujianese immigrants, accusing them of drug trafficking, gang membership, and crime (Lii 1994a). The longtime residents also accuse the Fujianese of taking over parts of Chinatown, especially along East Broadway, where they have established restaurants, businesses, and Fujianese-serving social service agencies and advocacy organizations (Lii 1994b). Political divisions also exacerbate the uneasy relationship between older and newer Chinese immigrants. Many Cantonese immigrants tend to support the Taiwanese nationalist movement, whereas Fujianese immigrants are often sympathetic to the mainland communist government (Lii 1994b).

Organization leaders express uncertainty about how the diversity will affect the community's future development: said one, "In my day, we had Toishanese and Toishanese, and now we have everybody. Nowadays, the faces are all different. I mean we have northern faces, and the food. It's wonderful. An amazing explosion. And we have Fukianese [Fujianese] with their associations. There are going to be a lot of differences, and I don't know if that will be better or worse, because it may end up splitting us, which is even worse."

Although Chinatown remains a major settlement area for Chinese immigrants, many also settle in other parts of New York City, such as the multicultural Flushing and Elmhurst-Corona neighborhoods in Queens and Sunset Park in Brooklyn. Recent immigrants from Hong Kong and Taiwan (about 17 percent of all Chinese immigrants to New York) are attracted to other areas because they consider Chinatown to be overcrowded and do not speak its dominant dialects, Cantonese and Toishanese (H. Chen 1992; Hum and Zonta 2000, 214). Neighborhoods outside of Chinatown tend to be more diverse and less commercial, and their Chinese residents tend to rank slightly higher socioeconomically than Chinatown's residents (Hum and Zonta 2000).

In Flushing, for example, students who could not afford Manhattan's high rents were among the first Chinese immigrants to settle there (H. Chen 1992). Today, it is characterized by Chinese businesses, including grocery stores, restaurants, garment factories, health clinics, banks, bookstores, and the offices of major Chinese-language newspapers (H. Chen 1992). By the late 1990s, more than 55 percent of Flushing's eighty thousand residents were Asian American, with most coming from northern China and Taiwan (J. Kim 2002, 155). Mandarin is the community's dominant language (Deutsch 1994, 1).

Roger Sanjek, author of a major study on Elmhurst-Corona (1998), another important Chinese community in Queens, notes that more Chinese live there than in Flushing, although the media often touts Flushing as the city's "second Chinatown." His research reveals that as early as the 1960s, large numbers of Taiwanese immigrants were settling in Elmhurst. In a 1999 interview with a New York City newspaper, Sanjek emphasized the racial and ethnic diversity found in Flushing and Elmhurst-Corona in contrast to Manhattan: "There is no street in Queens that is 100 percent Chinese" (Ruiz 1999, 3). Chinese immigrants who reside in Queens are likely to live in integrated neighborhoods, perhaps with immigrants from Korea, Latin America, or the Caribbean (Sanjek 1998).

The press also often labels Brooklyn's Sunset Park a "new Chinatown." However, like its counterparts in Queens, Sunset Park is actually multiethnic rather than exclusively or even majority Chinese American. Chinese speakers in New York often refer to the Sunset Park community as Bat Dai Do, or Eighth Avenue, where much of the Chinese commercial strip is located. Since the opening of a single Chinese grocery store on that street in the 1980s, thousands of Chinese immigrant families have moved into homes between Fifth Avenue and Eighth Avenue and along the side streets from Fiftieth Street to Sixty-second Street. However, just blocks away, along Sixth and Seventh Avenues, the shops are no longer mostly Chinese but an ethnic mix, including many that sell groceries and products from Central and South America (Ruiz 1999).

Over the past twenty-five years, Sunset Park has experienced rapid demographic change. In 1980, the neighborhood was mostly Scandinavian. Today, it is one of the largest Chinese immigrant neighborhoods in New York City. In fact, Brooklyn's Chinese population grew almost 300 percent during the 1980s, and Sunset Park was one of the most popular destinations for newcomers (Ruiz 1999). By 2000, the census recorded approximately thirty thousand Asian American residents in Sunset Park, the vast majority of them Chinese (Brooklyn AIDS Task Force 2003). However, most scholars and activists in the Brooklyn community argue that the number is higher than sixty thousand (Mustain 1997). Many of those who live in Sunset Park are Cantonese speakers from Hong Kong, but Mandarin or Fujianese speakers live there as well.

Ethnic change has sparked some resentment among longtime residents. For example, one man complained to a local newspaper that the Chinese immigrants in his neighborhood do not frequent his pizzeria: "I don't mean this in a racist way, but it's just a fact we've become a Chinatown, which I resent. In this country, we are supposed to assimilate, but they don't. We are supposed to be a melting pot, but they aren't in it" (Mustain 1997, 34). Despite that sentiment, it is important to note that Sunset Park is not a Chinatown in the traditional sense. Asked to speak about an exhibit focused on Sunset Park, Cynthia Lee, an associate with the Museum of Chinese in the Americas, said, "People look at the growth of the community in Sunset Park, and think it is another Chinatown. . . . Yet, it is different. It never was as self-contained as Chinatown, for instance. One of the reasons is that Sunset Park still is a destination for immigrants of many nationalities" (Ruiz 1999, 3).

Chinese Immigrants in Los Angeles

When downtown Los Angeles's original Chinatown was demolished in the 1930s to make way for Union Station, Chinese merchants and Anglo activists lobbied for the development of "New Chinatown." It was built between North Hill Street and North Broadway, its architecture a combination of Hollywood kitsch and modern, 1930s design: "While the architecture of New Chinatown might invite criticism for being a stereotype of authentic Chinese architecture, the cluster of pseudo-Chinese stores and restaurants gave the 1940s community some ethnic identity where none had existed. The result was the nation's first planned Chinatown. At the time, the architecture was described as not an exact representation of native Chinese buildings, but as 'Chinese-American,' a blend of Chinese elements and modern buildings" (Heimann 1998, 1). The development was intended to attract tourists as well as to provide a residential and shared community environment for Chinese Americans in Los Angeles.

Until the 1960s, Chinatown remained the center of Chinese cultural and traditional life in southern California. Originally, mostly Toishanese immigrants lived and worked in Chinatown, and the main dialects were Cantonese and Toishanese. Following reforms in immigration law in 1965 and the Vietnam War, a large wave of ethnic Chinese from Southeast Asia began to settle in Chinatown. By 1990, twenty-five thousand people lived there, and U.S. Census reports indicated that 43.5 percent identified themselves as Chinese and 11 percent as Southeast Asian. Many of those who identified themselves as Chinese, however, were not born in China but were ethnic Chinese born in Laos, Cambodia, or Vietnam. Kevin Ng, who was born in Cambodia and now lives in Chinatown, explained to a reporter, "In 1975, we were looked down upon as refugees. But after a few years, the business community started to develop and the older Toishan couldn't compete" (Torres 1996, 1).

In 1970, there were about 22,000 immigrants from China, Taiwan, and Hong Kong in the Los Angeles metropolitan region. By 2000, the number of immigrants from China, Taiwan, and Hong Kong in the region had grown to more than 200,000 (Sabagh and Bozorgmehr 2003, 107). This influx of new immigrants led to the development of new concentrations of Chinese Americans outside the central city. Today, the San Gabriel Valley, a suburban swath in Los Angeles County that includes the cities of Monterey Park, San Gabriel, Rosemead, Alhambra, Hacienda Heights, and Rowland Heights, is a major focal point of Chinese American life in Los Angeles. Some cities in the San Gabriel Valley have experienced dramatic changes. Notably, while Monterey Park's total population grew from 54,000 in 1980 to 61,000 in 1990, the Asian American portion of the population grew from 34 percent to 58 percent, an 85 percent increase (Asian Pacific American Legal Center 1998; Harney 1992). The Chinese American population alone accounted for 41 percent of Monterey Park's residents in 2000 (Zhou and Kim 2003, 129).

During the late 1960s and 1970s, Chinese began moving out of downtown Chinatown and, concurrent with national suburbanization trends, began to settle in the San Gabriel Valley. This settlement pattern was further reinforced when immigrants from Asia began arriving in large numbers in Monterey Park after a real estate agent began to advertise homes in the area in Taiwanese and Hong Kong newspapers in the 1970s (Harney 1992; Saito 1998). Thus, not only was secondary migration occurring as residents moved from Chinatown to suburban Chinese communities, but new immigrants began to move directly to the suburbs, bypassing Chinatown and the central cities of Los Angeles County (Li 1999; Zhou and Kim 2003).

The post-1965 Chinese immigrant settlers in suburban enclave communities are notably diverse in both national origin and class background. In his 1995 study of Monterey Park, John Horton reports that 38 percent of the community's immigrants were born in mainland China, 24 percent in Vietnam, 11 percent in Hong Kong, 7 percent in other Southeast Asian nations, and the remainder in Latin America and other countries (22–23). Although many Chinese immigrants were born on the mainland, a large number immigrated from Hong Kong and Taiwan after leaving the mainland during the communist revolution. More than one-third of Chinese immigrants to Los Angeles identify themselves as Taiwanese (Hum and Zonta 2000, 214; Zhou and Kim 2003).

In terms of class, the Chinese population in the San Gabriel Valley is bifurcated along income and educational lines. This reflects the twin prongs created by the "professionally trained" and "family reunification" preference categories in post-1965 U.S. immigration policy. Because many of the original immigrants from China were from poor rural backgrounds, their relatives who arrive as part of the family reunification program and settle in the San Gabriel Valley are likely to come from similar circumstances. Nevertheless, a growing number of immigrants are professionals (Zhou and Kim 2003). Los Angeles and in particular the San Gabriel Valley are the primary destination for immigrants with professional and managerial backgrounds from Taiwan and Hong Kong (Hum and Zonta 2000). Therefore, it is not surprising that studies find both "high education and income and high levels of poverty" among the Chinese population in the San Gabriel Valley (Horton 1995, 25). Min Zhou and Rebecca Kim (2003, 142) report that Chinese immigrants as a group tend to exhibit higher levels of education than Los Angeles County's population.

Researchers and residents have described Monterey Park and other San Gabriel communities as "suburban Chinatowns" (Arax 1987; Harney 1992; Fong 1994). Like Chinatown, these communities are characterized by Chinese-owned stores and restaurants selling Chinese products and advertising in Chinese. One Chinese American who owns a real estate agency in Monterey Park told a reporter, "You might say that Monterey Park is a second Chinatown, a Chinatown in the suburbs. A lot of businesses that began there—including ours—now have branches here. If people can buy whatever they need here, why go to Chinatown?" (Harney 1992, 8). Chinese speakers and Chinese-language signs abound, so that speaking English is often unnecessary. Wei Li, a scholar studying the Los Angeles Chinese community, asked one woman who moved to Monterey Park in the 1980s why Chinese people chose to settle there: "Because of living here we feel just like home. There are so many Chinese people and Chinese stores, restaurants, banks, newspapers, radios and TV, almost everything you need. . . . Those [Chinese] born in the U.S. do not care whether to live close to Chinese or not. But we do care as new immigrants with poor English or no English skill at all" (1999, 14).

However, like the Chinese communities in Flushing and other New York suburbs, cities in the San Gabriel Valley are not as ethnically or racially homogenous as traditional downtown Chinatowns. As Li notes, "the ethnic concentration in the San Gabriel Valley is not just another Chinatown, but is, instead, different from previously identified ethnic settlements" (1999, 2). Although Monterey Park's population is mostly Asian American, especially Chinese American, it is also clearly multiracial and multiethnic. According to Leland Saito (1998), in 1990 Latinos made up 30 percent of the area's population and whites about 12 percent. Chinese were the largest Asian American group in the area during the 1990s, but Japanese (17 percent) and Vietnamese (8 percent) also made up a large proportion of Monterey Park's Asian community.

Comparison between Chinese Immigrants in New York and Los Angeles

The demographic and social differences in the Chinese American populations in New York and Los Angeles shape their political participation. The Los Angeles community is more diverse economically and occupationally than is its counterpart in New York (Waldinger and Tseng 1992; Hum and Zonta 2000). On average, though, the Chinese population in Los Angeles is better off in terms of education, income, and occupational status than the Chinese population in New York (Zhou and Kim 2003, 128). In 1990, most immigrants from Taiwan (42 percent of whom entered under the "professionally trained" preference category) had Los Angeles as their destination. In contrast, New York was the most popular destination for immigrants from the People's Republic of China (Waldinger and Tseng 1992; Hum and Zonta 2000; Zhou and Kim 2003). Of those from mainland China entering the United States in 1990, more than 80 percent did under family reunification provisions, and 60 percent were from working-class backgrounds (compared to only 15 percent of those from Taiwan) (Waldinger and Tseng 1992). Class differences in the Chinese migration flows to New York and Los Angeles have led to differential economic development in the two cities' Chinese communities (Waldinger and Tseng 1992; Saito 1998). In Los Angeles, many Chinese-owned businesses provide services aimed at professional clients, such as real estate, technology, and financial services, whereas in New York, restaurants and garment factories dominate the Chinese ethnic economy (Waldinger and Tseng 1992).

A continuous flow of new migrants has important implications for political organizing in the Chinese community. More migrants increase the community's overall demographic power, but the political mobilization of newcomers—who may not speak English, be familiar with the political system, or be naturalized—also requires more resources than does incorporating the native-born. Another factor that is likely to shape the evolution of immigrant political involvement is internal ethnic diversity within the larger Chinese community. For example, a desire to understand his identity within an increasingly heterogeneous Chinese community led one immigrant to become involved in an ethnic organization that is active around both Taiwanese culture and Asian American issues:

> There was a time [when] I started to think about things and I realized that I had not socialized with people or talked to people that I have a tie to from my ancestry. People asked me, "Are you Chinese?" And I'd say, "Yeah, I'm Chinese." And "Where are you from?" "I'm from Taiwan." And then they'd ask questions about what it means to be a Chinese person from Taiwan and Taiwanese and what the difference is. Apparently, there is a political debate. And I had a hard time, really, trying to communicate what it means to be Taiwanese, making sense of who I am. So I figured I wanted to do something like volunteer just to get myself back in learning about what the perception of the public is about being Taiwanese and Chinese as well. And this can be reflected through interacting with people, who have this experience with this every day. I mean, I can tell my personal story, but [it is] never the same as when you hear from another person who kind of has the same background. So that's why I decided to join.

Residential mobility patterns also may pose a challenge to political organizing in the community. Chinese immigrants in New York City are more likely to move to surrounding suburbs than are those in Los Angeles. New York's Chinese immigrants in both the suburbs and the central cities generally live in areas with a relatively high density of Chinese residents (Fang and Brown 1999). The greater city-to-suburbia mobility of New York's Chinese is attributed to the ethnic job market for Chinese immigrants in New York, where competition for entry-level jobs for those without English-language fluency can be very high (Fang and Brown 1999). One Chinese American activist in New York suggested that Chinese settlement dynamics in New York City make political organizing particularly hard: "The difficulty for our community, the Manhattan Chinatown community, is that they turn over. After they stay [in Chinatown] a while, then they move out. They get enough money to go to Queens, and they go straight to Queens. So we have a lot of transients."

Political experiences in the countries of origin also affect immigrants' political involvement in the United States. One Chinese American leader attributed Chinese immigrants' reluctance to affiliate with a U.S. political party to suspicions of political involvement developed in mainland China: "When we do [voter] registration, unfortunately we have a very high number of people who do not register for parties. Difficult. And some of it is because they had had the Communist Party before. And if you joined, you had obligations. They're not sure what the obligations are. But also, there's just a suspicion." Similarly, a Chinese immigrant claimed that because the political system in China is not a democracy, recent Chinese immigrants to the United States might not understand the U.S. system. Lack of familiarity with a more democratic system might prevent some Chinese immigrants from taking part in such activities as voting: "New immigrants come from places that are not a democracy. People are not used to one man, one vote. . . . There is no tradition of an open vote. People are not used to it. The U.S. system is complicated, and people are put off by that complication."

Despite their growing numbers, Chinese Americans have been slow to achieve elected representation in both Los Angeles and New York. However, there is a longer history of electing Chinese Americans to local and state offices from the Los Angeles region compared to the New York region. Elected in 1985, Michael Woo became the first Chinese American to serve on the Los Angeles City Council. He remained in that office until 1993, when he lost a bid for mayor of Los Angeles to Richard Riordan. Several Chinese Americans have been elected to the Monterey Park City Council (which has a rotating mayor system) over the past two and half decades. In 1983, Lily Lee Chen became the first Chinese American mayor of Monterey Park. Judy Chu, elected to the Monterey Park City Council in 1988, served as a council member for thirteen years, three times as mayor. Chu was elected to the California State Assembly, representing a district that encompasses much of the San Gabriel Valley, in 2001. She joined another Chinese American assemblywoman from the San Gabriel Valley, Carol Liu, elected to the state assembly in 2000, after serving as mayor of La Cañada Flintridge. The first Asian American elected to office in New York City was John Liu, who won a seat on the city council in 2001, representing a district in Queens, New York, that includes Flushing. It was not until 2004, when Jimmy Meng, a Democrat and also from the Flushing area, won office, that the first Asian American was elected to the New York State legislature.

Community Profiles of Mexican Immigrants in Los Angeles and New York

As with the Chinese community, the Mexican community encompasses many diverse elements. Comparing the communities in New York and Los Angeles highlights some critical internal differences. For example, Los Angeles was originally a Mexican settlement, and a well-established Mexican presence constitutes one of the city's important historical features. In sharp contrast, Mexicans are a relatively new population in New York City, beginning to settle there in large numbers only recently. Consequently, a significant proportion of Los Angeles's Mexican population is U.S.-born, whereas a majority of New York's Mexican population consists of immigrants. The Mexican population in Los Angeles includes people from a wide range of socioeconomic status groups, whereas New York's population as a whole occupies a more tenuous socioeconomic position. These geographic, historical, and socioeconomic differences influence how Mexican immigrants are incorporated into the U.S. political system. Community organizations that recognize these differences are better able to do outreach and mobilize particular segments of the Mexican immigrant community.

Mexican Immigrants in Los Angeles

The history of Los Angeles is tied intimately to Mexican settlement in California. El Pueblo de la Reina de Los Angeles was founded in 1781 by an expedition from colonial Mexico. During the Mexican-American War, U.S. forces occupied Los Angeles despite strong resistance by the region's residents. The war ended with the signing of the 1848 Treaty of Guadalupe, under which Mexico ceded all of Alta California to the United States. By the 1860s, Anglos began to outnumber Mexicans in Los Angeles, but Spanish remained widely spoken (Ríos-Bustamante and Castillo 1986, 98). By the end of the nineteenth century, according to Antonio José Ríos-Bustamante and Pedro G. Castillo, Mexicans were "concentrated in specific areas of the city, . . . relegated to a second-class status that belied their ancestral claim to the City of Angels. Economically and politically, Los Angeles became a two-tiered city. Anglos lived, worked, prospered, and grew self-satisfied on the top rung of a mythical social ladder, while Mexicans operated from a position of imposed subservience. These are the disturbing realities of the history of Los Angeles, but they undeniably constitute a cornerstone of the experience of the city's Mexican population—then and now" (1986, 104).

By the late 1800s, Los Angeles's Mexican population comprised not only the descendants of Spaniards and the later Mexican colonizers of Alta California but also newer immigrants from Mexico and their descendants. This community had become concentrated in a part of the downtown area west of Main Street and bounded by Short, Main, Yale, and College Streets (Ríos-Bustamante and Castillo 1986). Mexican households were found sprinkled throughout downtown until the 1920s (Sanchez 1993; Laslett 1996). Between 1900 and 1915, as the city grew and the Mexican population downtown became denser, the community began to move into East Los Angeles, an area that today remains one of the most concentrated in terms of Mexican population (Valle and Torres 2000). Some areas, such as Boyle Heights, eventually developed into multicultural neighborhoods (although Boyle Heights has again become predominantly Latino).

By 1930, more than 165,000 Mexicans lived in Los Angeles County, making it home to more Mexicans than all but a few of the most populous cities in Mexico. The community experienced the greatest growth in the Central Plaza District downtown, Lincoln Park, and Boyle Heights (Ríos-Bustamante and Castillo 1986). Rapid growth in the 1920s was followed by a period of population loss during the Great Depression, when the U.S. federal government began to impose repatriation policies and to severely limit Mexican immigration (the yearly average, which had been 58,000 entrants, fell to 16,000 nationally in 1930). In 1931, in response to lack of jobs, anti-Mexican sentiment among Anglo Americans, and forced repatriation by local governments, 7,500 individuals returned to Mexico from Los Angeles alone (Ríos-Bustamante and Castillo 1986, 153). Throughout the 1930s, more Mexicans would return to Mexico than would immigrate to the United States.

Nevertheless, during the 1940s the Mexican community constituted at least 10 percent of the total Los Angeles population (Ríos-Bustamante and Castillo 1986, 154). In addition to the primary concentrations in downtown and East Los Angeles, the cities of Santa Monica, Azusa, Burbank, Glendale, Monterey Park, and Culver City now had Mexican enclaves. However, according to Ríos-Bustamante and Castillo, "These new Mexican residence patterns were closely related to housing, income, and employment discrimination. Although Mexicans lived in most every city in the county, they were inevitably segregated into specific areas of those cities" (1986, 156).

In 1942, the United States initiated the Emergency Farm Labor Program, later known as the Bracero Program, through which it would recruit

4.6 million temporary agricultural workers from Mexico (Durand, Massey, and Parrado 1999). Although initiated as a temporary "emergency measure," it was renewed continuously until 1964. As John Laslett notes, "With time, an increasing number of migrants dropped out of the Bracero stream, heading for better jobs in Los Angeles, San Francisco, and other urban areas. By 1964, when Congress abolished the program, networks between the United States and sending villages throughout Mexico's central plateau were already in place, providing all the information and connections needed to keep the migrants coming, whether or not they had legal documents in hand" (1996, 10).

In the 1950s and 1960s, Mexicans in Los Angeles began to integrate into previously all-white suburbs. By the 1970s, the Mexican community had established a significant presence in suburban areas such as San Fernando, Long Beach, and El Monte. Laslett (1996) attributes suburbanization among Mexicans to the passage of the 1968 Open Housing Act, which abolished the racial covenants that had excluded Mexican and other minorities from many Los Angeles neighborhoods, as well as to the development of a growing Mexican American middle class, which included third- and fourth-generation Mexicans who could afford suburban homes.

In 1986, Congress passed and President Ronald Reagan signed into law the Immigration Reform and Control Act (IRCA), which included four main provisions: employer sanctions, resources for Border Patrol expansion, amnesty for long-term residents, and a legalization program for agricultural workers. IRCA offered amnesty to undocumented residents who could prove that they had been living continuously in the United States since 1982. The separate agricultural program provided legalization specifically for workers who could show prior employment in U.S. agriculture. More than 75 percent of those who received legal residence under these two provisions were immigrants from Mexico—more than 2 million people (Massey, Durand, and Malone 2002, 90).

By the 1990s, more than 2.5 million people, or 40 percent of Los Angeles County's residents, were of Mexican origin, and about half were immigrants (Ortiz 1996; Allen and Turner 2002).[5] The community had moved south and west of traditional settlements in downtown and East Los Angeles into South-Central Los Angeles and "into the previously white heartlands of the San Fernando Valley south and west, the Santa Clarita Valley to the north, and even the newly developed exurban settlements on the county's very northern boundaries" (Ortiz 1996, 267). Most Mexicans in Los Angeles come from the central states of Guanajuato, Michoacán, México, and Jalisco. Since 1965, many have also arrived from the southern state of Oaxaca (Gutierrez 1999).

Despite their long presence in the region, Mexican immigrants today remain at the bottom of Los Angeles's economic hierarchy, earning significantly less on average than either U.S.-born Mexicans or whites (Ortiz 1996; Sabagh and Bozorgmehr 2003). The wage gap between Mexican immigrants and U.S.-born whites narrows as an immigrant's duration of residence lengthens, allowing time for an enlargement of language and other skills. However, Mexican immigrants are concentrated in the city's lowest-paid and lowest-status occupations. Allen J. Scott's work on Los Angeles's manufacturing economy finds that "in particular, foreign-born Hispanics of both sexes now occupy the least favorable labor-market positions in the region's economy" (1996, 228).

Mexican Immigrants in New York

Mexicans constitute a growing presence in the New York area (Gutierrez 1999; Sabagh and Bozorgmehr 2003). However, in comparison to Los Angeles, New York City's Mexican population is relatively small, although it constitutes the third-largest Latino group in the city, after Puerto Ricans and Dominicans (Alonso-Zaldivar 1999). Immigrant-rights advocates note that Mexicans are the city's fastest-growing immigrant group (Mollenkopf, Ross, and Olson 1999, 4; McHugh 2000). In Mexican-origin population, New York is the sixth-largest U.S. metropolitan area, after Los Angeles, Chicago, Houston, San Francisco, and Dallas/Fort Worth (Alonso-Zaldivar 1999). New Jersey and New York together form the twelfth-most-popular U.S. receiving region for Mexican immigrants (Durand, Massey, and Parrado 1999). The 1990 Census counted 69,495 Mexican-origin individuals in New York City, almost 300 percent more than were found in 1980; the 2000 Census counted 186,876, for another 250 percent increase (Inter-University Program 2002). Because estimates hold that about half of New York's Mexican population lacks documentation, most researchers and observers believe these figures are an undercount and that the number is now closer to 250,000 and possibly as high as 300,000 (Mollenkopf, Ross, and Olson 1999). Moreover, experts believe that the Mexican-origin population will double again by 2010 (Getlin 2003, A-10.)

Compared to other ethnic groups in New York, Mexicans are recent arrivals. That is, most Mexican immigrants in the city arrived after 1985, and about half of the Mexican population migrated after 1990 (Robert Smith 1996; Gonzalez and McCoy 1998). Robert Smith (1996), an expert on New York's Mexican community, has traced its origins to two Mexican men brought to New York to work during World War II. These two men began a chain of migration from their native state of Puebla, in Mexico's Mixteca region, that still continues. Today, most immigrants to New York come from one of three states in that region: Puebla, Oaxaca, or Guerrero (Gonzalez and McCoy 1998).

When settling in New York, Mexican immigrants have usually moved into existing Latino neighborhoods, including the South Bronx; Jackson Heights, Queens; East Harlem; and Sunset Park, Brooklyn (Gonzalez and McCoy 1998; Getlin 2003). Sunset Park, for example, is home to a growing number of Mexican immigrants who work in the area's garment and manufacturing establishments (Gonzalez and McCoy 1998). However, Mexican immigrants are beginning to change the neighborhoods in which they settle. In Manhattan, on Third Avenue along East 116th Street, by the late 1990s Mexicans owned and ran more than ten stores selling tacos, cactus fruit, flowers, and even cowboy boots (McCoy 1998). Fifth Avenue in Sunset Park is dotted with Mexican-owned stores that sell tortillas and other Mexican foods. One Mexican immigrant woman explained to a *New York Daily News* reporter, "We began settling in Sunset Park because we didn't have to take the subway to get to work in the factories by the water and were far from *la migra* [immigration officers]" (Gonzalez and McCoy 1998, 6). By 1998, more than one-third of the two hundred students at Rafael Cordero Junior High School, a bilingual school on First Avenue in Manhattan, were Mexican immigrants (McCoy 1998, 35).

Although a middle-class population is emerging, many Mexican immigrants in New York are economically and educationally disadvantaged. Almost half have completed only nine or fewer years of school, and many are also young. The men tend to work in restaurants, storefront delicatessens, or construction. The women often work at home raising families or in factories. Labor statistics show that the median income for Mexicans in the city is $10,231, compared to the $22,402 for the average New Yorker (Getlin 2003). David Herszenhorn, for example, has noted that Mexican workers in New York are likely to "hold the lowest-paying jobs in the service industries—in kitchens, as cooks and dishwashers; in groceries, as clerks and stock handlers; behind the counters of delicatessens and pizza shops; in factories, or among construction and cleaning crews" (1998, 51). Close to one in three Mexicans in New York live at or below the poverty line (Getlin 2003). According to a reporter who interviewed Mexicans in New York City in 1999, many Mexican immigrants describe their lives as *esclavizante* (enslaving) because they work such long hours for little pay. One advocate for Mexican immigrants in New York explains, "Life is a kind of slavery that doesn't permit them to enjoy the things New York has to offer" (Alonso-Zaldivar 1999, A-1). It also permits little time or energy for civic involvement.

Religion plays a strong role in the lives of many Mexican immigrants in New York. Every year on December 12, the Feast of Our Lady of Guadalupe is celebrated, and in 1998 an estimated five thousand Mexicans attended a mass for that occasion held in St. Patrick's Cathedral (Claffey, Rafferty, and Singleton 1998). A Jesuit brother who directed one of the few social service organization that targets Mexican immigrants in New York emphasized the feast's importance: "This is the biggest religious holiday of the year. We say that we are more Guadalupanos than Mexicans. We say that because Our Lady of Guadalupe is our symbol, our identity. Our Lady of Guadalupe is stronger in the United States because she is the mother of the oppressed people, of the people who are being discriminated against. She is the protector, and so in New York City, when we are feeling we are suffering that kind of situation, she becomes a stronger symbol to follow" (Herszenhorn 1998, 51).

Some neighborhoods in New York have seen the development of hometown associations, a type of ethnic voluntary association that forms around specific communities in the sending region (Gonzalez and McCoy 1998; for an extensive study of the development and maintenance of such associations, see Robert Smith 1996, 1998). Mexican migrants from Chinantla, Puebla, meet regularly in Sunset Park to discuss the new schools and water systems that their U.S. wages are helping to build in Chinantla. More than five thousand of the town's population of seven thousand live in New York, which, according to some observers, has created "two societies that operate in tandem" (Alonso-Zaldivar 1999, A-1).

Comparison between Mexican Immigrants in New York and Los Angeles

The most prominent difference between the Mexican communities in New York and Los Angeles has to do with length of settlement. Whereas the Spanish-speaking community dates back several centuries in Los Angeles, Mexicans have had a significant presence in New York City only since the 1990s. The implications of this contrast are important: "Snapshots of *mexicano* New York reveal an experience much different from the one in Southern California, with its centuries of Mexican tradition and generations of Mexican Americans. In New York, all Mexicans are pioneers, facing jarring adjustments thousands of miles from home in a city that can be as treacherous as a February ice storm" (Alonso-Zaldivar 1999, A-1).

Thus it should come as no surprise that organizational life for Mexicans in the two cities is quite distinct. Mexicans in the West and Southwest have a long history of organizational development. Voluntary associations were very much a part of life there for the Spanish-speaking community in the early twentieth century, with the Alianza Hispano-Americana, the Club Anajuac, and the Sociedad Moctezuma providing social support and mutual aid. The Alianza Hispano-Americana was founded in 1894 in Arizona to provide life insurance as well as social activities to Mexican Americans in Tucson (Acosta 2002). The organization quickly spread throughout the Southwest, reaching as far as Texas and California. During the early 1900s, the Alianza annually sponsored a Mexican Independence Day celebration (Sanchez 1993).[6] "Indeed, the combination of rapid growth and increased importance of these organizations stands as one of the most striking features of Mexican social life during the period" (Ríos-Bustamante and Castillo 1986, 122–23). The Alianza Hispano-Americana remained active until the 1970s, although its national membership peaked at 17,366 in 1939. Furthermore, the organization established lodges in Mexico as well as the United States (Acosta 2002). The Federation of Spanish-Speaking Voters was the first explicitly political group established by the Mexican community in Los Angeles (Ríos-Bustamante and Castillo 1986). In 1930, it ran candidates for state and local offices, although none were elected.

In contrast, and in part because of their relatively short length of residence in New York, Mexicans there have not established a wide net of community organizations, and no Mexican-origin candidate has ever been elected to office. Interviews conducted for this study suggest that the disparity in the development of community institutions and candidate organizations serving Mexicans affects the level of political involvement in the two cities. Mexican immigrants in the Los Angeles sample were much more likely than were those in New York to have been contacted by an elected official. This finding is not surprising, given that representation by

Mexican-origin elected officials is so much greater in Los Angeles than New York. Although a causal relationship cannot be drawn as a result of the limited sample size, the connection between political mobilization of immigrants and elected representation by members of the same ethnic group deserves further study.[7]

Mexican immigrants in New York are also much farther away from their county of origin than are those residing in the western United States. Because of the proximity to Mexico, Mexican migrants in California, Arizona, New Mexico, and Texas often engage in circular migration. Mexicans who want to reach New York must first cross the U.S. border by land and then make the arduous trip by plane or land transportation (bus) to the East Coast (Alonso-Zaldivar 1999). As a result, Mexican immigrants in New York may not return to Mexico as frequently as do those residing in western and southwestern states. As their length of residence increases, Mexican immigrants in New York may find themselves naturalizing at higher rates than do those who live near the U.S.-Mexico border and who are thus able to travel back and forth more easily. This would allow the New York population to become a significant voting bloc in local elections. Despite their distance from Mexico, Mexican immigrants in New York maintain strong ties to their hometowns, especially by raising money for hometown civic projects (Robert Smith 1996).

Longer length of settlement among Mexicans in Los Angeles has also contributed to a longer history of Mexican American elected representation in that city compared to New York. As previously mentioned, no person of Mexican origin has ever been elected to citywide office in New York City. Nor are any New York State Assembly members from the city of Mexican origin. However, other, non-Mexican Latinos have won local and state elected offices in New York, including Puerto Ricans and a growing number of Dominicans (Graham 2001).

In contrast, Los Angeles has become a symbol of Latino electoral power. In 2005, Antonio Villaraigosa, son of a Mexican immigrant father and U.S.-born mother of Mexican origin, was elected mayor of Los Angeles. He defeated incumbent James Hahn to become the city's first Latino mayor since 1872. The two candidates were also opponents in 2001. According to an exit poll conducted by the Center for the Study of Los Angeles at Loyola Marymount University (2005), Villaraigosa received overwhelming support from Latino voters and strong support from whites and blacks. Although a majority of Asian Americans voted for Hahn, Villaraigosa's support among Asian Americans increased significantly between 2001 and 2005. Villaraigosa served as a member of the California State Assembly and as a member of the Los Angeles City Council before becoming mayor. Villaraigosa joins several other prominent Latino elected officials representing Los Angeles, including Speaker of the State Assembly Fabian Nuñez (D-Los Angeles), county sheriff Lee Baca, school board president José Huizar, and city council president Alex Padilla.

The growing number of Latino elected officials in Los Angeles, many of Mexican ancestry, can be attributed in large part to legal action by the Mexican American Legal Defense and Education Fund (MALDEF). In 1985, MALDEF and the Justice Department sued the city for violating the Voting Rights Act with a reapportionment plan that discriminated against Latinos. Five years later, MALDEF and the Justice Department challenged a redistricting plan adopted by the Los Angeles County Board of Supervisors, arguing that it diluted Latino voting strength (Weinstein 2005). Following MALDEF's victory in that case, the first Latina, Gloria Molina, was elected to the Los Angeles County Board of Supervisors. Although Latinos have made great strides in achieving political empowerment in Los Angeles over the past two decades, their electoral power continues to lag behind their demographic power. Latinos made up almost half of the population of the city of Los Angeles in 2005 but accounted for less than 30 percent of voters in the 2005 mayoral election (National Association of Latino Elected Officials 2005).

Similarities and Differences between Mexican and Chinese Groups

The Mexican and Chinese immigrant populations in the United States can be compared along a number of dimensions, particularly in terms of settlement histories, size relative to the general population, average socioeconomic resources, challenges of adapting to U.S. life, and attitudes toward the U.S. political system. Both groups have long histories in the United States. Whereas the first Chinese immigrants had to travel a long distance to arrive here, however, Mexicans already occupied territory that the United States absorbed through expansion, conquest, and colonization. In terms of population size, immigrants from Mexico and their descendants are the largest Latino group in the United States, and immigrants from China and their descendants are the largest Asian American group. However, the Mexican population greatly exceeds the Chinese population. Today, more than 25 million people in the United States are of Mexican origin, including 9 million immigrants, compared to only 2.7 million Chinese, 1.5 million of them immigrants (Malone et al. 2003, 2). Both are geographically concentrated in specific regions of the United States. Within each group, however, perceptible regional differences exist, especially in terms of socioeconomic status and duration of residence in the United States.

The groups differ in their attitudes toward the U.S. political system, undoubtedly influencing their political involvement. In the interviews, Chinese immigrants were much more likely than their Mexican counterparts to claim that they do not participate in U.S. politics because the system is difficult to understand. As a fifty-three-year-old Chinese immigrant woman who had lived in New York for thirty years explained, "Language. Number one problem. Because if you don't understand what is going on, how can you get involved?" A forty-eight-year-old Chinese immigrant man who had lived in Los Angeles for more than twenty years said that "culture has a lot to do with it. Because I don't quite understand that type of culture. Political culture. What is their motive being active in a political party? I have a hard time seeing myself becoming involved." And an eighty-year-old man who had lived in Los Angeles for thirteen years noted that "It's very hard. . . . The government makes it hard for us to learn about [the political system]. I mean, they don't even allow bilingual education in the schools. How do they expect us to know or learn?" It is likely that lack of familiarity with a democratic system, parties, and voting contributes to many Chinese immigrants' feeling that the U.S. political system is complicated. In contrast to the Chinese immigrants, only a few Mexican immigrants said that they had difficulty understanding the U.S. political system. This is not surprising, given Mexico's proximity to the United States and the resulting flow of information across the border. Further, the Mexican Constitution was modeled in part on the U.S. Constitution, and the government is a federal system with a president and a bicameral legislature.[8]

In their countries of origin, Mexican and Chinese immigrants have had distinct experiences with civic and community institutions, which may influence how they respond to opportunities for political involvement in the United States. Past political participation in the country of origin may facilitate an immigrant's willingness to join local organizations. In the interviews, Mexican immigrants were much more likely than their Chinese counterparts to have belonged to local organizations or clubs (sports club, women's group, church group, or political organization) before migrating to the United States. This study's sample is too small to infer causal relationships, but it is interesting that those Mexican immigrants who appear to have been the most active in organizations in Mexico were also active in organizations in the United States. For example, one immigrant woman who had been active in her church choir in Mexico also sang in the choir in New York, participated in a folk dancing group, and was active in a women's organization. Analysis of the Los Angeles Survey of Urban Inequality, a quantitative survey that includes a large sample of Chinese and Mexican immigrants, indicates that the Chinese in Los Angeles are much less likely to belong to community organizations (including religious institutions, unions, or political organizations) than are Mexicans, even when the factors of age, education, income, length of residence, English proficiency, and gender are taken into account (J. Wong 2000).

These similarities and differences as well as the growing U.S. presence of both groups make Chinese and Mexican immigrants ideal populations to study. In terms of identifying factors that influence immigrants to become politically engaged, a comparison of the two groups may facilitate the determination of which factors are specific to a particular group and which are influential across groups.

Conclusion

Individuals from Asia and Latin America account for the vast majority of today's U.S. immigrants. Moreover, newcomers from those areas enter the United States not only as immigrants but also as members of racial minorities. The conceptualization of these groups as racial minorities emerged through a process of racial formation, which Michael Omi and Howard Winant define as the social and historical process by which racial categories are created, changed, destroyed, and experienced (1994, 55). Throughout American history, the U.S. government's laws and policies and native-born Americans' biases have been deeply implicated in the process of racial formation for immigrants from Asia and Latin America. For example, the Naturalization Law of 1790 distinguished free "white" immigrants from others and helped to both create and support the development of racial categories in the United States. The racial minority status of Asian American and Latino immigrants has influenced their political incorporation, which has occurred in ways that are quite distinct from that their European counterparts. Thus, it is important to understand how the two groups have been racialized and how their racialization has affected their relationship with American civic institutions.

Studying Mexican and Chinese immigrants can lead to a better understanding of the political mobilization of racial minorities and the immigrant members of these minorities more generally. Chinese and Mexicans account for a large part of the U.S. immigrant stream. The largest group of Latinos consists of people of Mexican origin, and the largest Asian group consists of people of Chinese origin. Chinese and Mexicans in the United States share many experiences but also differ in their social histories and characteristics. Thus, an examination of these groups is likely to yield insights about which factors associated with political mobilization affect a particular national-origin group versus the factors that affect immigrants more generally.

Many immigrants, like those from China and Mexico, share a history of exclusion from the political system. Common characteristics, including lack of English language skills, citizenship, and acculturation may challenge political involvement in the United States for a great number of immigrants. Despite these similarities, different immigrant ethnic groups possess unique characteristics that are likely to affect their mobilization. For example, immigrant ethnic groups differ in size and geographic settlement patterns. In addition, internal diversity along economic, religious, and national-origin lines distinguish different immigrant ethnic groups. How do U.S. civic institutions help to mobilize immigrants into the political system? Do these institutions take into account the unique features of particular immigrant communities? Given that unprecedented numbers of immigrants are entering the United States and participating in U.S. politics at much lower rates than the general population, these are critical questions for the future health of the American democratic system.

3 Institutional Mobilization in an Era of Local Party Decline

*H*ow do U.S. civic institutions shape contemporary immigrants' political mobilization and participation, especially in the case of the majority of immigrants who are arriving from Asia and Latin America? Said a Mexican American community leader in East Los Angeles, "Stop anybody walking down the block, ask them, 'Can you please tell me where is the local chapter or the local office of the Democratic Party in your neighborhood?' Everybody will look at you with bewilderment: 'What is this crazy guy talking about?'" This comment illustrates party organizations' low profiles in immigrant neighborhoods. Immigrants are well aware that contemporary mainstream political parties are uninterested in mobilizing newly arrived minorities. When asked whether she felt like a part of the political system, a Chinese immigrant in Los Angeles responded, "No. We won't be elected officials, and they don't want our votes. How can we feel a part of the system? Besides, I don't even vote or participate in their functions. Of course I don't feel part of it." Mexican immigrants also feel that they have no say in and are not taken seriously by machines or local party organizations. In New York City, where neither the two major political parties nor local party clubs has conducted any substantial outreach to the Mexican population, a Mexican immigrant man said that it was difficult to get involved in the U.S. political system because it "doesn't care about us."

It is not merely the newly arrived who perceive the absence of political parties. According to a Latino leader, the political advocacy organization he heads in Los Angeles was established because the two major political parties were not supporting Latino political participation. His organization, which exists outside of the mainstream political machine or party structure, assisted nearly ninety thousand legal permanent residents in the 1990s with obtaining U.S. citizenship. The organization was started, he explained, "because a number of Latino elected officials saw the need for a networking organization of Latino elected officials, especially in light of the fact that the political party structures would not support Latinos." In sharp contrast to the experiences of past waves of European immigrants, political machines and party organizations today are no longer the driving force behind minority immigrant political mobilization.

Such perceptions might seem at odds with recent political campaigns that appear to have targeted the growing Latino population through Spanish-language campaign advertisements in Latino media markets and the inclusion of high-profile Latino elected officials and entertainers at campaign and party events. However, the outreach efforts in the 1990s—undertaken by the Democratic and Republican Parties in an attempt to attract Latino and Asian American immigrant populations—were largely symbolic and limited in their scope and for the most part fell short. In the 2000 presidential race, expectations that the two major political parties would court the Latino vote were dashed when, in the waning days of the campaign, the parties turned their attention to midwestern and southern battleground states, where, with the exception of Florida, the immigrant population is relatively small. In 2004, both parties claimed to be paying attention to Latinos, but members of the Latino community continued to express disappointment in party outreach efforts. The number of Latino delegates at the 2004 Democratic Convention actually declined from 2000, as did the time allotted to Latino speakers during prime time, leading Loretta Sanchez, a Democratic member of the House of Representatives, to complain that Latinos did not receive enough time at the podium (Ratcliffe 2004, A-3).

Mainstream political parties today generally have been slower to respond to contemporary immigrants than had been the case with earlier groups. The nature of political party campaigning at the beginning of the twenty-first century is different than it was one hundred, fifty, or even twenty-five years ago. The party structure is weak at the local level, and outreach strategies have shifted dramatically. Today, parties primarily use direct-mail and media campaigns that target only those registered voters who are the most likely to vote, a group that includes few immigrants. The potential for mass-mobilization efforts—including the type of face-to-face mobilization at the neighborhood level that in the past was standard practice for reaching European immigrants—has been overlooked in favor of party activity confined primarily to the airwaves.

Parties also have incentives to distance themselves from minority immigrants, including the desire to maintain existing party coalitions and to appeal to median voters and assumptions about apathy among immigrants. Because whites are overrepresented among voters, parties and candidates may be reluctant to fully embrace newcomers who trigger hostile attitudes among that mainstream electorate. This disincentive is reinforced by popular and even academic perceptions that immigrants are apathetic about taking a role in politics or that even if they did take an interest, there are no guarantees about how they might vote. Facing such uncertainties, parties are unwilling to expend scarce resources to cultivate relatively unpredictable groups. As Asian American and Latino immigrants gradually become more powerful demographically and more involved in the political system, the two parties may turn their attention to these groups. Current evidence, however, raises the possibility that their efforts to appeal to immigrants will be limited in terms of mass mobilization.

The Historical Role of Parties & Immigrant Mobilization

The widespread perception among immigrants and immigrant-community leaders that the Republican and Democratic Parties are not doing much to mobilize immigrants is surprising given what we know about the past political mobilization of European immigrants. The role of machines in mobilizing turn-of-the-century European immigrants is well documented in historical accounts and is firmly entrenched in the popular imagination (Cornwell 1960; Dahl 1961).[1] The late 1860s to the early 1890s is considered the golden age of political parties (Reichley 1992).[2] For the 1868 New York gubernatorial campaign, the Tammany machine recruited more than forty thousand immigrant voters (Erie 1988, 10). By the first decades of the 1900s, the political recruitment of immigrants had become the center of American party politics. Parties and politicians offered immigrants patronage jobs and social services in exchange for their participation and loyalty in the voting booth (Dahl 1961). "In a nonbureaucratic manner that placed a premium on personal loyalty and left much room for corruption, the party served its constituents by facilitating naturalization, finding jobs, offering relief in times of distress, and acting as an intermediary with higher authorities" (Archdeacon 1983, 100).

In a competitive two-party system, parties usually compete for the loyalty of potential voters in an attempt to expand their electoral bases. Whatever else European immigrants lacked in the late 1800s and early 1900s, they possessed numerical power (Dahl 1961). Kristi Andersen notes that "a half million to a million potential voters . . . disembarked in this country every year between 1890 and 1910," and the Democrats actively recruited these new potential supporters (1979, 22, 25). These numbers may have helped European immigrants overcome the racial biases of the turn of the last century. The mobilization of immigrants was so great that Andersen attributes the New Deal partisan realignment to the Democratic Party's political incorporation of the foreign-born. Politicians made it easy for immigrants to become citizens, encouraged them to register to vote, put them on the party rolls, and aided them in meeting the challenges of poverty, distance from their homelands, and low social position (Dahl 1961; Andersen 1979). To obtain and hold the votes, political leaders rewarded newcomers with city jobs (Dahl 1961, 34). As goods and services were exchanged for votes, political machines became the mediating institution between immigrants and the U.S. political system (Skerry 1993).

That role, while a historic fact, is somewhat exaggerated (Erie 1988; C. Stone 1996). In reality, parties often worked in concert with local organizations, such as unions and churches (Sterne 2001). The inclusive nature of political machines has also been romanticized. Parties mobilized some groups of European immigrants when it was to their advantage but failed to mobilize others when no obvious benefit existed. Political competition and the quest for votes, not commitments to inclusion, drove outreach to immigrants (C. Stone 1996). Moreover, immigrants have never been passive recipients of political mobilization. Ann Chih Lin (forthcoming) argues that European immigrants did not occupy the submissive role accorded them in the traditional story of urban machines that incorporated newcomers politically while simultaneously exploiting them for votes. She points out that immigrant groups developed their own community institutions, such as ethnic social clubs, which existed outside of the machine structure and furthered the group's interests. Lin also reminds us that "machines acted strategically to suppress immigrant votes when it was in their interest to do so" (10). Political machines were quite capable of abandoning their potential immigrant constituencies when expediency demanded it. Despite these significant revisions to the classic political-machine narrative, machines and parties clearly played a critical role in politically incorporating European immigrants until the middle of the twentieth century.

Thus it is natural to assume that political mobilization and immigrant political mobilization in particular are the purview of the mainstream parties (Dahl 1961; Banfield and Wilson 1963; Glazer and Moynihan 1964). Parties are characterized as critical institutions for ensuring democracy and representation for diverse elements in American society (Rossiter 1960; Ladd and Hadley 1975). In their overview of American parties, Samuel J. Eldersveld and Hanes Walton Jr. (2000, 9) described a party as "a group that competes for political power by contesting elections, mobilizing social interests, and advocating ideological positions, thus linking citizens to the political system." Similarly, Samuel Huntington (1968, 401) describes the party system as an important foundation of a stable polity, "capable of structuring the participation of new groups in politics." This view suggests that powerful incentives exist for political machines and party organizations to bring potential voters or blocs of voters, such as immigrants, into the political system to build winning coalitions. It also suggests that a failure to do so would have serious consequences for the American polity.

Contemporary Political Parties: Changing Contexts, Strategies, Incentives, & Constraints

Despite parties' importance for the stability of the polity, their historical involvement in immigrant political mobilization, and their seeming incentives to mobilize immigrants, it is unlikely that even the limited pattern of mobilization experienced by European immigrants in the early twentieth century will repeat. Why are the Republican and Democratic Parties so absent today? There are at least three factors: (1) weakened local party structure and changing campaign tactics; (2) selective mobilization strategies and maintenance of existing party coalitions; (3) assumptions about political attitudes among immigrants and median voters.

1. Weakened Local Party Structure and Changing Campaign Tactics

The golden age of political parties coincided with the height of European immigration to the United States. From 1850 to 1930, the foreign-born population of the United States increased from 2 million to 14 million, and by 1890 immigrants accounted for nearly 15 percent of the entire U.S. population (Gibson and Lennon 1999, 3). From that year until 1910, party machines governed 75 percent of major U.S. cities (Reichley 1992, 174). Indeed, European immigrants and their children were the lifeblood of many urban party machines (Andersen 1979). A general decline in local party strength was set in motion by Progressive Era reforms and continued through the 1960s and 1970s, just as immigrants from Asia and Latin America were entering the country at unprecedented levels (Ceaser 1978; R. Scott and Hrebenar 1984; Wattenberg 1994; Skocpol 1999a; J. Green and Farmer 2003). The absence of local political machines and parties in the lives of contemporary immigrants distinguishes their experiences from those of their European predecessors. How did this change in political context come about?

Although they did not undermine local party strength immediately, Progressive Era reforms had a cumulative weakening effect on parties, particularly in the western states. One of the most critical changes in election procedures introduced by Progressive Era reformers was the introduction of the Australian ballot in 1880. The Australian ballot, printed with all of the candidates' names and marked by voters in secret, encouraged more split-ticket voting. Coupled with the widespread implementation of nonpartisan elections for local office, this electoral reform reduced parties' control over ballot procedures and election outcomes (Reichley 1992). The introduction of direct primaries in the early 1900s further diluted local party control over nominations, prompting political scientist David Truman to assert that "The direct primary has been most potent in a complex of forces pushing towards the disintegration of the party" (quoted in Reichley 1992, 170).

Many urban machines survived an earlier wave of assaults by Progressives, but a new wave of reformers seeking to eliminate inefficiency and corruption by attacking state and local machines emerged in the aftermath of World War II. They pressed for the professionalization of state and local workforces by implementing merit-based systems, undermining the machines' most powerful resource—local patronage (R. Scott and Hrebenar 1984; J. Green and Farmer 2003). Local party decline is attributed to several other factors, including the federal government's expanding role in social and economic redistribution programs and the growth of alternative political organizations, such as interest groups (R. Scott and Hrebenar 1984; Reichley 1992).

The rise of candidate-centered campaigns has also contributed to a weakening of local party organizations (Wattenberg 1994). In 1913, the adoption of the Seventeenth Amendment, allowing for the direct election of senators, encouraged campaigns around specific candidates, rather than a party label. Building on support by the general public and political activists for reforms to encourage more participatory democracy, the parties, particularly the Democrats, adopted new rules of nomination in the 1970s that gave increased power to individual candidates and their campaign organizations, rather than to local party leaders. These rule changes coincided with larger social trends that weakened local political machines throughout the 1970s, including suburbanization that moved people outside of the cities and traditional machine territories. Technological changes increased the importance of mass media marketing and further focused the American public on the image and characteristics of individual candidates. Finally, lack of electoral competition exacerbated this decline. In 2004, only 10 percent of elections for the House of Representatives were considered competitive, a drop from previous recent elections (Page 2004). Redistricting that creates a bias in favor of incumbents has led parties, which are already oriented toward national politics, to devote their energies to a handful of competitive congressional races, while paying far less attention to the majority of Americans who live in noncompetitive districts.[3] Lack of competition is also related to low rates of turnout in local elections (Hajnal, Lewis, and Louch 2002). Parties do not need to mobilize voters when the outcome is assured.

The end of the twentieth century witnessed a limited revitalization of political parties driven by the expansion and institutionalization of the national committees rather than by state and local party organizations (J. Green and Herrnson 2002). The Democratic and Republican National Committees acquired permanent headquarters and larger professional staffs, and they are now major fund-raisers and the purveyors of critical campaign services (Reichley 1992; J. Green and Herrnson 2002; Dulio and Thurber 2003). However, the parties' strategies for revitalization focused on technical and professional sophistication rather than grassroots organization (Reichley 1992). Both parties built sophisticated production facilities at their national headquarters, instituted large-scale direct-mail campaigns, and hired professional pollsters and consultants (Dulio and Thurber 2003). By the end of the twentieth century, personal contact by neighborhood party activists had become largely a thing of the past, replaced by "selective voter activation" that uses sophisticated phone and direct-mailing techniques and media advertisements to narrowly target those individuals most likely to support a particular candidate or policy issue (Conway 2001, 84).

These new high-tech outreach strategies stand in unmistakable contrast to those of the past. Machines were effective because party activists spent the time and effort to become familiar with residents of a precinct and consequently were able to mobilize immigrants through personal contacts, make ethnic appeals based on knowledge of a particular neighborhood community, and work closely with community-based institutions (Skocpol 1999a; Conway 2001). However, direct-mail and mass-media campaigns are much less effective in mobilizing the electorate at the local level. With a few exceptions, such as the 1992 and 2000 elections, vote turnout and other types of political participation are characterized by a dramatic and ongoing pattern of decline (Shea 2003, 292–93).[4]

Local party organizations and machines were hit hard by these changes, and although the midcentury reforms addressed the corrupt practices associated with traditional machines, they also exacted a price in terms of citizens' personal contact with parties, one of people's primary connections with the larger political system. Writing in the 1980s, Ruth Scott and Ronald Hrebenar describe the consequences of these changes for the population as a whole and for immigrants in particular: "Contemporary parties have lost their historical role of socializing Americans into the political system. . . . The replacement of the patronage system with the merit system has further reduced the parties' opportunities to function as socializers. People no longer rely on parties for their initiation into politics, for ombudsman services, or for large numbers of patronage jobs. . . . Are any of today's immigrants introduced to American politics and political traditions through the medium of the Republican or Democratic parties?" (1984, 15–16).

Despite these broad changes in the party system, urban machines remain active in some regions, including New York City (Mollenkopf 1992, 77; Jones-Correa 1998; Sanjek 1998). James Q. Wilson notes that "the political machines, once a conspicuous feature of urban and country life, are now found in relatively few places . . . but party organizations do exist . . . and they perform a variety of functions, ranging from candidate endorsement through fund raising to systematic canvassing" (1995, 95). However, given the changing political environment, even in places where local party machines remain, they are on the defensive, fighting for their survival (Shea 2003).

2. *Selective Mobilization Strategies and Maintenance of Existing Party Coalitions*

In their quest to exploit new technologies and implement national-level strategies, parties have failed to develop a mass base of active members (J. Green and Herrnson 2002). These developments weaken the connections to the political parties for all but the most elite citizens, a particularly serious and harmful development for contemporary immigrants, whose connection to the political system is even more tenuous than that of other Americans. When deciding whom to mobilize, political leaders focus their efforts strategically to expend the least effort and resources to achieve the greatest effect. According to Steven J. Rosenstone and John Mark Hansen, "The wealthy, the educated, and the partisan are more likely to be targeted for mobilization than the poor, the uneducated, and the uncommitted" (1993, 33). In the political system, having few economic and educational resources is clearly a detriment, and it weighs heavily on immigrants because they are among the least advantaged members of society.

Many immigrants also lack citizenship (and therefore voting power), English language skills, and an understanding of the U.S. political system, all of which makes them even less desirable targets for mobilization by parties and political leaders.[5] In general, parties focus on upcoming elections to the detriment of long-term planning that would have to consider changing demographics. When taking this short-term approach, cultivation of a group that contains a large number of people who are ineligible to vote is not likely to seem to be a viable tactic. Reuel Rogers (2000b) has witnessed this in central Brooklyn, where the Democratic organization selectively mobilizes traditional supporters under the assumption that they are the segment of the population most likely to vote and to vote as they have done in the past—for Democrats. The organization shuns the city's many Afro-Caribbean residents, who are perceived as noncitizens (and hence ineligible to vote) or newcomers to the political system (and hence unorganized or uninterested or, worse yet, unaligned with a party and thus open to non-Democratic recruitment).

Especially where interparty competition is low, entrenched machines may be indifferent or even hostile to immigrant mobilization because they anticipate that newcomers will disrupt the existing power structure and coalition base (Mollenkopf 1992, 79; Jones-Correa 1998; Rogers 2000b). In his study of political participation of Afro-Caribbean immigrants in

New York, Rogers (2000b), observes that although the Democratic Party in Brooklyn dominates the borough, its growing Afro-Caribbean population has the potential to cause an insurgency within the party; as a result, few attempts to mobilize these newcomers occur. The executive director of a political empowerment organization in New York's Chinatown suggested that neither party in New York wants to mobilize Asian American immigrants because of a fear of disrupting existing coalitions: "The Republicans are afraid to register more people. It's a five-to-one Democratic city; there'll be more Democrats registered. But for the [Democratic] City Council, they'd rather keep it the same way that it is, because they got elected this way, so why should they change?"

3.   *Assumptions about Political Attitudes among Immigrants and White Swing Voters*

The stereotype of minority immigrants as apolitical individuals may also dissuade parties from mobilizing immigrants. Perceptions that certain racial or ethnic minorities are apathetic or preoccupied with homeland politics have served to discourage parties from mobilizing those groups. An elected official's staffer has described Afro-Caribbean immigrants in Brooklyn as "docile" (Rogers 2000b, 95). Michael Jones-Correa, who studies Latinos in Queens, observes that the entrenched Democratic Party there long ignored Latinos because they were perceived to be apolitical. He spoke with politicians in Queens who made it clear that they would not mobilize Latinos until they became registered voters: "Claire Shulman, the Queens borough president, reportedly asked one Latino activist why Queens politicians should pay attention to Latinos when they don't vote. She said she would deal with Latinos when they voted, and they don't vote now." He also quoted a Democratic district leader who said, "For years I have heard talk about [Latinos] delivering votes. . . . In all my years as district leader, I haven't seen anyone deliver more than a pizza" (1998, 79). Such comments fail to acknowledge the possibility that Latinos were not voting because they were not being mobilized and place the blame for lack of participation on immigrant attitudes alone rather than on the political system and political leadership.

Furthermore, immigrants, especially those from Latin America and the Caribbean, are often assumed to be loyal to the Democrats; consequently, little is done to woo their votes. Jones-Correa observes that limited resources are not wasted on the already committed: "The Democratic

Party could register and mobilize Latino voters, but mobilization would only mean additional competition for scarce resources" because the Latinos who do participate tend to be Democrats anyway (1998, 80).

Scholars—perhaps inadvertently—also perpetuate the idea that immigrants are politically apathetic. Peter Skerry (1993, 222) describes the Mexican American community in Los Angeles as "relatively unorganized" and "passive." These descriptions help to wrongly attribute minority immigrants' lack of participation to cultural characteristics while avoiding the tough question of whether the lack of mobilization by political institutions might be at the root of the problem. In fact, the long history of political activism within Asian American and Latino immigrant communities counters assumptions about apathy. Although many are barred from voting because they fail to meet eligibility requirements, both groups have participated in politics through civil disobedience, civil rights litigation, and boycotting (see Muñoz 1989; Perea et al. 2000; Lien 2001). Latino and Asian American immigrants have historically worked for political change through their participation in the labor movement (K. Wong 1994). More recently, members of the two groups have worked together on issues related to political redistricting (Saito 2003).

Political parties may also make assumptions about white swing voters' attitudes about racial minorities and tailor behavior toward those minorities accordingly. Although the political science literature on traditional party structure contends that minorities will be represented in a competitive party system, political parties historically have failed to incorporate racial minorities (Pinderhughes 1987; Jones-Correa 1998; Frymer 1999; Rogers 2000a, b). Paul Frymer notes that the mainstream U.S. parties developed in part to minimize divisive racial issues among white voters. Martin Van Buren created an electoral coalition that emphasized the distribution of power and was neutral on slavery as a means of uniting southern slave owners and northern voters indifferent or opposed to slavery. In reaction, Whigs also sought to minimize the issue of slavery (1999, 36). During the 1930s, black voters joined the Democratic Party, often providing critical votes in close state and local elections. Yet party leaders sought to preserve whites' political dominance within the party and to defend their position vis-à-vis the black newcomers (Reichley 1992, 259). In the case of Latinos, before the late 1980s, the parties paid scant attention to the group and even worked to actively depress Latino political participation (de la Garza and DeSipio 1996).

Racial division and exclusion continue today, and white racial attitudes remain strong determinants of party behavior. To build their electoral bases, parties appeal to moderate whites because white voters make up the majority of the electorate. Party leaders believe that if they appeal to blacks, whites will defect as a consequence of hostility toward programs perceived as benefiting blacks. "The behavior of party leaders reflects their belief that the nation is divided along racial lines, and that the prominence of racial issues is bound to disadvantage one of the parties in a system of two-party competition. . . . The stakes of a winner-take-all electoral system only heighten this ambivalence, since it is crucial for party leaders to respond to the opinions of the median voter. These concerns lead party leaders to attempt to manipulate the two-party system in a manner that denies the primacy of race, all the while confirming that very primacy" (Frymer 1999, 34). To preserve their coalitions and appeal to (white) swing voters, the Democratic and Republican Parties marginalize black interests. Both give preference to white voters, who are perceived as being ambivalent or even hostile toward blacks. Thus, the parties make little effort to represent policy perspectives that would benefit blacks or to mobilize the black community toward political participation.

Because antiblack attitudes are closely associated with hostility toward other racial minority groups and immigration (Burns and Gimpel 2000, 218), we can extend Frymer's argument to minority immigrants. This is not to say that discrimination against Latinos and Asian Americans mirrors that against African Americans. Each group faces distinct stereotypes as well as different forms and levels of racism (C. Kim 1999; T. Lee 2000),[6] but white hostility toward Asian American and Latino immigrants is well documented (R. Lee 1999; Santa Ana 2002). As levels of immigration to the United States have increased, so have negative attitudes toward immigrants, and this hostility is not race-neutral. Public opinion surveys conducted from 1984 to 1995 suggest that Americans believed that immigration from Europe was "at about the right level" but that immigration from Asia and Latin America was "too high" (Lapinski et al. 1997). Further, racial stereotypes of Latinos are associated with negative attitudes toward immigration (Burns and Gimpel 2000). The racial minority status of many immigrants and the racial stereotypes that they face are likely to influence party organizations to distance themselves from the Asian American and in some cases Latino immigrant communities. The parties are especially likely to distance themselves from those immigrants who generate negative attitudes among voters—that is, those who are poor or without documents.

In the case of Latino immigrants, fears of alienating white swing voters might explain why the parties and candidates shied away from discussing legalization for undocumented immigrants during the 2004 campaigns. Instead, the candidates opted to reach out using symbols of inclusion and emphasized traditional family values and education. This rhetorical and symbolic strategy allowed them to appeal to Latinos generally without offending white swing voters by offering substantive policies that would benefit undocumented Latinos, an unpopular group. Although party leaders are not likely completely to reject the growing Latino community, beliefs about white swing voters' racial attitudes may cause officials to distance themselves from some unpopular segments of the community.

California illustrates the incentive for parties to distance themselves from racial minorities. The state has some significant gaps in public opinion between whites and other racial groups (Hajnal and Baldassare 2001). Whites (24 percent) are more likely than blacks (14 percent), Asians (13 percent), or Latinos (13 percent) to agree that ethnic and racial change is bad for their region. When asked whether immigrants today constitute a burden on California, 22 percent of Latinos, 29 percent of Asians, and 45 percent of blacks responded in the affirmative, whereas a majority of whites (53 percent) did so. Moreover, the public-opinion divide was exacerbated by the fact that although whites made up just 54 percent of all adults in California in 2000, they accounted for 70 percent of all voters.

Rogers makes the important point that "whatever the impetus for the party's practice of selective mobilization, then, it only reinforces racially stratifying trends and patterns of participation—New York's political insiders are preponderantly white, while the outsiders and marginal players are mostly nonwhite" (2000b, 98). Though parties may not discriminate against immigrants based on race, the fact that the majority of all immigrants are nonwhite (from Latin America, Asia, Africa, and the Caribbean) means that lack of mobilization in immigrant communities is likely to lead to political outcomes that are unequal across racial groups. In short, even when race issues do not directly determine party behavior, they can negatively affect mobilization in immigrant communities of color.

Party Outreach: Symbolic Politics versus Mass Mobilization

Influenced by the three factors that act as disincentives and constraints impeding mainstream parties from mobilizing immigrant communities, the national mainstream parties have largely ignored minorities and especially minority immigrants. Gradual changes have been apparent since the late 1980s, but efforts continue to be limited primarily to symbolic gestures rather than the type of mass mobilization of immigrants that was apparent in the nineteenth and early twentieth centuries. In 2000, researchers and pundits proclaimed that a genuine change in party behavior was taking place because, it was believed, the Democratic and Republican Parties were finally taking minority populations seriously. In retrospect, it appears that the efforts in that campaign represented merely more of the same, and 2004 also saw no significant changes. An analysis of national party strategies and activities clearly demonstrates how the nationalization of parties has contributed to lack of immigrant mobilization at the local level. Neither major party has paid attention to the specific characteristics of Asian American or Latino immigrant populations, nor have the parties expended resources on face-to-face mobilization. Although both the Democrats and the Republicans emphasized mobilization during the 2004 campaign, the vast majority of their resources went to media campaigns rather than mobilization (J. Green 2004). The failure is most apparent in the political parties' treatment of the Latino community.[7]

Political Party Outreach to Latinos

Despite Latinos' long presence in the United States, political parties have throughout most of the nation's history worked actively to demobilize Latinos from participating in the political system, using such measures as English-literacy requirements and blatant discrimination (de la Garza and DeSipio 1996, 14; DeSipio 1996). With the exception of the 1960 presidential race, notable for the Kennedy campaign's effort to reach Latino voters via local Viva Kennedy! clubs, mainstream party interest in Latinos was virtually nonexistent before 1988 (DeSipio and de la Garza 2005). That year, Latino leaders and organizations worked to develop a more positive relationship between Latino communities and the political parties by attempting to influence party policy priorities and asking the parties to heed Latino concerns (DeSipio and Rocha 1992).

The 1988 election proved to be a harbinger of future party response to the Latino community. Both parties claimed to be making an effort to recruit Latino voters. Although they granted Latinos greater visibility, neither party addressed Latino issues or invested resources in mobilizing or increasing Latino voter turnout. Most party appeals to Latinos consisted of symbolic outreach requiring minimal time, resources, and policy commitments (DeSipio and Rocha 1992, 15). Democratic candidate Michael Dukakis spoke Spanish on occasion and emphasized his immigrant ancestry (DeSipio and Rocha 1992). The Dukakis campaign ran Spanish-language advertisements and established Viva Dukakis clubs, but these were underfunded and controlled primarily by Dukakis staffers in Boston (DeSipio and Rocha 1992, 16, 175). Republican presidential candidate George H. W. Bush emphasized his family's ties to the Latino community through his son, Jeb, who is bilingual, and Jeb's wife, Columba, who is Mexican American. The party recruited Latinos as state-level party organizers and tried to improve the party's image among non-Cuban Latino groups, which had traditionally shunned the Republicans (DeSipio and Rocha 1992).

In 1992, the Republican Party again used the Spanish-language media, and Bush, now the incumbent, continued to emphasize his familial ties to the Latino community. The Republicans again chose a prominent member of the Latino community, Gloria Gonzalez-Roemer, to second the presidential nomination. Latino participation at the national convention was greater than in years past, yet no Latino-specific issues were included in the convention messages (de la Garza and DeSipio 1996). Instead, the Republican Party platform included strong support for increased border control, and convention speakers voiced their concerns that immigrants were abusing the American social welfare system (Elder 1999).

The Democrats, for their part, condemned the Republican policies that Latinos viewed as hostile, but the party did not break from tradition in terms of advocating for Latino-specific issues such as more inclusive language policies and immigrant rights (Elder 1999). Instead, much of Bill Clinton's campaign revolved around the rhetoric of inclusion while deemphasizing the party's links with specific minority communities: "Clinton downplayed traditional Democratic party efforts to seek minority votes with specialized messages" (DeSipio, de la Garza, and Setzler 1999, 12). This would prove a new strategy (de la Garza and DeSipio 1996; DeSipio, de la Garza, and Setzler 1999).

Although proposals of specific interest to the Latino community were absent, symbols of Latino inclusion were quite apparent. For example, Clinton introduced his national education plan at the predominantly Latino East Los Angeles College. In terms of substantive efforts, a few high profile and prominent Latinos received key or leadership positions:

Gloria Molina was Rules Committee cochair, and Edward Roybal served as convention cochair. However, the Latinos who spoke at the Democratic National Convention did so only outside of prime time. Adelante con Clinton y Gore (Forward with Clinton and Gore) clubs received party support in the most competitive states but were not effective for mobilization elsewhere. Perhaps the most substantive Democratic efforts were the monitoring of polling places to ensure that Latinos were not unfairly disqualified from voting and the establishment of a national Hispanic voting rights hotline. The lack of consistent mobilization in Latino neighborhoods by either party was apparent throughout the campaign. Indeed, fewer eligible Latinos voted in 1992 than had voted in 1988 (de la Garza and DeSipio 1996).

By 1996, the Republican Party had given up efforts to win Latinos on the basis of substantive policy appeals (Elder 1999). Instead, following close on the heels of congressional Republicans' adoption of the Contract with America and the passage of the Republican-supported Illegal Immigration Reform and Immigration Responsibility Act, the Republican platform contained measures Latinos opposed. The offending proposals included termination of the automatic citizenship accorded U.S.-born children of undocumented immigrants and the right of those children to a public education (Elder 1999; DeSipio 2001). This hard-line stance made it difficult to employ symbolic outreach at their national convention, where, not surprisingly, Latino delegates were noticeably absent (DeSipio, de la Garza, and Setzler 1999, 21). By 1998, most of the anti-immigrant policies had been reversed, but in the eyes of many Latinos, the Republicans' image had suffered (Elder 1999; Neal 2003; R. Ramirez forthcoming).[8]

In 1996, the Democratic Party sought to persuade Latinos to join by arguing that Republican attacks could best be countered by a Democratic president. Laurel Elizabeth Elder's interviews with Democratic Party leaders reveal that the party's strategy throughout the 1990s was to "exploit the Republican Party's alienation of Hispanic voters, without [offering] any specific policies to further the interests of Hispanics themselves" (1999, 271). Even though Latinos already occupied key positions in the Clinton administration, on the Democratic National Committee, and as Democratic elected officials at various levels of government (DeSipio, de la Garza, and Setzler 1999), the Democrats implemented decidedly mixed policies. They opposed Republican attempts to completely dismantle bilingual programs and services but avoided addressing immigrant-rights issues and even called for stronger border controls and helped to enact laws that denied legal immigrants government benefits (Elder 1999).

The 1996 Democratic campaign was, once again, heavily symbolic. A memo circulated among Latino Democratic National Committee members emphasized that "visually, Latinos needed to see the president standing in Latino neighborhoods; viscerally, they needed to see themselves or people who looked like them in party ads" (Subervi-Vélez and Connaughton 1999, 53). The Democratic Party established the Office of Latino Outreach, staffed by Latinos, which coordinated the party's outreach strategy, as well as Adelante con Clinton clubs in twenty locales nationwide, and it committed $2.5 million (out of a $217 million war chest) to run a Spanish-language media campaign. However, these efforts targeted registered Latino voters. Federico A. Subervi-Vélez and Stacey L. Connaughton note that the strategy during the Clinton reelection campaign was "to have the president's carefully constructed messages repeatedly disseminated only to those registered Latino voters most likely to influence the campaign by tipping the electoral college balance in their respective states" (1999, 62).

Despite the use of Spanish-language media by both parties, campaign strategies were largely devoid of mass mobilization efforts aimed at Latinos. A correspondent for Univisión, the largest Spanish-language television station in the United States, noted that during the 1990s, top officials from both parties contacted the station, a dramatic change from the 1980s, when "no one in Washington would return our calls" (Armando Guzmán quoted in Elder 1999, 285). However, the campaigns continued selectively to target constituencies, and in the case of Latinos, the focus was on Latinos who were already mobilized. The 1996 campaign failed to make voters out of Latino nonvoters (DeSipio, de la Garza, and Setzler 1999, 12–13).

In sum, despite the Republican Contract with America in the middle of the decade, the 1990s saw the Democratic and Republican Parties gradually paying greater attention to the Latino population, but this development manifested primarily in terms of symbolic visibility at the state and national levels. However, consistent with their tendency to selectively mobilize voters, both parties continued to shun mass mobilization and to target those Latinos most likely to vote. Despite the utilization of Spanish-language media, parties did not expend resources in an attempt to connect with Latinos not yet mobilized, preferring instead to focus on partisan supporters through increasingly centralized and high-tech strategies. Further, perhaps because they feared alienating white swing voters, neither party offered substantive policy benefits aimed directly at the Latino community. Consequently, the Republican and Democratic Parties played a minimal role in facilitating the political involvement of most Latinos and particularly Latino immigrants.

In 2000, researchers and pundits proclaimed that the Latino population, long considered a sleeping giant in American politics, had awakened, and the Democratic and Republican Parties were going to heed the realities of demographic change. For the first time in history, Latinos outnumbered black Americans, becoming the country's largest minority at more than 12 percent of the population. Voter-registration rates for Latinos had been rising consistently for the previous twenty years, as had their share of the national electorate. In 1976, Latinos comprised 2.4 percent of the national electorate; by 2000, that figure was estimated at 7 percent, an increase of 300 percent over twenty-four years (Fraga and Ramirez 2000). Significantly, Latinos were concentrated in the states with the largest numbers of electoral votes.

Analysts of the 2000 election tend to agree that "more than in any previous national election, Latinos gained the direct attention of the major Democratic and Republican candidates for president" (Fraga and Ramirez 2000, 1). The campaigns utilized the Spanish-language media more than ever before, and both presidential candidates used Spanish in their speeches. George W. Bush addressed Latino crowds with, "Mi corazón es Hispano" (My heart is Hispanic), and Al Gore introduced himself by saying, "Llamáme Alberto" (Call me Alberto). A Ganamos con Gore! (Let's Win with Gore) subcampaign organization was set up. The Bush team hired Sonia Martinez, a Mexican American immigrant, as its bilingual public-relations spokesperson (DeSipio and de la Garza 2005). At the conventions, Latinos and Latino symbols were very visible. California's lieutenant governor, Cruz Bustamante, one of the country's most prominent Latino politicians, spoke during prime time the night that Gore accepted the Democratic nomination, and Abel Maldonado, a Republican member of the California Assembly, gave a speech in Spanish on the Republican Convention's final night. The Mexican American band Los Lobos played for the Democrats, and Mexican singer Vicente Fernandez entertained the Republican delegates. Although the Democrats had four hundred Latino delegates on the floor compared to the GOP's seventy-three, Latino Republican delegates reported that they sensed a new openness their party (LeDuc and Melton 2000).

In marked contrast to the 1990s, anti-immigrant and anti-Latino rhetoric did not characterize the policy debates in the 2000 election, which was a step—albeit a weak one—toward greater inclusion. Both Gore and Bush underscored tolerance toward immigrants. The Bush campaign proposed new resources for processing naturalization claims, and although it did not put forth policies that aimed to benefit Latinos in particular, the campaign sought to appeal to the group by emphasizing compassionate conservatism and family values (DeSipio and de la Garza 2005, 44). The Gore campaign supported the Latino Immigrant Fairness Act, a legalization program, and proposed more liberal education and healthcare policies that would likely appeal to Latino voters (DeSipio and de la Garza 2005). Luis Fraga and David Leal contend that the Bush campaign in particular engaged in a strategy of rhetorical and symbolic inclusion that was designed reach out to Latinos without alienating median white voters: "There are demonstrations of understanding and respect for Latinos and their communities. However, the material interests of many of these voters, such as for English language training, long-term immigration reform, increased access to adequate health insurance, and greater opportunities for home ownership, are rarely mentioned, if at all. When they are mentioned, such as with early descriptions of educational reform resulting in the No Child Left Behind Act and the need to rethink temporary guest worker programs, the details of funding and implementation are not specified" (2004, 309).

Latino leaders and community members welcomed the parties' long-awaited efforts to reach out to the group. However, disappointment in the parties' efforts set in quickly. As the campaign proceeded, outreach efforts by the candidates and parties dropped off dramatically: "The sense of disappointment among Latino activists [was] deep, especially given the promise of the primaries and the summer conventions, when both sides declared this would be the year in which the Latino vote was vital" (Tobar 2000, A-17). Commenting on the election, Cecilia Muñoz of the National Council for La Raza said, "We seem to have made one transition, which is that candidates get it, that they need to be campaigning in our community. And that's been reflected in their use of the Spanish language and in the overall tone and tenor of the campaign, and in the extraordinary amount of marketing that is being aimed at our community." But she also went on to say that "for the most part, the focus has been on marketing and not on policy. We would note that Latinos didn't come up in any of the presidential debates" (Fountain 2000, A-26).

Asian American Immigrants: Left Behind?

Although the 2000 election represented a change in the parties' relationship with Latinos, non-Latino immigrants remained on the perimeters of party outreach efforts. In particular, the Republican and Democratic Parties did not target Asian Americans during the 2000 elections. The Democratic Party's lack of commitment to that community was apparent on its campaign Web site, where the page focused on outreach to the Asian American community was available in English only. This is surprising given that the 2000 Census shows that nearly 80 percent of Asian Americans speak a language other than English at home.[9] Although it may be unrealistic for the parties to make outreach efforts accessible in every Asian language, it would not require immense resources to translate their materials from English into three or four of the Asian languages most commonly spoken in the United States. Despite the best efforts of Asian American campaign staffers, the outreach efforts of both the Democratic and Republican National Committees remained nearly invisible.

Selective mobilization strategies were one of the reasons that the parties failed to target Asian Americans during the 2000 campaign. Although Asians are one of the fastest-growing major racial or ethnic groups in the country, the 2000 Census showed that fewer than 5 percent of the U.S. population identified itself as Asian; of Asian American adults, approximately 40 percent were noncitizens (Jamieson, Shin, and Day 2002). Like their Latino counterparts, Asian Americans are geographically concentrated in a few electoral-vote-rich states, such as California, New York, and Illinois, but these were not battleground states in the 2000 election.

Perceptions of Asian American voting and partisanship patterns may have been another factor. Furthermore, it is unlikely that Democrats or Republicans see Asian Americans, even eligible Asian Americans, as likely voters. Despite exhibiting higher education and income levels than the population as a whole, Asian Americans have some of the lowest voting rates of any racial or ethnic group. Only one out of every four adult Asian Americans voted in elections throughout the 1990s according to Current Population Survey data (Lien, Conway, and Wong 2004). In terms of partisanship, those Asian Americans with a party preference tend to lean slightly toward the Democratic Party. In the 2000–2001 Pilot National Asian American Survey, 36 percent of Asian American respondents self-identified as Democrats, 14 percent as Republicans, and 13 percent as independents. Notably, however, about 20 percent did not think of themselves in partisan terms, and 18 percent claimed that they were uncertain about their party identification or refused to give a response.

Thus, half of Asian Americans in the survey did not identify with an American political party. If the Democratic or Republican leadership believes that Asian Americans are not likely to vote, it is reasonable that they would also believe that spending resources to mobilize that group would be unwise. Given the uncertain partisan attachments of Asian Americans, a campaign may also hesitate to mobilize Asian Americans because it is not clear what candidate those mobilized voters would ultimately support. Accentuating this point, Kathay Feng of the Asian Pacific Legal Center in Los Angeles says, "I think politicians are very savvy and very calculating about how they spend their education or marketing dollars. A politician's greatest fear is . . . to wake up the voters who are going to come out and vote for someone else" (quoted in Somashekhar 2002, 1).

Yet small population size and weak partisan attachments do not explain fully the parties' marginalization of the Asian American population. Historically, other small population groups, such as Jewish Americans and African Americans, have received more (if still limited) party attention. In some places, such as California, exit polls and surveys show consistently that Asian Americans make up the same proportion of registered voters as do African Americans. Further, rather than view Asian Americans' lack of commitment to a particular party as a problem, parties might consider Asian Americans an important swing vote, open to party recruitment and influence (Nakanishi 1991). Asian Americans represent a ripe opportunity for parties to appeal to a constituency through issue mobilization. Garrett Yee, president of an organization that encourages Chinese Americans to get involved in local politics, argues that Asian Americans "make their decisions based on the person and the issue, not the party. Most people philosophically want to think that, but Asian Americans actually do that" (quoted in Somashekhar 2002, 1). Thus it seems that community organizations, which mobilize around issues rather than partisan platforms, may be well positioned to assist with Asian American political mobilization.

Race may be yet another reason parties do not court Asian Americans, who are stereotyped as foreigners with no legitimate place in the political system. This hypothesis is consistent with American public opinion. A random telephone survey of 1,216 Americans, conducted in January and March 2001 by the Committee of 100 (an Asian American advocacy organization) and Yankelovich Partners (2001), found that more people would reject an Asian American presidential candidate (23 percent) than would reject a black candidate (15 percent), a woman candidate (14 percent), or a Jewish candidate (11 percent). According to community leaders, both parties distanced themselves from the Asian American community following allegations in 1996 that the Clinton administration improperly accepted donations from Asian nationals living in the United States. The racialization of the campaign scandal was epitomized by a *National Review* cover illustration featuring President Clinton, Hillary Rodham Clinton, and Vice President Al Gore as yellow-faced caricatures. Shortly after the allegations arose, the Democratic National Party began doing background checks and audits on all donors with "Asian-sounding" surnames. The perception that during the campaign finance investigations, the media, and the Democratic National Committee targeted Asian Americans because of their race has led some to speculate that "the fund-raising scandal will have a 'chilling effect' on Asian Pacific American participation" (Nakanishi 1999b, 35).

Although immigrants from Latin America and Asia began arriving in the United States in significant numbers in 1965, party mobilization over the past forty years has been the exception rather than the rule. Whether parties' behavior will shift toward a more sustained effort to mobilize contemporary Asian American and Latino immigrants depends on changes in the political environment and institutional incentives as well as demographic changes.

Election 2004: More of the Same?

The three factors discussed earlier (changing campaign tactics as a result of party nationalization, selective mobilization strategies, and assumptions about political attitudes among immigrants and median voters) help to explain the parties' limited effects in terms of mobilizing Latinos during the 2000 and 2004 presidential campaigns. First, a nationalized campaign strategy focused on winning the electoral vote in specific battleground states and reduced the incentive to woo Latino voters because the majority are not concentrated in most of those states (Florida, New Mexico, and

Arizona do contain significant Latino populations, but the vast majority of Latinos live outside of these states). In 2000, as it became clear that Gore would take California, the campaigns of both candidates focused their attention elsewhere. At the end of October, a reporter from the *Los Angeles Times* wrote, "The battle for Latino hearts and minds is a lesser sideshow to the all-out push to win centrist voters in states such as Michigan, Wisconsin, and Pennsylvania" (Tobar 2000, A-17). Hector Orci, a Latino activist and founder of La Agencia, a New Mexico advertising agency targeting Latinos, commented, "The circumstances of this election have led both candidates to ignore the Latino vote almost completely, because tactically, they don't see it as important" (quoted in Tobar 2000, A-17).

In 2004, the battleground states remained largely unchanged from 2000.[10] Thus, the two parties failed to target mobilization efforts at California (home to about one of every three Latinos in the nation), New York state (one of every eight), and Illinois (one of every fifteen). Only 20 percent of all U.S. Latinos but 40 percent of all non-Latino whites live in the battleground states. Consequently, Latinos are about half as likely as whites to live in the states that were the focus of the past two presidential campaigns. In 2004, as a result of these demographics, the vast majority of the parties' resources were directed toward states that are disproportionately white. Adam J. Segal of the Hispanic Voter Project at Johns Hopkins University observed in late September 2004, "Most of the Hispanic voters across the nation will never see or hear a paid advertisement by the campaigns and will likely never see the candidates at events in their state. Limited resources force the campaigns to make trade-off decisions based on this year's election. This short-term strategy unfortunately does little to contribute to broader, long-term national political gains for the Hispanic community" (Segal 2004, 3).

Second, the shift in mobilizing tactics to the use of sophisticated media, direct-mail, and market-research techniques at the expense of local outreach meant that in a handful of battleground states, both parties targeted only the most likely Latino voters. Louis DeSipio and Rodolfo de la Garza conclude that in 2000 both parties were "narrow in their focus, seeking only to reach Latinos who [were] likely to vote. Although this segment of the Latino electorate continues to increase, the number of eligible nonvoters continues to grow as rapidly. As a result, campaign and party investment in outreach did not necessarily mean that presidential campaigns at the end of the twentieth century had become more likely to increase Latino turnout" (DeSipio and de la Garza 2005, 21). The campaigns and parties spent record amounts of money courting the Latino vote via Spanish-language media outlets in 2004. By late September of that year, the Kerry campaign had spent more than the Gore-Lieberman campaign and the Democratic National Committee combined in 2000 (Segal 2004, 2). In an interview, Rosalind Gold, senior director of policy, research, and advocacy at the National Association of Latino Elected Officials (NALEO), acknowledged in late October 2004 that the parties were spending money on advertising and field operations in the battleground states, but she also observed that the "parties are very, very heavily media-oriented. . . . I don't know how much of their fieldwork is being targeted specifically toward Latinos, except in the battleground states."[11] The Bush-Cheney campaign also set records, devoting $3 million to Spanish-language advertisements by August 2004 (Segal 2004, 3). However, for the majority of the campaign, patterns of party outreach appear to have remained similar to those of 2000. Despite the unprecedented amounts of money that both groups contributed toward Spanish-language advertising, Latino outreach efforts remained mostly limited to the airways and focused on the battleground states (where fewer Latinos live). Both parties failed to mobilize Latino participation at a mass level.

Third, in the face of statistics that showed that the voting rate for all Latino adults in the United States is less than 30 percent (compared to 55 percent of the general adult population), the parties may have believed that courting the Latino vote, especially outside of key battleground states, was not worth the effort and expenditure of resources. However, although almost 40 percent of adult Latinos were ineligible to vote because they were not citizens, 79 percent of registered adult Latinos voted in 2000, which compares favorably with the 86 percent rate for the registered population as a whole (Jamieson, Shin, and Day 2002). DeSipio and de la Garza observe that although "electoral institutions have increased their sophistication at reaching out to Latinos and the number of Latinos voting has increased, there is still no pattern of overall Latino electoral mobilization that reaches more than a small share of Latino adults" (2005, 16). Had the parties expended the effort, they might have belied the misperception about Latino political apathy.

The parties also made little effort to address Latinos' substantive policy concerns and instead discussed those concerns superficially. This strategy allowed the parties to try to appeal to Latinos without alienating white swing voters who might not support more direct measures that would benefit Latinos. During 2004, both candidates sought to reach out to Latinos by emphasizing substantive policy priorities in the areas of education, health care, and job creation generally, which a series of town hall voter forums organized by NALEO had revealed were the most salient issues for Latino voters. However, when asked in an interview whether the two candidates were doing a good job of addressing these issues, NALEO Director of Communications Erica Bernal answered,

> No. And I'll give you a perfect example about why. We visited eight communities, talked to over six hundred Latinos ranging in age, socioeconomic status. We didn't hear one person who thought that No Child Left Behind was working. . . . Latino voters are saying, "50 percent of our kids are not graduating, our schools are overcrowded, our teachers are underpaid, they're not credentialed properly, so who's going to give me something that's going to fix my child's education and make sure that they're successful?" So there's a particular perspective that the Latino communities are facing. Even though education is thrown around, Latinos are not hearing any substantive policy that's going to ensure their children's success.

Although the two candidates may have addressed issues important to Latinos, they did not offer specific policy recommendations that addressed core Latino concerns about the issues. Further, a *Los Angeles Times* reporter observed that although the GOP featured more minority delegates at its convention than had previously been the case, its "bid for minority votes is . . . hindered by the animosity that some of Bush's policies and decisions have stirred up in black and Latino communities. . . . Many Latinos question Bush's no-citizenship program for illegal immigrants, and stricter rules on travel to Cuba are dividing the Cuban American vote in Florida" (Neuman 2004, A-26).

As the size of the Latino population has grown and its voting potential has become more apparent, the Republican and Democratic Parties have shown greater interest. In the future, they may continue in this direction and recruit votes in Latino communities, but party efforts to this point have been primarily symbolic. The focus has been on recruiting Latinos into key party positions, adopting policy platforms that appeal to (or at least are not perceived as hostile to) Latino interests, and targeting only those members of the Latino community already registered to vote. Noncitizen immigrants and other major ethnic groups, including Asian Americans, have been ignored.

Asian Americans received far less attention than Latinos in 2004. During the campaign, Karen Narasaki, president of the National Asian Pacific American Legal Consortium, commented, "In this election season, I think we've been fairly invisible" (*USA Today* 2004, 1). Echoing these sentiments, David Lee, executive director of the Chinese American Voters Education Committee, said of the 2004 campaign, "Traditionally, neither party has spent much effort reaching out to Asian Americans. . . . As a result I think you have a very large untapped population" (Schwartz 2004, A-21). One reason for this is that parties and candidates do not understand the contours and internal diversity within the Asian American community well enough to conduct effective outreach efforts. "Asian votes should be courted, not taken for granted," Cao K. O, executive director of the Asian American Federation in New York, told an Associated Press reporter in July 2004. "At the same time, politicians and the political parties don't know how to court the Asian vote" (Armas 2004). That same month, a coalition of Asian American media representatives complained that the Kerry campaign and Democratic National Committee were overlooking Asian American media outlets (Hua 2004).

Although they broke records in their campaign fund-raising, the parties seemed reluctant to devote more than scant resources to the mobilization of Asian Americans in 2004. The Republican National Committee included more Asian American delegates at its convention than ever before and created a steering committee of 175 Asian Americans, encouraging them to host house parties and participate in phone banks. The committee also included Asian Americans in its Team Leader program, implemented to recruit Republican supporters. In October 2004, the Democratic National Committee initiated APIA Voice, a get-out-the-vote campaign that targeted Asian American voters and involved the hiring of Asian American field directors and organizers, the production of multilingual materials, and in-language phone banking and canvassing efforts. Nevertheless, most community members were disappointed in the two parties' outreach efforts (Armas 2004; Schwartz 2004).

In the last months of what was shaping up to be a close campaign, it was clear that undecided voters represented the holy grail for the parties and candidates. In theory, they should have targeted Asian American registered voters because, as late as August 2004, fully 20 percent of Asian Americans were undecided about their candidate choice (New California Media 2004). In fact, Asian American likely voters included a much larger proportion of undecided voters than did their Latino counterparts. By July 2004, only 3 percent of Latino likely voters remained undecided about the two presidential candidates (Greenberg et al. 2004). Further, the number of Asian Americans who actually cast a vote grew at a tremendous rate from 1996 to 2000—22 percent, compared to 19 percent for Latinos and just 4 percent for whites (Passell 2004). Yet the two major parties failed to mobilize most Asian Americans, in part because of selective mobilization strategies that focused on likely voters in battleground states. The Democratic National Committee's APIA Voice campaign focused almost exclusively on the battleground states and was not well funded compared to other aspects of the campaign. Like their Latino counterparts, only about one out of every five Asian Americans lives in a battleground state.

The parties' shift to mass-media and direct-mail tactics, use of selective mobilization strategies and need to maintain existing coalitions, desire to appeal to white swing voters with moderate views on race, and misperceptions about immigrant apathy have led the Democratic and Republican Parties to avoid mass mobilization strategies, which had been the normative strategy in the first half of the twentieth century (see Escobedo 2002; de la Garza and DeSipio 2004; see also DeSipio, de la Garza, and Setzler 1999). The behavior of the major parties in the presidential campaigns since 1988 shows that minorities and especially immigrants cannot yet count on parties as primary sources of political mobilization.

Local Politics in New York and Los Angeles

Many of the constraints and disincentives experienced by the Democratic and Republican Parties at the national level are also in evidence at the local level, although these forces manifest differently on the neighborhood stage than they do in presidential campaigns. An examination of local politics in New York and Los Angeles illustrates the problems arising from weakened local party structures and changing campaign tactics, selective mobilization strategies and the need to maintain existing party coalitions, and assumptions about political attitudes among immigrants and median voters.

Turning to an overview of politics in New York and Los Angeles, it is apparent that mainstream political structures at the local level, such as community boards or local political organizations, have been slow to recognize or incorporate Asian American and Latino immigrants. Instead, labor organizations, workers' centers, advocacy and social service organizations, ethnic voluntary associations, and religious institutions have partially taken on the responsibility of mobilizing Asian Americans and Latinos to participate in the political system.

The Political Context in New York City

New York City is often described as a one-party town (Arian et al. 1991). Democratic Party organizations are part and parcel of the history of politics in New York. From the nineteenth century through the 1960s, Tammany Hall, a classic, big-city machine based in Manhattan, dominated the city's political life. Machines developed in the other counties as well, drawing on the city's resource pool of public-sector jobs and social services to maintain control of local elections. In the contemporary era of candidate-centered and media-driven campaigns, however, politics in New York has been described as more "fragmented" than in the years before reforms and changing urban demographics weakened the political machine (Wade 1990). The city is made up of five counties created by an 1898 charter; each county is characterized by a unique political context, with "its own party rules, identity, political dynamics, and county leader" (Mollenkopf 1992, 77). Despite this fragmentation, the Democratic Party retains control of most state and local elected positions despite the conservatism exhibited by recent New York City mayors such as Rudolph Giuliani and Michael Bloomberg.[12]

The most important municipal election is for mayor (Arian et al. 1991; Mollenkopf 1992, 69). The Democratic Party no longer determines who will win that office but still influences lower-level positions (Mollenkopf 1992, 78). The city's smallest units of political-party organization are assembly districts, which function as wards, although the assembly districts are not the most critical offices. In general, two leaders are elected in each district, and those district leaders elect a county leader, who is similar to a party boss. New York City district leaders seldom face reelection challenges, and many are legislators or the relatives of legislators. Although reformers and insurgents have challenged the party organization at the local level, the city's political organization remains based on Democratic clubs that nominate the local leadership and produce the candidates for city council and state assembly seats (Arian et al. 1991). John Mollenkopf notes that the influence of the party clubs has declined since the mid–twentieth century: "Most observers would agree that the grass-roots organizational base of New York's political parties has decayed. Evidence to support this view may be found in the weakness of the regular Democratic political clubs compared to the 1920s or even the 1950s. They are fewer, have smaller and more elderly memberships, no longer provide the sole access to political careers, and play a smaller role in citywide political campaigns" (1992, 77).[13] Despite their declining influence, party clubs retain some power, especially in terms of controlling how the city grants government contracts and, in the assembly districts where clubs are most active, providing a healthy margin of victory to candidates (Mollenkopf 1992, 80, 122).

Despite the rapidly growing numbers of Latino and Afro-Caribbean immigrants, which make them a rich source of potential votes in several New York assembly districts, the weakened local party organizations have not reached out to these groups, preferring instead to protect existing coalitions. In his study of Latino immigrant political participation in Queens, Michael Jones-Correa asserts that "given that the political machine in Queens is long established, and has only token competition, machine politicians have little interest in disrupting the status quo" (1998, 82).[14] As a result, Latinos in Queens receive little attention from the local party organizations (see also Mollenkopf 1992, table 4.1). Reuel Rogers identifies a similar phenomenon, noting that the Brooklyn Democratic Party has made virtually no effort to mobilize Afro-Caribbean immigrants and has failed to sponsor voter-registration drives or to support Afro-Caribbean candidates. Rogers attributes this phenomenon to the party's desire to avoid "bringing new unpredictable voters into the electorate" (2000b, 93). In the past, however, Afro-Caribbeans had a stronger presence in the city's political life (Kasinitz 1992).[15]

The need to protect the status quo intersects with selective mobilization strategies and the need to appeal to moderate white swing voters in surprising ways. Both Jones-Correa and Rogers note that because the Democratic machine is firmly entrenched in Queens and Brooklyn, it has little incentive to expend resources to attract votes from immigrants, who tend to be unregistered and nonvoters. Rogers notes, "To be sure, party gatekeeping and selective mobilization can be explained as a purely rational, race-neutral strategy that allows Democrats to maintain their hegemony and the political status quo. But the practice undeniably produces racially stratified patterns of participation. The party's core of traditional voters turns out to be more white and native-born than the overall population, while the nonvoters on the political margins are mostly nonwhite immigrants from the Caribbean, Latin America, and Asia" (2000b, 97).

In terms of shaping the political landscape in New York, civic associations represent another set of important local institutions. These associations frequently have connections to local party organizations—in some cases, they are in fact the same organization or have overlapping leadership. Most focus on quality-of-life issues having to do with street safety, zoning regulations, garbage removal, and local politics. Here again, the need to appeal to white swing voters proves a disincentive to immigrant political mobilization (Sanjek 1998). Like the party clubs, most associations until recently were composed primarily of established white residents, who often exhibited ambivalence toward new immigrants in their communities and consequently have done little to bring immigrants into the organizations.

The dynamics in Elmhurst-Corona provide a good illustration of the weaknesses of civic associations in mobilizing immigrant communities. According to Roger Sanjek (1998), during the 1970s and 1980s, residents of Elmhurst-Corona, which was fast becoming one of the most ethnically diverse parts of New York City, began establishing civic associations. Yet "only in small numbers, or in the outer layers, did any Latin American, Asian, or black newcomers appear" (263). When someone suggested adding Spanish and Chinese pages to the Newtown Civic Association's newsletter, several members reacted strongly against the proposal, and none were in favor.

Community Board 4, representing Elmhurst-Corona, had forty-five members in 1980. Despite the district's racial diversity, only two members were African American, three were Latino, and none were Asian (Sanjek 1998, 300). At times, the board's leadership has demonstrated outright racial hostility toward new immigrants, further diminishing the likelihood that immigrants will turn toward civic associations or local government institutions for help with getting involved in politics in New York City. For example, Sanjek recalls the comments of the board's chair during a discussion of applicants for a new low-income housing development for seniors: "Everybody's name is Wang. . . . I know how to solve their housing problem—call the INS. We want our own people. Chinese have some nerve, saying we don't speak Chinese. We were here first. We want our neighbors in first" (1998, 303).

Since the 1990s, local civic associations and community boards have become more open to immigrants in terms of both membership and leaders. For example, Ron Casey, the chair of Community Board 2's veterans' affairs committee, expressed concern at an April 2001 board meeting about the fact that only three Latinos served on the board despite the fact that 35 percent of the area the board serves was Latino. "I'd like to see diversity," Casey said, noting that the board was made up mostly of third-generation whites (quoted in Becker 2001, 2). However, perhaps because of their initial reluctance to incorporate newcomers and the slow embrace that followed, other local institutions such as labor organizations, workers' centers, advocacy and social service organizations, ethnic voluntary associations, and religious institutions are taking the lead in the political mobilization of New York's immigrants.

The Political Context in Los Angeles

In contrast to New York, Los Angeles is the "prototypical western metropolis" (Sonenshein 2004, 19). In the early twentieth century, the city's leaders were committed to clean government, supporting reforms designed to increase citizen participation and discourage corruption. As Raphael Sonenshein points out, "Los Angeles is a model of the newer, western cities [that] developed in the late nineteenth and early twentieth centuries, shaped by Midwestern Protestant migrants who hoped to devise an urban alternative to the 'old, corrupt' cities of the East and Midwest. The antiparty norms of the Progressive movement found their greatest expression in the West and were central to the development of the Los Angeles political community. Party organizations have been virtually non-existent in Los Angeles" (1993, 230).

This reform culture has received strong support from the city's voters, who hold strong antimachine attitudes. To select the mayor, the city holds a nonpartisan primary followed by a runoff between the two most successful candidates. The city's strong council model requires that the mayor share power with the fifteen city council members, each of whom is elected every four years from single-member districts. Power rests in part with the "permanent government" in Los Angeles, a coalition of progrowth business executives, developers, and members of the bureaucracy (Sonenshein 1993). The city council is small compared to other cities, such as New

York or Chicago, and is an important structural feature of Los Angeles politics that affects Asian American and Latino political mobilization. Because there are fewer seats on the city council, racial minorities have limited opportunities to achieve local political power (Mollenkopf, Olsen, and Ross 2001). A small city council means fewer electoral opportunities for coethnic candidates to mobilize Asian American and Latino immigrants (Sonenshein 2004, 255).

The historical weakness of the party structure is another notable feature of Los Angeles (Fogelson [1967] 1993). Although the New York example provides little evidence that minorities can rely on machines for political mobilization, the historical absence of a political-machine culture in Los Angeles has stringently limited the mobilization of Asians and Latinos. As Sonenshein notes, "There were no political party organizations to recruit precinct captains and mobilize minority voters. The doctrines of homogeneity and conservative reform left little incentive for elite groups to incorporate new groups though balanced tickets" (1993, 33).

Despite the absence of a traditional big-city machine culture, Los Angeles is home to the Waxman-Berman political organization, run by westside politicians and fueled by money from Hollywood and developers rather than by city patronage jobs and strong grassroots mobilization strategies (M. Davis 1992; Fulton 2001). Indeed, rather than relying on grassroots strategies, the Waxman-Berman organization led the country in developing direct-mail and targeted-media campaigns and drew its strength from fund-raising and mailing lists. Until the 1990s, when term limits and Republican redistricting sharply limited its effectiveness, this machine had been somewhat powerful in city politics, though never absolutely dominant. The machine would slate candidates and promote them through direct-mail campaigns, eventually dominating Los Angeles's west side (Sonenshein 1993). The Waxman-Berman political organization and its strategies illustrate how both weak local party structures and a focus on large-scale direct mail campaigns rather than on grassroots mobilizing tactics discouraged immigrant mobilization in Los Angeles (Fulton 2001, 46). Minority immigrants are seldom the target of the superficial media campaigns that have come to dominate politics in Los Angeles and at the national level.

Peter Skerry associates organizations like the Waxman-Berman one with the "nationalization" of American politics, characterized by the decline of neighborhood-based, machine-style politics and the rise of "elite-network politics" (1993, 375). Elite networks are exclusive groups of elected officials, staffers, and in some cases advocacy organizations relying primarily on direct mail and television advertisements that tend to have weak ties to Los Angeles communities: "The clique may not have roots reaching down into Los Angeles, but it has plenty of branches extending widely across the state" (228). This trend has created a gap between local ethnic communities and the larger political system. Historically, immigrants have participated only at low levels in Los Angeles politics. Skerry notes that the available political institutions (national parties, elite networks, political consulting and polling organizations, and the media) "offer little help in negotiating the gulf between the traditional values newcomers bring with them and those of contemporary American society" (375).

New York and Los Angeles Compared

New York and Los Angeles are the two most populous U.S. metropolitan areas (Halle 2003, 1). Both have been characterized as *global cities* because of their dominant role in "national and international interactions" and their critical position in global systems (Abu-Lughod 1999, 400). Despite their similarities, the two regions are the product of distinct historical forces (Abu-Lughod 1999) and represent different urban development outcomes. New York is organized around a traditional urban core, while Los Angeles is organized around a constellation of decentralized urban clusters (Halle 2003; Fogelson 1993; Fulton 2001).

Immigrants from all over the world have settled disproportionately in the Los Angeles and New York City regions (Waldinger and Lee 2001). Immigrants from Mexico dominate the stream of immigrants entering Los Angeles, while New York's immigrant flow is more diverse (Cordero-Guzmán, Smith and Grosfoguel 2001; Waldinger and Lee 2001; Abu-Lughod 1999). New York has a longer history of immigration. The native white population in New York is composed of the descendants of earlier waves of Jewish, Italian, Greek, and Irish immigrants from Europe. In contrast, many native white Angelenos are the descendants of Western Europeans who settled first in small towns in the Midwest and then migrated west. Sabagh and Bozorgmehr (2003) assert that the latter group tends to be more nativist and that their presence in Los Angeles partly explains greater anti-immigrant sentiment in Los Angeles compared to New York. In addition, Mollenkopf (1999) argues that Los Angeles has been more hostile to immigration than New York because New York's demographic and political dynamics encourage greater collaboration among ethnic groups. For example, whites in New York need to form coalitions with other groups to govern, but that is not the case in Los Angeles.

One of the most striking differences in political organization between the two cities is that New York is a traditional machine-culture city whereas Los Angeles has developed in the reformist mode. However, in his study of urban reform, Sonenshein reminds us that both cities defy simple characterizations. New York City has not only been home to famous political machines and bosses but "has also been the cradle of the urban reform movement." And although it is held up as the quintessential reform metropolis, Los Angeles shares many of the attributes of "unre-formed big city government" (2004, 17). Further, New York and Los Angeles have some important commonalities. In the 1990s, white Republican candidates succeeded African American mayors in both cities, and both were challenged by secession movements, driven in part by white residents' negative attitudes toward an increasingly diverse metropolis. Yet there are differences between the two cities in terms of their general features (Mollenkopf, Olsen, and Ross 2001).

Political mobilization in New York is still based on local party organizations and neighborhood networks, whereas in Los Angeles, mainstream political parties rely heavily on direct mail and media campaigns for electoral and issue mobilization (Sonenshein 2003; Mollenkopf, Olson, and Ross 2001). As a result, in New York, a salient factor vis-à-vis immigrant political mobilization is the entrenchment of parties and coalitions that selectively mobilize traditional supporters but not new voters as a means of maintaining the status quo. In Los Angeles, the salient factor is selective voter mobilization using sophisticated phone and direct-mail techniques and media advertising aimed at narrowly targeted groups that are most likely to support a particular candidate or policy issue.

John Mollenkopf, David Olson, and Timothy Ross (2001) and others (Halle 2003; Sonenshein 2003) note additional differences: First, New York City's government is more organized and much larger than that of Los Angeles. New York's political system provides many more opportunities for people to get involved in politics, through election to local offices and low-level appointments, than does the system in Los Angeles (Mollenkopf 1999). Local political offices in New York City include representatives on the school board, city council, or assembly. An assembly member's constituency can include as few as 140,000 people. In contrast, the local office of county supervisor in Los Angeles represents more than a million constituents (Fulton 2001, 45; Mollenkopf, Olson, and Ross 2001, 37; Abu-Lughod 1999). Los Angeles has relatively few city council seats compared to New York City; consequently local races in Los Angeles County rely heavily on the ability to raise money and spend it on advertising and campaign professionals, whereas entry-level office seekers in New York City can still rely on networks based on friends, neighbors, and organizations. Minority immigrants have been running for the local school board in New York City with increasing success. However, representation is still limited. As mentioned earlier, despite Asian Americans' long history in New York City, it was not until 2001 that John Liu, representing northeast Queens on the city council, became the first Asian American elected to citywide office and not until 2004 that Jimmy Meng became the first New York City Asian American to serve in the New York State legislature.

Both New York City and Los Angeles have citizen advisory bodies. Community boards were introduced throughout New York City in 1969 to make recommendations on land use and budget decisions (Sanjek 1998). Their role is advisory, but at times they do wield power (Sonenshein 2003; Sanjek 1998). In 1999, Los Angeles voters approved charter revisions that provided for neighborhood councils that would monitor service delivery to local areas and make budget requests. Sonenshein (2003, 310) argues that neighborhood councils became "the main vehicle for enhanced citizen participation" in Los Angeles, while the community boards remained part of a collection of local organizations, including local party organizations, that could promote citizen participation in New York City. As noted earlier, community boards have a long history of racial exclusion but began to reflect New York City's diversity in the 1990s. The community boards have not served traditionally as a step toward elected office for residents of New York City (Sanjek 1998, 51). Los Angeles neighborhood councils were disproportionately white in June 2004, although Latino, black, and Asian American representation increased in areas of greater non-Latino-white population (Musso et al. 2004).

Finally, opportunities for political mobilization for minority immigrants may be affected by the presence and political calculations of minority political elites. Mollenkopf, Ross, and Olson (1999) note that many elected officials in New York City, including those who are Jewish, black, and

Latino, have a large number of immigrant residents in their districts. However, "like all local elected officials, these incumbents and their local county parties like the electorate which put them in office and are in no hurry to enlarge, and perhaps destabilize, that electorate or encourage new political competition from immigrant office-seekers" (8). In Los Angeles, second-generation immigrants often run for elected offices. For example, Xavier Becerra and Antonio Villaraigosa, both Mexican Americans, emerged as two of the top six contenders in the 2001 mayoral primary election. Becerra's mother is from Guadalajara, Mexico, and his father was born in Sacramento, California, but grew up in Tijuana in Baja California. Villaraigosa's father was born in Mexico, and his mother was born in the United States. Villaraigosa was elected mayor in 2005 (see chap. 2). However, given that most Latino elected officials in Los Angeles represent safe seats, mobilization of immigrants—which might disrupt existing coalitions—is often not a priority. In their comparison of immigrant political participation in the two cities, Mollenkopf, Ross, and Olson conclude that "neither New York nor Los Angeles County suggest that native minority politicians will help to promote active citizenship among and develop a political synergy with even closely related immigrant groups" (1999, 9).

Conclusion

Mainstream political parties' long-standing involvement in immigrant political mobilization has been undone during the past forty years, and the parties' absence at the local level can be explained by at least three factors: (1) weakened local party structure and changing campaign tactics; (2) selective mobilization strategies and maintenance of existing party coalitions; (3) assumptions about the political attitudes of immigrants and white swing voters. Since the 1960s, political machines and party organizations have shown little interest in organizing immigrants to participate in the U.S. political system. The Democratic and Republican Parties have nationalized, to the detriment of local party structures. To get out the vote, today's candidate-centered campaigns rely on direct mail, radio, and television—not face-to-face interactions or neighborhood grassroots activity. The parties tend to engage in selective mobilization of those who have the most resources in terms of income, education, and language skills because those are the people who are most likely to vote. Parties will not expend their scarce resources on noncitizens, who cannot vote in federal, state, and most local elections. The two-party, winner-take-all structure of the American political system intensifies party reliance on an appeal to the median voter. Moderate views on race in that bloc of voters represent an incentive for parties to distance themselves from racial minorities or unpopular groups within those minorities and from policies that might be construed as benefiting those minorities. Because entrenched and reliable blocs of party support might vanish in response to appeals to minorities and especially to unpopular segments of minority groups such as undocumented immigrants, such appeals are discouraged. In the context of these many constraints and disincentives, immigrant enclaves—particularly the majority located outside of battleground states—are ignored. Thus, parties are not mass mobilizing immigrants, especially when they are poor, lack citizenship, do not speak English, and are from a racial minority. Nor are the parties likely to do so in the near-term future. However, this may be a mistake and may be less rational than party leaders seem to believe. By appealing to immigrants—even those who are not citizens—parties could build their future bases and political power.

Would immigrants participate more if parties appealed to them? A long history of research by political scientists has shown that mobilization is one of the most influential determinants of political participation for Americans generally (Gosnell 1927; Eldersveld 1956; Verba, Schlozman, and Brady 1995). In their classic study of mobilization and political participation, Rosenstone and Hansen (1993, 170) find that people mobilized by the two major parties over the course of presidential election campaign are more likely to vote, to try to persuade others to vote, to work for a party or candidate, and to contribute money to a campaign. Other studies show that mobilization can substantially affect voter turnout among those who are disadvantaged in terms of socioeconomic resources (Cain and McCue 1985; Rosenstone and Hansen 1993, 173). Mobilization is positively associated with participation among Asian Americans and Latinos. Jan Leighley (2001) shows that mobilization has a positive effect on Latinos' political participation, and Lien, Conway, and Wong (2004) find that mobilization by parties increases political participation among Asian Americans. R. Ramirez (forthcoming) finds that mobilization increases turnout among Latino immigrants, although the effects of that mobilization depend on the type and quality of contact. Using an experimental field research design, J. Wong (2004) finds that mobilization increased turnout among Chinese (immigrants and nonimmigrants) in Los Angeles County. Thus, a wealth of research suggests that increased efforts to mobilize immigrants would significantly affect political participation.

The relationship between American civic institutions—parties and community-based organizations in particular—and political mobilization is not relevant for immigrants alone. Parties are no longer bridging institutions between government and constituents; instead, the parties operate at the national level, and their reliance on the mass media and sophisticated direct-mail strategies means that most Americans, not only immigrants, are not targeted for direct mobilization. Face-to-face, personal contact—a factor that is strongly associated with political participation (Verba, Schlozman, and Brady 1995; Gerber and Green 2000; Leighley 2001)—is no longer the primary feature of political organizing. Lack of mobilization by parties is exacerbated by features of the American political system, including redistricting practices that have led to a decline in competitive elections, that also undermine mobilization.

In the gap, community organizations are critical, especially because they can reach those who are resource- and skill-poor, the group that parties are the least likely to target because, according to traditional criteria, it is the least likely to participate. Labor organizations, workers' centers, advocacy and social service organizations, ethnic voluntary associations, and religious institutions are directly connected to immigrant and poor communities and can engage in ethnic-specific mobilization strategies and practices. Community organizations are reaching out to involve day laborers, noncitizens, and non-English speakers in the U.S. political system. That makes those organizations crucial in terms of helping the country move closer to fulfilling its ideals of political equality. Community-based organizations may represent a more promising source of mobilization than political parties, not just for immigrants but also for the population as a whole (Verba, Schlozman, and Brady 1995; Leighley 2001).

4 The Role of Community Organizations in Immigrant Political Mobilization

Organizations that do community-based work—labor organizations, workers' centers, social service organizations, advocacy organizations, ethnic voluntary associations, and religious institutions—appear to have great potential for politically mobilizing Asian American and Latino immigrant communities. When asked which civic institutions had been important for involving the Chinese community in the U.S. political process, a Chinese American leader, active in a campaign for a Chinese American candidate in Los Angeles, revealed the role that these organizations have in immigrant politics. Rather than mentioning a traditional political party or even the elected official for whom he had campaigned, he named a nonprofit legal-advocacy organization serving Asian Americans: "I think the Asian Pacific American Legal Center has done a great job of getting people to register to vote and helping people in the community."

Community organizations have long been active in politically mobilizing immigrant groups (Skerry 1993; Skocpol 1999a; Hall 1999; Sterne 2001; A. Lin forthcoming), but their centrality to the process is something new. During the first half of the twentieth century, political machines and party organizations courted immigrant groups, running consistent, committed mobilization efforts at the neighborhood level. In those efforts, the political institutions worked closely with churches, fraternal organizations, and other community organizations. Since the 1960s, however, the collaboration between parties and community organizations has weakened notably. Community organizations are more likely to focus on promoting immigrants' and minorities' civil and economic rights than on getting out the vote. The proliferation of nonprofit organizations (Berry 1997) incorporated under the 501c(3) section of the Internal Revenue Code, which precludes participation in any political campaign on behalf of a candidate

89

running for public office, has also undermined collaboration between parties and organizations. A third factor is that the political parties have shifted their focus to the national level and no longer have a presence in neighborhoods (Conway 2001). The relative absence of political parties has created a vacuum in terms of immigrant political organizing at the local level. Community organizations are stepping into the breach.

Community Organizations: Incentives & Strengths for Mobilizing Minority Immigrant Communities

Local community organizations have certain strengths and incentives for politically mobilizing minority immigrant groups. Three stand out: (1) the desire for organizational maintenance, (2) connections between the leadership and immigrant constituencies and leaders' resulting expertise regarding the immigrant group, and (3) transnational connections.

The first incentive is shared with organized groups everywhere: community organizations seek to expand their membership and constituencies to build a base and increase effectiveness (Hrebenar and Scott 1990; C. Thomas and Hrebenar 1999). In contrast to political parties, community groups are often interested in the power of numbers of individuals rather than in absolute voting power alone. Thus, community organizations have an incentive to reach out to noncitizens and others who may not be obvious potential voters as a means of increasing the organizations' influence, clout, and ability to achieve policy goals. Immigrants represent a sizable bloc of potential constituents. By claiming to represent a large number of people, a community organization can increase its influence and policy-making power. As one community activist explains, having more immigrant participants at events, such as demonstrations, contributes to the success of those activities by generating more attention from the media, elected officials, and the public.

> My personal feeling is that there is still a lot to be said about mobilizing large numbers of people to take action and to show support for a specific issue or policy or whatever concern they have. I think about the time of Proposition 187 [the mid-1990s], when immigrant rights, including legal immigrants, were being attacked. In [California, there] was the largest march and rally I had seen in the whole time I've lived in L.A. I think upwards of twenty-five thousand people or maybe more—

it might have been many, many more—marched through the streets of L.A. for immigrant rights, primarily led by the Latino community. And that really changed the tone in the city of L.A. . . . The tone was set that attacks on immigrants—immigrant bashing—was not going to be accepted, and this was because tens of thousands of people were in the streets.

Further, to expand its membership base, the organization must create activities and provide services that will attract and solidify its potential constituency. An obvious approach is to provide a group with what it lacks. In the case of immigrants, this can include education (English as a second language and citizenship training), services (health care, legal advice), information (logistical, work-related, political), and a reinforcement of positive self-identity (through ethnohistorical commemorations, religious rites, and social events such as soccer games), among other things. Organizations provide immigrants with the tools explicitly needed for naturalization (such as English proficiency and a knowledge of U.S. history and civics). Furthermore, by providing services, sharing information, and reinforcing group identity, organizations help to give their constituents some of the traits that are generally characteristic of civically active segments of the population—social and economic stability and positive self-identity. Finally, the provision of these things builds a connection between the organization and its constituency so that the organization is positioned to mobilize people around relevant issues.

A second strength of community organizations for working with immigrants is that the organization leaders often have close ties to immigrant communities and are committed ideologically to immigrant and minority rights. It is not uncommon for leaders to be first- or second-generation immigrants who have grown up in—or have parents who grew up in—immigrant communities. All of the forty community leaders interviewed in the fieldwork for this book were immigrants or the children of immigrants. Because of these close personal affiliations and common concerns, leaders may be impelled to involve immigrants in the organization's work and activities. For example, when asked why he decided to organize Asian Americans, one leader mentioned his commitments to the community: "I think once you have a better understanding of your cultural heritage and the stark conditions your community is facing in this country, it makes you want to do something about it, to be part of a legacy that was started by farmworkers and laborers who struggled at the turn of the century. Being exposed to that developed that consciousness in me and has got into my work." The transmission of historical knowledge and cultural identity bolsters positive group identity and helps to create a community within the United States that is vital and anchored rather than bleak and temporary. These are significant steps along the slow path that over time leads to full political incorporation. In the past, political parties provided some of the resources needed to move along that path, but today community organizations appear to have replaced parties as the source of tools that immigrants must acquire to participate in politics.

Because leaders have or develop strong social and cultural connections to immigrant communities, they may be more effective in terms of mobilization. They can engage in culturally sensitive strategies and reach out to immigrants in their native language. One community organizer emphasized the importance of linguistic skills and ethnic awareness for achieving successful mobilization.

> Unless you have that language capacity, it is going to be impossible to make inroads in these communities. It's not even so much [that] you need to understand culturally the community, because you can learn that once you have the language access and once you can talk to actual members in the community and go into their neighborhoods and meet with them, and that's where these organizations have an advantage. They tend to be staffed by second-generation and even later Asian Americans, but people who have consciously tried to maintain their language heritage or who have just learned on their own or who have hired other folks—first-generation immigrants who do have a language capacity—they've made that a priority. And so I think that's the single-most important factor in being able to mobilize these communities.

In contrast, for the most part, mainstream political leaders have at best tenuous connections to the local community. This does not bode well for political parties' ability to mobilize locally because leadership is key to group mobilization (Cigler 1985; Nownes and Neeley 1996). Even if the mainstream parties made an effort to balance their national-level, mass-media-driven strategies with some efforts at more local and personal appeals, they would be hard-pressed at present to find people who are not already community organization leaders but would be positioned to move immigrants along the road toward naturalization and voting. In his study of Latino politics, Louis DeSipio observes that "electoral and institutional politics appear only after a foundation of mutualist, civic, and community-focused politics is laid" (2002, 1).

In addition, organizations are run by individuals who have or develop extensive expertise in and familiarity with immigration policy and law, labor laws, naturalization procedures, minority-health-care issues, civic and language education, economic and development problems, and other social-service concerns. Involvement in these areas is a strength because these issues frequently become points of political contention and mobilization in communities. The leadership and staff of community organizations are well positioned to organize and mobilize politically around these concerns. They can do that because they have firsthand experience with these issues and because they have the cultural sensitivity and direct, personal contacts needed to reach the people who will respond to challenges in these areas. That experience, coupled with years of providing immigrants with services and information, can endow an organization with strong legitimacy that helps it to mobilize immigrants. In contrast, political party organizations, especially local chapters, are much less likely to have teams of experts in place to work on a day-to-day basis on mobilization around issues of concern to immigrant communities.

Anecdotal evidence gathered during interviews with Chinese and Mexican immigrants demonstrates that many immigrants continue to have a deep interest in the politics and events relating to their homelands. Thus, in terms of fostering a strong base of immigrant support, it is not surprising that a third strength for community organizations lies in their transnational connections and work.

Immigrants have been the agents in creating new transnational philanthropic organizations and in instituting transnational practices within existing organizations. Migrants just from the Mexican state of Zacatecas have created more than 250 clubs located throughout the United States. In terms of new organizations created by immigrants, hometown clubs are a prime example of groups that use transnational practices to mobilize immigrants to participate in politics not just in their homelands but also in the United States. Associations in the Federation of Zacatecan Clubs of Southern California are active regarding hometown issues, and their members lobby Mexican political authorities on these topics, but they have also sponsored scholarships for students in Southern California and protested Proposition 187, the 1994 California ballot measure that aimed to restrict services to illegal immigrants (Levitt 2002).

The Support Committee for Maquiladora Workers in San Diego, which organizes Asian immigrant women to document unsafe working conditions in maquiladoras near the U.S.-Mexican border and to provide social services to the predominantly female Mexican maquiladora workforce, provides another example of an organization that uses transnational organizing to engage immigrants. For immigrant and native women working in subsistence-wage jobs, these partnerships have helped to build cross-border solidarity and communication that transcends ethnicity. Lisa Lowe, who has studied the support committee, notes, "Labor organizing projects are changing both in response to the modes of global restructuring and to the changes in immigration and immigrant communities over the last two decades; new strategies aim to take on the difficult work of forging understanding and political solidarity between women and men across racial and national boundaries" (1998, 41).

Implications of Mobilization by Community Organizations

With the decline of a strong political party presence at the local level, contemporary community organizations are poised to take an even more prominent role in the political lives of immigrants than has been the case in the past. If community organizations continue to take on this role, they are likely to (1) provide multiple channels of political socialization; (2) increase the opportunities for noncitizens to participate in the U.S. political process; (3) develop single-issue-based political agendas; and (4) foster the retention of ethnic identity as a component of organizational strategy.

First, community organizations are likely to mobilize immigrants around a wide range of political activities, both electoral and nonelectoral. Involvement of noncitizens in nonelectoral activities raises questions about the relative effectiveness of electoral versus nonelectoral participation. Many political scientists consider electoral participation to be the cornerstone of political participation (Wolfinger and Rosenstone 1980; Rosenstone and Hansen 1993; Verba, Schlozman, and Brady 1995). Parties and elected officials also tend to focus on electoral participation because votes and electoral victories are the source of their power. Although the value of nonelectoral activities remains an open question, the research for this book indicates that participation in activities other than voting and campaigns, especially if that participation occurs through an array of different types of community organizations, may represent an easily overlooked element of immigrants' involvement in politics, as acknowledged by others who have studied nonelectoral participation

(Piven and Cloward 1978; Echols 1989; Wei 1993; Kelley 1994; Verba, Schlozman and Brady 1995; Wrinkle et al. 1996). Robin Kelley writes eloquently about the "need to break away from traditional notions of politics" preoccupied with voting and participation in formal social movements (1994, 4). He claims that to understand the full scope of political participation, we must look beyond traditional political institutions and focus on oppressed groups' efforts to organize through institutions outside of the mainstream as well as their ability to transform both mainstream and more marginalized institutions (10). Further, he encourages greater attention to unique forms of political participation beyond voting or such traditional grassroots activities as protesting.

Second, because community organizations seek to expand the size of their bases (unlike political parties, which single-mindedly pursue the vote among a narrow group of likely voters), community organizations are more likely than are parties to focus their energy on noncitizens. As they mobilize immigrants generally, community organizations will also mobilize noncitizens, giving that group—which mainstream parties have traditionally ignored because they cannot vote—an opportunity to participate in certain aspects of American politics, such as protesting, picketing, and testifying at public hearings.[1]

Third, while mobilization by political parties is likely to lead to organization around a party platform or comprehensive agenda, mobilization led by community organizations is likely to be driven by issue-specific and issue-oriented strategies. Parties are the vehicles of America's two competing ideological agendas, republicanism and liberalism (Reichley 1992). The two parties mobilize around broad sets of policies reflecting these ideological agendas, which are framed in more universal terms to appeal to people at the state or national level. In contrast, the policy concerns around which community organizations mobilize their constituencies tend to be much narrower and more specific in scope. They are likely to mobilize around a single issue or set of related issues affecting an immigrant community—for example, legalization, worker rights, or language policy. It may be easier to mobilize around a local issue or specific issue that is related to concerns that directly affect people. A personal concern may prompt individuals to become politically involved. The degree to which community organizations mobilize around a specific set of community concerns may vary considerably, but most do so to a greater extent than the two major parties.

Finally, a distinguishing feature of contemporary community organizations is that they allow for a strong retention of ethnic identity and a role for it in organizing. Political parties may periodically engage in symbolic outreach to immigrants based on perceived aspects of immigrant culture such as language and ethnic foods, but because they must also appeal to white swing voters, they are not deeply committed to supporting or recognizing diverse cultural practices or traditions. Community organizations, in contrast, often simultaneously offer political activities (such as citizenship classes) and cultural activities (such as ethnic-language instruction for children, training in traditional dances, or traditional ethnic festivals). Community organizations also seek to protect immigrants from cultural or ethnic discrimination. For example, the Asian Pacific American Legal Center in Los Angeles has fought several legal battles to ensure language rights for immigrants and to change language policies at the Los Angeles Police Department. Some organizations have launched public education campaigns to teach the wider community about the specific traditions of the represented group. The dual nature of the activities that today's community organizations promote not only distinguishes them from political parties but also sets them apart from the community organizations of the first half of the twentieth century, such as settlement houses, which were assimilationist in orientation.

The extent to which these four implications are associated with any specific type of organization varies. Nonetheless, understanding those implications helps us to distinguish the ways in which community organizations' role in immigrant mobilization is likely to affect the future direction of immigrant participation.

Community Organizations in the Absence of Parties

Contemporary community organizations are taking responsibility for many types of immigrant activities that used to be associated with political machines, including applying for citizenship and naturalization, voter registration, voter education, and getting out the vote. They have not entirely replaced political parties, however, because the community groups have an array of responsibilities. Only rarely can an organization be involved consistently or full time in political activities. They also face serious limitations in terms of financial resources, as comments by a leader of a nonprofit that focuses on voting rights in the Latino community illustrate.

How we try to situate ourselves with that kind of mission is by organizing the community around elections. We do that by doing voter education, voter registration, and get-out-the-vote [work]. We work within a very specific moment of the political process. That defines a lot of our organizing, but it's also required because our community is so large, and money-wise, there's no way to sustain ourselves. There's a whole question of continuity, because we don't have the money to work continuously. We practically work within different windows of opportunities, within certain conjunctures, political conjunctures.

Some community organizations have had surprising success in politically mobilizing their constituencies. In certain instances, community organizations have mobilized the least advantaged segments of the immigrant community, those individuals who have few resources, do not speak English, and are not citizens—day laborers, garment workers, and undocumented immigrants among others. According to traditional theories of political participation (especially socioeconomic theories), this segment of the U.S. population is the least likely to participate politically. Understanding how organizations have mobilized those people may provide important insights about how civic institutions could mobilize immigrants more generally and potentially even other segments of the U.S. population.

Immigrants acknowledge community organizations' importance in motivating newcomers' political participation. Mexican and Chinese immigrants interviewed in New York frequently connected their level of participation in U.S. politics to their level of involvement in community-based advocacy organizations. For example, a thirty-nine-year-old Mexican immigrant who had lived in New York City for sixteen years claimed that since he had never belonged to an organized community group in the United States, he didn't "have the experience" needed to participate in politics. In contrast, a twenty-nine-year-old Mexican who had been living in New York for only three years had joined a Mexican workers' organization there and had recently attended two protests, one outside the Immigration and Naturalization Service offices to call for amnesty for undocumented immigrants and another outside a New York City restaurant calling for workers' rights. He claimed that he had joined because of the group's goal of protecting immigrants from labor exploitation and abuse.

Chinese immigrants who were interviewed in Los Angeles also tended to view involvement with an organization or group as key to their political involvement in the United States. One forty-nine-year-old Chinese immigrant who had lived in the United States for thirteen years claimed that he was not very involved in U.S. politics because he did not know people willing to work with him to address the issues about which he cared. In contrast, a Chinese immigrant woman who had lived in the United States for only a year said that she was interested in getting involved in politics and seemed to believe that participation in a group would be an important step in that direction: "I'm still new. I'm working on forming a group and getting involved."

The community organizations that I studied covered an array of forms and missions. The work and strategies of (1) labor organizations and workers' centers, (2) advocacy, social service, and ethnic voluntary organizations, and (3) religious institutions highlight community organizations' contributions to immigrant mobilization. These three groupings do not suggest rigid analytical categories. Instead, they help to describe the variety of community organizations that mobilize immigrants into politics. The specific organizations described loosely fit under each grouping.

Data collected in part through fieldwork consisting of participant observation, gathering materials from community organizations, and in-depth interviews conducted in New York City and Los Angeles with Chinese and Mexican immigrants and individuals affiliated with organizations that provide social, legal, political, or issue-oriented services for these immigrants inform the descriptions. I conducted interviews with forty individuals affiliated with organizations that provide social, legal, political, or issue-oriented services for Chinese or Mexican immigrants in New York or Los Angeles, including the Southwest Voter Registration Education Project, One-Stop Immigration, the Asian Pacific American Labor Alliance, the Chinatown Service Center, the Coalition for Humane Immigrant Rights, and the Asian Pacific American Legal Center in Los Angeles and the Chinese Voter Education Alliance, the Chinese Staff and Workers' Association, the Catholic archdiocese, the Latino Commission on AIDS, and the Asociación de Tepeyac in New York. These research methods provided a rich source of qualitative information about the ways that community organizations mobilize Chinese and Mexican immigrants as well as the challenges they face. Interviews with organization leaders revealed some of the motivations and political commitments driving institutional activities and the strategies that are bringing immigrants into the political system. (The methods used in the study are described in greater detail in the appendix.)[2] My observations are intended to provide a personal, descriptive, and process-oriented view of how certain leaders have come to understand their organizations' roles vis-à-vis immigrant communities. The observations also allow for an assessment of how community institutions, local mobilization efforts, and neighborhood settings structure opportunities for immigrant political mobilization in the United States.

Labor Organizations and Workers' Centers

It is surprising that national labor unions[3] and their local affiliates are mobilizing immigrants because labor organizations have often taken an ambivalent—if not overtly anti-immigrant—stance toward racial minorities (Takaki 1989, 199; K. Wong 1994). At the beginning of the twentieth century, the American Federation of Labor did some selective immigrant organizing, "appealing to the early arriving Irish and Germans and to skilled labor, but openly and vituperatively opposing newer, unskilled immigrants from Eastern and Southern Europe and from Asia" (A. Lin forthcoming, 17). Labor organizations' contemporary efforts to include immigrants partly reflect changing demographic and economic realities. At the end of the twentieth century, the increase in immigrant workers within the U.S. manufacturing and service sectors coincided with an overall decline in union membership. In response, labor leaders began actively to recruit Latino and Asian immigrants (Greenhouse 2000a, b). A high-ranking member of the California Federation of Labor even claimed that "immigrant workers from Mexico and Central America . . . are the strongest part of the workforce for us" (Cleeland 2000, A-1).

Nevertheless, not all unions or sectors of the labor movement have embraced immigrants. Even though the American Federation of Labor–Congress of Industrial Organizations (AFL-CIO) has recently made efforts to include Asian and Latino immigrant workers, Alicia Schmidt-Camacho notes that "the institutionalized labor movement still privileges the skilled, male, white labor force in both its structures of representation and in its vision for combating the erosion of labor rights under the globalization of capital. The crisis of international trade unionism is a direct result of the hyper-differentiation of workers along lines of race, gender, nationality, and immigration status" (1999, 92). An example is the slowness with which traditional unions have responded to the needs of restaurant and garment workers in New York's Chinatown (Kwong 1996). National trade unions and their local affiliates undeniably continue to struggle with their commitment to fully incorporate and represent immigrants, women, people of color, and other marginalized groups. Thus, building a strong relationship between unions and immigrant workers remains a challenge (K. Wong 1994).

There are, however, significant signs of progress. Racial minorities and women are slowly gaining leadership positions within the "new labor movement" (M. Chen and Wong 1998; Mantsios 1998; Milkman and Wong 2000). This new generation of leaders demonstrates a greater commitment to inclusion of nonwhite immigrants than did their mostly white, mostly male predecessors. This new vision has translated into some encouraging, tangible activities.

The AFL-CIO created the California Immigrant Workers Association in 1989 to help Latino immigrants with citizenship and English acquisition. In addition, in February 2000, the AFL-CIO called for amnesty for undocumented immigrants. In October 1999, at a major labor event at the Staples Center in Los Angeles attended by many Latin Americans, immigrants were symbolically welcomed with the availability of simultaneous English-into-Spanish translation. The September 2003 Immigrant Workers Freedom Ride (IWFR) was spearheaded by labor. Modeled on the 1960s freedom rides, immigrants from all over the United States embarked on bus journeys to Washington, D.C., and New York City, stopping at places throughout the country where local communities were facing labor, immigrant, or civil rights struggles. After reaching Washington, participants lobbied Congress for immigration reforms, including an amnesty program and more liberal family-reunification policies (see Greenhouse 2000c; Goldman 2003, A-25).

Today, unions are essential to immigrant political mobilization (Milkman 2000). A Chinese American labor leader who works with a New York union local 90 percent of whose members are Chinese immigrant garment workers noted that the city's proposal to build a jail in Chinatown catalyzed union members' political organizing:

> In 1983, the city decided to build a jail in Chinatown. And the reason they decided to build it was because they said that "Nobody votes in Chinatown. We can get away with it." And the union joined with a lot of the groups to actually get all of the shops to stop working. We had a

rally of ten to twenty thousand people out there. . . . Stories of the '80s, of the union after the strike, was really heavily building alliances around political action. And encouraging voter registration. So in '84, we did really massive voter registration; the first Chinese judges were elected. The union has been involved in a lot of the voter registration drives and the first efforts to elect Chinese into office, also in spearheading a lot of the lobbying efforts, like how do you lobby political officials. On the immigration issues, we'll send buses to Washington and stuff like that. . . . Since we are working now with an Asian population, I think we're able to do quite a lot of strong education to the community as to how to do some of this stuff . . . the nuts and bolts of politics. And I think we're able to impart that back to the community in a way that's got people much more involved. And not just the workers, and not just our members, but also the community at large.

That particular union has organized more than twenty thousand Chinese immigrant garment workers in New York's Chinatown and mobilized more than a thousand workers to rally in Sunset Park, Brooklyn, in 1995, in that neighborhood's first large political rally.

As one union leader in Los Angeles noted, "For unions to be successful, they have to embrace a much broader vision of who they are and what they do. . . . They see the necessity of addressing all aspects of workers' lives, from the political arena to the social arena to [the] economic. And it's the same type of organizing skills whether you are bargaining for a contract or leading an organizing campaign, or fighting Proposition 187 or 209. . . . So I think that most successful unions have been able to skillfully combine both political mobilization and organizing."[4] This statement represents an approach to labor organizing that takes seriously immigrant involvement in the U.S. political system.

Some unions provide immigrant members with a space to receive and share information about how the U.S. political system works and about the basics of politics in this country. The few Chinese and Mexican union members interviewed for this book all stated that their unions had provided them with information about U.S. politics.

Political organizing by unions is also noteworthy because some unions build bridges across "city trenches," to use Ira Katnelson's (1981) term.[5] Whereas Katznelson and others contend that workers often view labor issues and community issues as separate and unrelated areas of struggle, today there are signs that the union's presence in immigrant workers' lives is not limited strictly to the workplace. The AFL-CIO held the Convocation for Working Families in Los Angeles in October 1999. The theme was "community alliance building," and it was followed by an AFL-CIO-organized a forum on hate crimes against immigrants, gays and lesbians, and religious minorities. Commenting on the forum, one organizer said, "Our message, in terms of why we organized that forum and why we set it up the way we did, was, once again, [that] we wanted unions, as critical institutions, to understand that they have a much broader role in society that extends beyond the workplace. And that it is imperative for unions to speak out against hate crimes, to mobilize community response, and to be at the forefront of fights against racism and for equality." In addition, the AFL-CIO sponsored town hall forums on immigration and immigration rights in Los Angeles, New York, Chicago, and Atlanta in which not only union members but also community organizations and immigrant-rights advocates participated.

Recent organizing campaigns by janitors in Los Angeles and New York indicate that immigrants see a strong link between workplace and political struggles (Waldinger et al. 1997; Greenhouse 2000b). That is, workers often see their fight for higher wages and benefits as political. One organizer for the Service Employees International Union's Justice for Janitors campaign in Los Angeles framed it as a fight for "rights, not just wages": "We said, 'There've been five demonstrations. It's probably very difficult for you, but we ask for your support as we fight for our rights.' And it turned out to have a positive impact" (quoted in Waldinger et al. 1997, 40).

Immigrant workers' centers also help to mobilize immigrants.[6] A few workers' centers are affiliated with unions, but most are independent, community-based organizations made up of low-wage workers. These organizations form to help protect workers' rights and wages and to give workers, many of them immigrants, a stronger voice in their communities. "Workers' centers pursue their mission through a combination of strategies: service delivery: such as legal representation to recover lost wages, English as a Second Language classes, and job placement, advocacy: speaking on behalf of low-wage workers to local media and government, and organizing: building an association of workers who act together for economic and political change" (Fine 2003, 1). Examples of workers' centers include the Chinese Staff and Workers' Association (CSWA) in New

York City, Korean Immigrant Worker Advocates in Los Angeles, and the Workplace Project in Long Island, New York. Workers' centers also exist in Chicago; Minneapolis; and Alexandria, Virginia.

The CSWA, with offices in Chinatown and Sunset Park, organized a petition drive and several demonstrations outside the New York State Workers' Compensation Board to call for an overhaul of the workers' compensation system. Despite their long and hard hours and the risk of apprehension, about one hundred immigrant workers made the effort to attend one demonstration. CSWA played a key role in organizing workers to testify at hearings for state legislation aimed at protecting garment-industry workers from employer exploitation. One worker recalled that after she joined the center's Women's Project, she became active in challenging the gender discrimination and substandard conditions for female garment-industry workers.

Labor unions and workers centers represent a unique and potentially potent space for political coalition building because although many community organizations are segregated, it is possible in some cases for "African Americans, Latinos, Native Americans, Asian Pacific Americans, and European Americans to work side-by-side" (K. Wong 1994, 340). The involvement and cooperation of a range of ethnic groups may fortify the unions' and workers' centers' efforts to mobilize immigrants politically. It is too early to know if these organizations will remain a source of political mobilization for immigrants, but their efforts to construct community alliances and develop a relationship with immigrant communities may allow them to build a sustained mobilization in some areas (for further examples, see Bonacich 1999; Saito and Park 2000). In addition, if unions in particular remain committed to recruiting more women, immigrants, and people of color into leadership positions, they are likely to become even more effective at political mobilization.

The implications of labor organizations' and worker centers' involvement in immigrant political mobilization are clear. Unlike the two major parties, these organizations are not primarily interested in getting candidates elected to office and so they are more likely than parties to involve non-citizens in a wide range of political activities. For example, the 2003 IWFR organized by labor unions drew attention to the struggles of immigrant workers. Along the bus route, workers and their supporters took part in rallies, and IWFR members wrote letters and columns advocating immigrant worker rights, which were printed in major newspapers across the country. IWFR organizers invited noncitizen workers to take part in the activities, and a number of them traveled on the buses. Significantly, better working and living conditions for noncitizens was an important demand made by the riders. The IWFR is an example of labor organizing workers beyond narrowly defined worker rights to address immigrant rights as well. However, compared to most political party platforms, worker and immigrant rights represent a specific and narrow set of concerns.

Given the declining role of mainstream party machines and organizations in mobilizing immigrants, it is important to consider the relationship between political parties and the labor movement in particular. Some argue that labor is an "ancillary organization" of the Democratic Party because the labor movement has long shown strong financial and logistical support for Democratic candidates (Schattschneider 1957; see also Greenstone 1969). Nevertheless, the strength and viability of the relationship between the Democratic Party and labor remains controversial. Organized labor has put tremendous resources and energy into supporting Democratic candidates, but "historically, the Democratic Party has given labour more symbols than substance" (Chang 2001, 384). For example, in its fight to reform labor-relations laws, the labor movement has failed to win strong Democratic support.[7] Not surprisingly, on occasion, the labor movement has supported Republicans who take a moderate stand on labor issues (Dark 2000). In 1998, the AFL-CIO endorsed twenty-seven Republican candidates for the U.S. House of Representatives (Greenhouse 1998a). The president of the AFL-CIO commented on the endorsements by saying, "If we're going to maintain credibility with our rank and file as well as with elected officials, we have to show that we're supporting candidates, regardless of party, who have supported us" (Greenhouse 1998b, A-20).[8]

Despite working closely together at times, the mainstream parties and labor unions do not share identical interests, and their mobilization activities reflect different concerns. Whereas parties are in the business of winning elections by gaining votes, the goals of unions include organizational maintenance and the adoption of policies that benefit labor. These distinct albeit sometimes intersecting interests affect the types of political activities around which the organizations try to mobilize. Parties aim to get out the vote on Election Day. To influence the policy responses of elected officials and the parties, labor organizations might mobilize individuals to participate by voting, but they also attempt to influence legislation by getting people to participate in nonvoting activities, including grassroots lobbying, rallies, and demonstrations. While mainstream parties have been turning much of their attention to raising funds and garnering support among business groups and large corporate contributors (Aronowitz 1998), unions have been directing their resources toward worker mobilization (Dark 2000).[9] Therefore, the labor movement is distinct from mainstream parties primarily because it engages workers, including immigrants, in a wide range of political activities.

Social Service, Advocacy, and Ethnic Voluntary Organizations

Nonprofit social service agencies, legal and voter-education advocacy organizations, and ethnic voluntary associations are among the most active institutions mobilizing immigrants politically today.[10] Because these organizations serve many immigrants and are often involved in community affairs, both immigrants themselves and community elites such as elected officials and government agency leaders have widely recognized the important role played by these institutions in the political mobilization of immigrants.

In the first half of the twentieth century, local community organizations such as settlement houses were assimilationist in orientation. Ethnic customs and practices were considered part of an Old World mentality that had little place in America (Kraut 1982). Organizations such as the Chicago-based League for the Protection of Immigrants sponsored programs to introduce and educate southern and eastern European immigrants to "American ways" (Fuchs 1990, 62). Reacting to assimilationist pressures, some groups established their own ethnic community institutions. For example, in Chicago, southern and eastern European immigrants created social clubs and developed cultural programs rather than attend the activities to which they were invited at Jane Addams's Hull House (A. Lin forthcoming, 15).

Social service and advocacy organizations currently incorporate community traditions and language into their mobilization strategies as a means of targeting particular communities. Most social service organizations that serve Asian American or Latino immigrants employ a multilingual staff and make educational materials available in multilingual or bilingual formats. Advocacy organizations commonly integrate community traditions into organizing strategies. For example, in December 2003, the

Mexican American Political Association, a Los Angeles–based advocacy organization, called for a labor and school strike, marches, and an economic boycott to protest the repeal of a law that would have allowed immigrants without legal documents to apply for drivers' licenses beginning on January 1, 2004. The actions were scheduled for December 12, to coincide with the traditional Mexican holiday honoring the Virgin of Guadalupe.

Some social service agencies not only provide information and resources to help immigrants find jobs, housing, and health care but also help them become politically active. Because these organizations provide direct services, often to thousands of immigrants, they are well positioned to mobilize large numbers of people. Three successful examples come from Los Angeles: the Chinatown Service Center, which assists more than twelve thousand Chinese immigrants a year; the Coalition for Humane Immigrant Rights of Los Angeles, which organizes domestic workers and day laborers in the Mexican community; and One-Stop Immigration, which provides citizenship-application preparation and legal education to more than forty thousand Mexican immigrants annually (*Directory* 1999–2000). All three have organized notable political demonstrations, marches, and petition drives.

Another New York organization, the Asian American Legal Defense and Education Fund, provides legal services for Chinese and other Asian immigrants. It organized approximately two hundred people to attend a teach-in for the National Day of Action for Dr. Wen Ho Lee, the Chinese American Los Alamos scientist incarcerated by the U.S. government for allegedly mishandling government secrets.

Although few community-based advocacy or social service organizations adhere to an explicitly political agenda, many leaders see their organizations as having a political role in immigrant communities. As one leader of a nonprofit Los Angeles social service center that targets Mexican immigrants said,

> The reason why I work at [the organization] is because I saw it as a space, as an opportunity where I could do a lot of work on behalf of the immigrant community. Because I understood that we have gone through cycles of very, very difficult political times. . . . We have touched the [people's] lives directly in actual services provided to them . . . both through our legal-services branch as well as our education

branch. . . . And we're very proud to have been—of the fact that we have been part of what rightfully can be called a social movement to empower formerly totally marginalized communities.

This statement indicates that some social service agencies see themselves as providing not just social services but also a space for political organizing.

One of the most interesting examples of political organizing by community-based advocacy groups involves the mobilization of immigrant day laborers. Because they are not concentrated in a traditional workplace, like a factory, but are dispersed at different street corners and work sites, it is often difficult for these laborers to organize collectively and share information. Traditional models that focus on socioeconomic status and assimilation would predict that day laborers would be one of the hardest groups to organize politically because they have few resources and little formal political power. However, certain advocacy organizations have begun to meet these challenges through innovative organizing tactics that create unique spaces in which immigrants can meet and talk. An organizer who works with Mexican immigrant day laborers in Los Angeles described how collective endeavors are promoted that create opportunities for workers:

> I think we've really done a lot of nontraditional things, like soccer. In every corner where we are organized, we try to make a soccer team. And we actually have a league. . . . They play soccer, and they love it. Getting people for soccer is never a problem. And after the game, when people are drinking water or refreshments and mingling and things come up, like, "At our corner, we have a minimum wage." "At our corner, the police came, but you know what, we filed a complaint." And things get shared like that. So that successes that have been happening on corners get shared in places where we're barely organized. That was the total intent of the soccer, and plus everyone loves soccer.

The executive director of a community-based voting rights organization that targets Los Angeles's Chinese American community also commented on his organization's desire to create space and opportunities for political awareness and education, noting how Chinese immigrants

> don't understand American politics, so you need to educate them. You need to empower them by giving them material, by providing opportunities for them, get them involved and get them interested. . . . But it takes a long time. . . . I mean, I will be talking to a Taiwanese group in

Mandarin—I have no problem giving a speech in Mandarin about U.S. politics. I will use some of my knowledge about their interests in Taiwan and play off that. Now, if I didn't have that understanding, I think it would be difficult.

Thus, ethnic appeals may be quite consistent with motivating interests in participation in American politics.

Regarding ethnic voluntary associations, Ann Chih Lin's forthcoming study of the political incorporation of nineteenth- and early-twentieth-century immigrants shows that immigrant-organized homeland associations made political demands, especially at the local level. Their successes included the creation of classes in native languages within some public-school systems. Even when homeland associations did not work to improve conditions for immigrant communities in the United States, the preservation of ethnic traditions and culture existed simultaneously with retention of homeland cultures and an interest in homeland politics could go hand in hand with the increase of interest and participation in American politics.

Today, homeland associations continue to aid their members' sending communities (Jacobson 1995). In 1999 in Los Angeles, Mexican immigrants from Oaxaca organized a fund-raising benefit to aid flood victims in their home state. A Mexican immigrant leader in New York who has organized several events for the Mexican community there explained how he had become an activist: although he had migrated to the United States nearly thirty years earlier, the boundaries of his community encompassed both New York City and his hometown in the state of Puebla (see Robert Smith 1998). Consequently, he organizes long-distance running races in both places. At first he had difficulty even knowing where to begin in organizing U.S. events: he would start by looking in a phone book and calling different government offices. Over time, however, he became familiar with the local government structure, and now he has friends in various city agencies and departments: "I started working with the organizers of the police department. They like me! You know, like the police department, now every time that I go up to the department [to do paperwork related to a community event], they know me like friends. The guy told me, 'Any time you just come, no problem. We just help you.'"

The interaction between homeland associations and government agencies is critical to political mobilization and empowerment. In the process of organizing events to benefit those in the sending community, members of homeland associations become more familiar with local government institutions in the United States and more comfortable with the people who work in them. This also works in reverse: contact with a homeland association gives individuals working in local government offices in the United States an opportunity to connect with the members of an immigrant community. One leader of another Oaxacan group in Los Angeles predicted, "Organizations like this are going to be more important in the next ten years because some of them are in the early stages and will mature in time. . . . Slowly some politicians, at least Latinos, are becoming aware of such organizations and are trying to tap into them to get political support." That prediction began to assume concrete form in 2003 when representatives from eighteen Mexican and Central American migrant organizations attended a series of leadership-building workshops under the auspices of the University of Southern California. One aspect of the series was an attempt to connect participants with officials and representatives from government agencies and philanthropic organizations (Rivera-Salgado, Rodriguez, and Escala-Rabadan 2004).

Most homeland associations engage in an array of activities to benefit or celebrate the region or hometown from which the immigrants came. At times, these activities have a political component. A festival in Los Angeles's Highland Park, attended by five hundred people, celebrated Oaxacan heritage by featuring music and dance from different regions. Vendors sold T-shirts, food, and juices, but there was also a table where those attending could register to vote in the United States. All of the literature and signs at the voter registration table were in both Spanish and English.

In the Asian American community, some ethnic voluntary associations sponsor explicitly political activities. For example, New York City's Chinese Consolidated Benevolent Association (CCBA) includes sixty associations, mostly based on home-country regional and district groups. The CCBA has been very active in Chinese politics. Historically, strong ties existed between the CCBA and the anticommunist (Nationalist) Guomindang party, and the CCBA has received financial backing from the party.[11] However, the CCBA has not focused its activities solely on homeland issues. It has assisted immigrants with housing, jobs, naturalization, and financial support (J. Lin 1998). The CCBA has also been involved in community politics in Chinatown. In 1974, for example, the CCBA and other Asian American community organizations helped to negotiate a settlement with the city over the hiring of Asian American construction workers at the site of Confucius Plaza, a Chinatown housing development. A year later, the CCBA mobilized a crowd estimated at twenty thousand for a demonstration at City Hall Park to protest police brutality against Asian Americans (J. Lin 1998, 136).

The CCBA's political power in the Chinese community has waned in recent years (Kwong 1987). However, immigrants I interviewed still mentioned the CCBA as an important institution for fostering political involvement. When asked about whether it was difficult for immigrants to get information about the U.S. political system, a Chinese man who had lived in New York City for thirty years responded that it is "difficult, unless under some guidance—for instance, the CCBA. . . . Because when you are in someone else's country, you don't know how the system works or how to get information."

According to Jan Lin, the importance of ethnic voluntary associations in the Chinese community should not be underestimated: "It would be misleading to assume that traditional associations are backward or obsolescent social institutions. . . . Traditional associations had a historical salience in assisting Chinese immigrants in their adjustment to life during the exclusion years and continue to play a significant role in their cultural lives and familial interactions. . . . There has been a continuing growth of new family, clan, and regional associations since the mid-1980s, particularly of the Fujianese variety, as emigration has accelerated out of Fujian province" (1998, 122). Lin also suggests that contemporary Fujianese clan associations are "institutionally comparable" to the older Chinese associations such as the CCBA. Like the members of many other ethnic voluntary associations, the members of Fujianese associations are concerned about homeland politics, but they are also likely to mobilize Chinese immigrants from Fujian in the United States, as when several Fujianese associations organized to resolve ethnic tensions in a Brooklyn neighborhood in 1996 (Lii 1996).

Because of their informal nature and organization, it is difficult to quantify the exact number and membership of ethnic voluntary associations. Although some hometown associations may have fewer than one hundred members, others are quite large. In Los Angeles, an organization representing immigrants from Jalisco has ten thousand members, and one representing immigrants from Oaxaca has two thousand (*Directory* 1999–2000). A nationwide federation includes more than 250 clubs representing Zacatecan migrants.

Ethnic voluntary associations offer immigrants a sense of belonging and self-worth that can lead to political empowerment in the United States. Immigrants are likely to experience a loss of status when they enter economic and social life in the United States, but this loss can be offset by their involvement in immigrant organizations. Within the immigrant organization, immigrants can "reconstruct the social networks and perpetuate socialization patterns of the home country. Ethnic organizations offer immigrants an alternative to adaptation to the receiving country by providing an environment which, like the ethnic enclave, recognizes their social standing in spite of whatever downward economic mobility they may have suffered in the United States" (Jones-Correa 1998, 333).[12]

Ethnic voluntary associations also represent the kind of institution that Sidney Verba, Kay Lehman Schlozman, and Henry Brady (1995) argue is important for the development of civic skills. Through their participation in homeland associations, immigrants improve their communication abilities and practice other civic skills such as organizing events. "Once honed," claim Verba, Schlozman, and Brady, "they are part of the arsenal of resources that can be devoted, if the individual wishes, to politics" (331). The formation of these associations requires tremendous organization-building skills. Organizational leaders develop skills in personnel management, time management, public relations, accounting, and grant writing, among many other areas. Many of these associations offer rank-and-file members educational and social services such as lessons in English, civics, health care, and maintaining cultural traditions. In addition, these organizations achieve some measure of a presence within the mainstream community through public events and the contacts they forge with social service providers and government personnel.

Despite their successes, ethnic voluntary associations also face significant challenges in influencing mainstream politics through mobilizing efforts. In her insightful study of the role of ethnic advocacy groups in the political incorporation of Arab immigrants, Ann Chih Lin (forthcoming) notes that because they operate outside the upper echelons of U.S. political circles and contribute only insignificant amounts to political campaigns, these groups find it difficult to influence elites. Still, given that political parties pay little attention to immigrant communities, especially those with the least resources, homeland and ethnic voluntary associations represent a significant source of mobilization for immigrants. Even when these associations fail to turn out massive numbers of voters, they have provided and will continue to provide a conduit for political expression by those who cannot vote. As the examples in this section show, their activities lay the groundwork for integrating future voters into the polity through activities that either directly involve political participation, understood broadly, or help immigrants to acquire the skills and experience needed for their political mobilization over the long term.

Social service, advocacy, and ethnic voluntary associations involve immigrants in a range of political activities beyond voting, and some of these organizations are very active in terms of working with and promoting participation by noncitizens. Unlike parties, which are more likely to mobilize generally by putting forth platforms describing their stands on a broad range of issues such as national security, education reform, and tax policies, advocacy, social service, and ethnic voluntary organizations are likely to organize around specific issues that directly affect immigrants, such as health benefits, hate crimes, amnesty for undocumented migrants, and naturalization. This more limited approach to issue advocacy further distinguishes the type of politics generated by ethnic voluntary associations from that of political parties. Social service, advocacy, and ethnic voluntary associations are also more likely than parties to reinforce ethnic identity among the immigrants they serve by providing information and services in the native language. While parties have made a major effort to reach out to Spanish-speaking voters, they have not been as attentive toward immigrants who speak an Asian language or other non-English-speaking immigrants. Social service, advocacy, and ethnic voluntary organizations working with immigrant communities also often participate in cultural events or celebrations that help to reinforce ethnic identity among immigrants. For example, to celebrate the traditional Mexican festival of the Día de los Muertos (Day of the Dead, or All Souls' Day), organizers with the Coalition for Humane Immigrant Rights of Los Angeles included an altar decorated with flowers, food, and candles at the tenth anniversary celebration of a coalition day-laborer site.

Religious Institutions

Religious institutions have always constituted a critical source of political mobilization for certain groups such as African Americans and Irish Catholics. In the past, however, some churches have been actively hostile to immigrants, especially those who were Roman Catholic or Jewish. Protestant social reformers demonstrated an unyielding assimilationist approach to non-Protestant immigrants and at times supported strong exclusionist measures against immigrants (Higham 1952; Kraut 1982; Katerberg 1995).

Similar tensions exist today. An increasing number of Protestant churches offer services in Chinese, Korean, and Spanish,[13] but several conservative Christian leaders have taken anti-immigrant stands (Abcarian 1996; Dart 1996). The Catholic Church, a significant institution in the lives of many previous immigrants, has seen its ranks swell with Mexican, other Latin American, and Asian immigrants. In heavily Latino regions, church leaders have even begun adopting Mexican indigenous ceremonies (Gold 1998; M. Ramirez 1999; Niebuhr 2000). Many Catholic Church officials and community members credit immigrants who arrived from Latin America during the 1990s with "revitalizing" the church (Christian 2000). The executive director of a major social service agency serving Mexican immigrants notes that "in the case of Los Angeles, for example, it didn't used to be, but now it is, the largest Catholic archdiocese in the entire United States. And the only reason it became that is because of the influx of immigrants. . . . And what did they cluster around? The one institution they knew—the church."

The Asociación de Tepeyac provides an important example of religion-based political organizing of immigrants. Mexican leaders suggest that the association is by far the most important organization for involving New York's Mexican immigrants in U.S. politics. The group was founded by a Jesuit brother from Mexico who was recruited by the New York archdiocese to provide outreach to the Mexican community. With more than half of its members having arrived after 1995, the Mexican community is among the newest immigrant groups in New York City (Robert Smith 1996; Gonzalez and McCoy 1998). The Asociación de Tepeyac is housed within the Catholic Church but is a citywide, neighborhood-based political network. Leadership, communication, and meetings are structured and formal. Most members are undocumented service workers with minimal economic resources, yet they have participated in more than fifty demonstrations for worker and immigrant rights. In the fall of 1999, they brought together busloads of people to participate in a march in Washington to call for amnesty for undocumented immigrants.

The members' socioeconomic profile is one of the most surprising features of the Asociación de Tepeyac. Traditional political-participation models tends to emphasize socioeconomic incorporation or citizenship as

key to political involvement (Skerry 1993; Portes and Rumbaut 1996).[14]
Association members are the type of individuals that those models would
predict to be the least likely to participate in U.S. politics, yet Tepeyac
leaders claim that 10,000 out of an estimated 250,000 Mexican immigrants living in New York attended one of the group's demonstrations.
The group is developing workshops on workers' rights, which will be
offered within the New York parishes. In addition, it emphasizes training
young people to be future U.S. political leaders.

New York's Catholic Church clearly illustrates a religious organization
that successfully mobilizes immigrants. There are other examples. The
Immigration and Refugee Division of Catholic Charities of Los Angeles
annually has contact with more than fifty-two thousand immigrants, primarily Latinos. The organization provides legal assistance as well as citizenship, literacy, and job-training classes (*Directory* 1999–2000). Clergy
and Laity United for Economic Justice (CLUE) is an interfaith organization that helps to organize low-wage workers in Los Angeles County. In
May 2002, religious leaders and workers affiliated with CLUE participated
in a downtown march for immigrant workers' rights.

Asian American evangelical churches appear to be very much a part of
the American Christian conservative movement. The reach of the church
into some Chinese immigrant communities is significant. Although only 2
percent of Taiwan's population is Christian, nearly 25 percent of Taiwanese immigrants in the United States are Christians (most convert after
migration) (C. Chen 2001). Two predominantly Asian American evangelical Christian churches in Los Angeles have shown signs of incipient political mobilization. A few months before the 2000 presidential election, the
pastor at one of these churches encouraged the congregation to register
and to vote for George W. Bush, emphasizing that the country needed a
"Christian" president. At another service, the same pastor urged congregation members to spread the antiabortion message to their friends, family members, and congressional representatives.

For Chinese immigrants, an evident link exists between political
involvement in the United States and membership in a religious organization. In separate interviews, two middle-aged immigrant Chinese
women living in Los Angeles mentioned the church as having played a
role in getting them involved in politics. One described opportunities for
political participation in the United States as being "easy because America is very free. I can do whatever I want. There's no limit. If I want to

join, I can. Easy to form groups to change problems in societies. Like in my church group, we discuss politics. If they wanted to change things, I think they can." She was one of the few immigrants interviewed who expressed a fairly positive feeling about opportunities for participating in U.S. politics.

In regard to politically mobilizing immigrants, religious organizations face two notable constraints. First, many are explicitly apolitical or even antipolitical in orientation. When political mobilization occurs, it may be the unexpected by-product of the pursuit of nonpolitical goals. Under such circumstances mobilization efforts will at best be sporadic. Second, ideological commitments, a fundamental aspect of religious life, may mean that a given religious organization is hostile to certain segments of immigrant communities, such as gays and lesbians; in other cases, the organization may be anti-immigrant altogether. Conversely, membership in a congregation can give immigrants an opportunity to meet and interact with nonimmigrants in their community, or membership in a congregation that consists primarily of immigrants can create a sense of belonging to a community of shared interest. In their report on *Immigrant Religion in the City of Angels,* Donald Miller, Jon Miller, and Grace Dyrness write that "for many immigrants religion continues to exercise a strong attraction simply because it provides a setting and a reason to be in contact with their fellow immigrants. Religion, in other words, is a source of community, a place to speak one's native tongue, eat one's native food" (2001, 35). In both cases, with or without the blessing of church officials, participation in a congregation provides opportunities and a setting for sharing information and ideas about U.S. life and politics.

Political mobilization by religious institutions is likely to affect how and which immigrants participate in politics. It leads to patterns of participation that are distinct from those that would result if parties were more involved. Like other types of community organizations, religious institutions are more likely than parties to involve immigrants in a range of political activities while encouraging their members to naturalize and to vote. For example, church leaders affiliated with CLUE organize Latino immigrant parishioners to take part in the immigrant rights march held in downtown Los Angeles each May. In contrast with parties, some religious institutions with large numbers of immigrant congregants have worked closely to provide support and services to undocumented immigrants and have advocated on their behalf. Finally, some religious institutions have proven to be much more attentive than are parties to immigrant members' cultural traditions. This is likely to reinforce the retention of ethnic identity while encouraging participation in political activities organized by their church or other religious institution.

Conclusion

Community organizations have long had an important role in helping to integrate immigrants into the political system. From the 1890s to the 1920s, when major migrations to the United States occurred and nativism flourished, community organizations such as ethnic voluntary associations proliferated at both the national and local levels. These organizations gave immigrants a voice and some measure of group representation in American political and social life (Skocpol 1999b; A. Lin forthcoming). They often worked directly with political parties, which had strong presences at the local or neighborhood level, to mobilize immigrants. By the end of the twentieth century, however, mainstream political parties, now focusing on national-level strategies and mass media and direct-mail campaigns, had become relatively absent at the local level. Community organizations have stepped into the breach.

Today, the labor organizations, workers' centers, social service organizations, advocacy organizations, ethnic voluntary associations, and religious institutions play a strong role in politically mobilizing immigrants even though some of these institutions have demonstrated ambivalence toward immigrants and ethnic and racial minorities. Community organizations bring certain strengths to immigrant mobilization, including a focus on outreach motivated by the desire for organizational maintenance; strong ties to immigrant communities and existing expertise related to the cultural traditions, language needs, and policy priorities of those communities; and in many cases a transnational orientation. In a fashion parallel to that of the political machines and the ethnic voluntary associations of old, today's community organizations often provide much-needed social services and sometimes material goods to Asian American and Latino immigrants (Skocpol 1999b). Community organizations often engage in mobilization around a single issue or set of issues while taking responsibility for a wide range of immigrant political activities, including applying for citizenship and naturalization, voter registration, voter education, and getting out the vote, all of which used to be associated with political machines. As did machines and voluntary associations in the past, contemporary organizations reach out to immigrants by making ethnic-specific appeals (Dahl 1961; Erie 1988; A. Lin forthcoming).

However, because their end goal is not necessarily influencing electoral outcomes, contemporary organizations also mobilize immigrants in ways that differ sharply from those that prevailed in the past. Mobilization manifests in nonelectoral activities, such as petition drives, demonstrations, and protests. In fact, because many of these organizations emerged during or after the civil rights movement, they are often more concerned with ensuring and promoting the civil rights of immigrants and racial minorities than in producing electoral outcomes. Community organizations' ability to engage immigrants in a wide range of political activities, especially those that take place outside of the electoral system, indicates a need to employ a broad definition of political participation when evaluating immigrant populations. Although immigrants participate in politics at lower rates than their U.S.-born counterparts, some newcomers participate in innovative ways (such as organizing through political theater groups or by becoming involved in transnational political campaigns) that should not be discounted. Finally, many community organizations have emerged in an era of multiculturalism, which shapes their notions of group representation and eases the assimilationist pressures present in the ethnic voluntary associations of the early twentieth century.

In the absence of strong political-party presence at the local level, contemporary community organizations have the space to take on an even more prominent role in immigrants' political lives than has previously been the case. If this opportunity is pursued, we are likely to see these organizations (1) providing multiple channels of political socialization; (2) increasing the opportunities for noncitizens to participate in the U.S. political process; (3) developing single-issue-based political agendas; and (4) fostering the retention of ethnic identity as a component of organizational strategy. Furthermore, if adopted on an even wider scale, these efforts would likely result in increased political participation for members of immigrant communities. Mobilization by community organizations has been shown to be effective in increasing Asian Americans' and Latinos' political participation. Janelle S. Wong, Pei-te Lien, and M. Margaret Conway's (2005) study of survey data regarding Asian Americans' political participation shows that mobilization by community organizations boosts participation, especially in terms of nonvoting political activities. In their analysis based on an experimental research design, Ricardo Ramirez, Alan Gerber, and Donald Green (2004) report that the National Association of Latino Elected Officials increased vote turnout among Latinos by using live phone calls.

Although the community organizations described here are bringing some immigrants into the U.S. political system, often through unique and creative strategies, this should not be misinterpreted to mean that all immigrants are suddenly participating at high rates. Further, only rarely can community organizations focus on political mobilization consistently or on a full-time basis. Immigrants frequently acknowledge that it is difficult to participate in the U.S. political system, citing as the main barriers language, lack of time, and the perception that major political institutions are simply not interested in them. Despite these barriers, some community organizations are politically mobilizing immigrants. Although most community organizations lack the financial resources required to engage in mass mobilization efforts, many are helping to lay the foundations of participation in immigrant communities through limited mobilization. They foster communication and organizational skills on a day-to-day basis that can be transferred to the larger political sphere. Surprisingly, this mobilization includes those immigrants who are usually thought to be the least likely to participate politically—non-English-speaking people who are racial and ethnic minorities, disadvantaged socioeconomically, and noncitizens. Their ability to mobilize new and often disadvantaged individuals could be built on to expand participation more generally.

Community organizations have not displaced political parties or achieved mobilization at the mass level. However, their activities and the role they play in immigrant communities illuminate potential strategies that, if adopted on a larger scale by parties or by community organizations, could lead to more political participation by Asian American and Latino immigrants.

5 Multiple Immigrant Identities & Community Organizations

*L*abor organizations and worker centers, advocacy organizations, social service organizations, ethnic voluntary organizations, and religious institutions are a key component helping to create the conditions under which immigrants will become involved in U.S. politics. These organizations do not necessarily have political mobilization as their primary motive, nor are they particularly influential within the larger political system. Yet whether through direct political mobilization or indirectly through broader measures of socialization, community organizations clearly constitute a component of immigrant political participation and should not be ignored.

Immigrants' characteristics influence the kinds of activities that these community organizations pursue. The members of ethnic and racial groups have multiple identities relating to nationality, gender, class, occupation, and even hometown. Immigrants experience the world not just as members of racial and ethnic groups but also as workers, residents, parents, women and men, and in a host of other ways. Even within groups, cleavages are apparent. Both the Chinese and Mexican immigrant communities have major internal divisions based on language, class, region of origin, length of residence, and religion. Although race or ethnicity is often an important starting point for mobilization, few community organizations mobilize solely around those identities. Instead, they choose to expand their constituencies through appeals to more than one identity. The multiple identities of an immigrant encompass ethnicity but are also fluid and evolving. In responding to those identities, the concerns of one community organization can (and often do) intersect with concerns of other organizations, giving rise not to ethnic or racial isolation but to coalition building as part of the effort to address issues politically. Contrary to the claims that activities of organizations serving immigrant communities reinforce ethnic balkanization and divisions in U.S. society, community organizations' activities apparently can cross-cut immigrant identities in surprising and sometimes powerful ways.

Whereas mainstream political parties appeal to voters only through the largest, most homogenizing of identities (Democrat or Republican), community organizations embrace and reinforce specific identities and their accompanying orientations and concerns. Diversity within an ethnic group is an important factor in political mobilization because internal cleavages within a particular community provide a heightened number of dimensions around which an organization can choose to mobilize and build coalitions.[1] Community organizations are thus well-positioned for issue-based mobilization.

The internal diversity within an ethnic group constitutes an important factor in immigrants' political mobilization. Further, the structures internal to specific immigrant communities drive the ways that community organizations choose to mobilize diverse elements within those communities. Attention to the key dimensions that define internal cleavages within a particular ethnic community reveal these structures. The activities of community organizations reflect the diversity of needs, resources, and identities of local immigrant communities and have led to new possibilities for immigrant political mobilization.

Organizing around Ethnicity: A Threat to American Democracy?

Do groups that organize around race or ethnicity threaten American democracy and civic culture? Some academics and journalists have voiced the opinion that the preservation and maintenance of ethnic ties threaten American civic culture, national identity, and social harmony (Skerry 1993; Geyer 1996; Connerly 2003). Samuel P. Huntington argues that since the 1960s, ideologies of multiculturalism and diversity have assailed "America's core Anglo-Protestant culture and its political creed of liberty" (2004, 17) . He suggests that the presence of a large number of Spanish-speaking immigrants who maintain a Latino identity may bifurcate America along linguistic and cultural lines. Among Mexican immigrants, "the rise of group identities based on race, ethnicity, and gender over national identity" poses a serious challenge to national identity and threatens to "divide the United States into two peoples, two cultures, and two languages" (30, 32). Other scholars fear that organizational elites impose a "minority-group perspective" on rank-and-file immigrants, which is likely to create divisions in society as a whole (Schlesinger 1993; Skerry 1993). From this viewpoint, organizations based on ethnicity overemphasize minority racial status, work against Americanization, and lead to ethnic conflict and competition. For example, Peter Skerry asserts that Mexican American community leaders are "tutoring Mexican Americans to define themselves as a victimized group that cannot advance without the help of racially assigned benefits" (1993, 7).

In response to the critics of identity groups, Amy Gutmann (2003) notes that such groups, in and of themselves, are neither bad nor good for America's democratic culture. Some may be problematic because they promote negative stereotypes and pursue unjust ends. For example, identity groups that raise group identity above justice are inconsistent with democracy. Others may occupy a legitimate place in the United States and may be "important, indeed even valuable, in democratic politics" (8). Identity groups may help to combat discrimination based on race, ethnicity, sexual orientation, and other group identities. Gutmann argues that "when they struggle for greater civic equality for a subordinated group, identity groups use their political power in defense of democratic justice" (193). In fact, Gutmann claims the failure of traditional interest groups gave rise to identity groups representing ethnic and racial minorities, women, gays and lesbians, and the disabled. Not only have these groups been at the forefront of the fight for their civil rights, but they have also defended "the application of universal and egalitarian principles—nondiscrimination, equal pay for equal work, equal opportunity, civic equality—to correct long existing injustices that interest group politics have passed by" (20). When ethnic organizations function in this way, they act as a powerful force for democratic inclusion rather than exclusion.

Critics see ethnic groups' demands for the right to organize around ethnicity as a threat to mutual solidarity. According to theorist Will Kymlicka, this view fails to recognize that such demands "are primarily demands for inclusion for full membership in the larger society. To view this as a threat to stability or solidarity is implausible, and often reflects an underlying ignorance or intolerance of these groups" (1995, 192). Those who believe that organization around ethnic or racial interests will divide American society also ignore ethnic organizations' and group-based claims' long history in American politics (Jacobson 1995). Political organizing based on group affiliations can be found throughout American history. European immigrant groups arriving at the turn of the twentieth century established ethnic clubs and voluntary associations (A. Lin forthcoming). As Lawrence H. Fuchs observes, "Nineteenth-century immigrant groups—particularly the non-Protestants—were not assimilated through friendships and intermarriage into American society. In large measure, they confined their primary relationships to members of their own groups (even through the second and third generations) throughout all stages of the life cycle. For the most part, their friends, dates, mates, and fellow churchmen and clubmen came from the same background" (1968, 3). The presence of ethnic associations does not preclude acculturation and may in fact be a necessary component of it in that such groups help to create an environment of viable social reproduction for immigrants by negotiating language issues, assisting with finding work and housing, and providing emotional support and validation.

One reason that groups emphasizing positive aspects of identity arise is to publicly organize against negative stereotypes based on ascriptive identity (Gutmann 2003, 11; Bedolla 2005). The arguments of Huntington, Skerry, and others overlook the possibility that an ethnic organization that may appear to be promoting a "minority-group perspective" instead might actually be reflecting an identity that mainstream society has imposed on the group the organization represents. Through policies such as Proposition 187 and through the perpetuation of stereotypes, American society marks groups such as Mexican Americans or Chinese Americans as racial outsiders. (For examples of the racialization of contemporary immigrants, see chap. 2.) Splintering occurs less as a consequence of self-identification than as a result of hostility and discrimination exhibited by mainstream society, which reinforces immigrants' self-perception as a racial minority.

Huntington (2004) and his colleagues likely would also view ethnic organizations with skepticism since many have their roots in the "deconstructionist movement." Prior to the 1960s, Huntington asserts, Americans were, or at least hoped to be, a nation unified by a shared Anglo-Protestant core culture, dedicated to the liberal-democratic principles of the American creed. The movements of the 1960s, which promoted group rights at the expense of individual rights, began to undo the core culture and belief system: "The deconstructionists promoted programs to enhance the status and influence of subnational racial, ethnic, and cultural groups. They encouraged immigrants to maintain their birth-country cultures, granted them legal privileges denied to native-born Americans, and denounced the idea of Americanization as un-American" (142).

However, a more nuanced view challenges the assumption that a zero-sum relationship exists between group rights and individual rights (Kymlicka 1995; Gutmann 2003). Kymlicka (1995) argues that the demands of ethnic groups are quite consistent with principles of individual freedom and social justice. He claims that membership in a societal culture such as an ethnic group provides a strong basis for individual identity and action: "Cultural membership provides us with an intelligible context of choice, and a secure sense of identity and belonging, that we call upon in confronting questions about personal values and projects" (105). Individuals make decisions about how to lead their lives in part through considerations related to cultural practices and associations (126). Therefore, an organization that supports an ethnic or a racial group can promote individual rights, such as the freedom of individual choice, as long as it does not allow the group to dominate other groups or oppress its own members. Consistent with this view, Gutmann claims that "free people mutually identify in many politically relevant ways, and a society that prevents identity groups from forming is a tyranny" (2003, 4).

Groups that organize around ethnicity can promote democratic inclusion in a manner consistent with democratic principles of individual choice, freedom, and social justice. Critics who claim that these groups threaten a unified American culture fail to recognize that mobilization occurs around multiple identities, not just around race or ethnicity alone.

Organizing around Multiple Identities

The belief that ethnic organizations may lead to balkanization at the expense of the common good is contradicted by mobilizations that crosscut ethnic, racial, and other identities. Many community organizations organize immigrants around their identities as workers, residents of a particular neighborhood, or individuals concerned about inadequate urban services. This strategy works for organizations because immigrants experience the world not just as members of racial and ethnic groups but also as workers, residents, parents, women and men, and in a host of other ways. In contrast to the assumptions of those who oppose ethnic-based organizing, immigrant participation in politics is likely to be based on a broad range of intersecting identities and issue concerns.

In New York, a Mexican man who had been in the country for only three years and did not have legal papers had joined the Catholic-affiliated Asociación de Tepeyac after hearing about it from members of his church choir who were active in the organization. He was acutely aware that Mexicans were discriminated against "because we're dark and short, and we don't speak English. Mexicans are one of the most discriminated in the United States because of race, lack of documentation, and because we don't speak English." His motivation for joining, however, was somewhat broader: "I'm supporting a political struggle in the United States even though I can't vote . . . because of its goal, for amnesty, and they help immigrants." As a member of the association, he had taken part in protests outside the U.S. Immigration and Nationalization Services Office to call for amnesty for those whose immigration status had not been regularized.

In California, many of the Mexican and Chinese immigrants I interviewed had become more interested in American politics when confronted with ballot propositions widely viewed as racist. However, in this case, in many of their aspects the propositions also indicated broader discrimination against all immigrants, regardless of race. Proposition 187, placed on the state ballot in 1994, sought to restrict undocumented immigrants' access to social services and nonemergency health care and to deny their children access to public education. Proposition 209 was a 1996 California measure that prohibited the state government; local governments; public universities, colleges, and school districts; and other government institutions from practicing affirmative action that used race or ethnicity as a criterion. These measures would have affected many of California's immigrant groups. A Chinese immigrant in Los Angeles said that discrimination was one of the most important issues facing Chinese immigrants, and he noted, "Propositions such as 187, that's the biggest problem." A Mexican immigrant college student in Los Angeles who had worked with a student group to promote affirmative action programs in California claimed that it was stressful and time-consuming to get politically involved, but he had become active because "some new laws, like Proposition 187 or 209, have affected me directly."

The power of intersecting identities and issue concerns is apparent in other cases. In New York, a Chinese immigrant with a strong professional identity as a lawyer joined an Asian American lawyers' association that supports Asian American candidates and elected officials as well as pursues the more predictable goal of lobbying the governor and state legislature on matters related to the law profession generally. Another Chinese immigrant revealed that her identity as a Christian drove her political participation. Despite a lack of interest in politics, she voted regularly because "I know that it's my duty. Every year I vote. The pastor challenged us. We should do it. It is the duty of the Christians." Several immigrants mentioned their role as parents. A Mexican in Los Angeles said that Proposition 187 had motivated his political involvement because he was concerned about how it would affect his children, while a Chinese immigrant there had become more interested in politics because "my children are raised here and I want to know [about] anything in America that might affect them." A Chinese woman in New York was active as a Boy Scout den mother, volunteered at her children's school, went to church regularly, and was a member of the Organization of Chinese Americans, which she described as a political advocacy association. She had become involved in this group because "it's an opportunity to show support for the community and kids and to have a voice. To act as an example for children to follow in community service."

Immigrants' interest in the American political system is clearly driven by multiple identities and a complex and overlapping set of concerns. Ethnic identity and perceptions of racial discrimination are part of that mix, as are other types of identities and issues. Because community groups—even those based on ethnicity or race—organize immigrants around multiple and often intersecting identities, there is little danger that the activities of these organizations will reinforce ethnocentricity or racial divisions in the United States. In the case of the immigrants interviewed in Los Angeles, it was clear that a local issue united Chinese and Mexicans along with many other nationalities in a political struggle against a local proposition.

How multiple identities are deployed in immigrant organizing is consistent with Seyla Benhabib's claim that no identity or culture is reducible to a single or discrete whole. Rather, cultures (and identities) are "complex human practices of signification and representation, of organization and attribution, which are internally riven by conflicting narratives" (2002, ix).[2] Members of a cultural group cohere because they "experience their traditions, stories, rituals and symbols, tools, and material living conditions through shared, albeit contested and contestable, narrative accounts" (5). Benhabib emphasizes that claims based on shared culture are not necessarily incompatible with recognition of internal distinctions and differences within that culture. Similarly, Gutmann suggests that "group identification is socially significant but not comprehensive of individual identity" and that "a person may make a group identification more or less comprehensive of his or her identity" (2003, 10). Individuals have multiple group identifications, and their individual agency modifies their group identifications just as group identifications shape individual agency. Individuals who mutually identify around a social marker often join together in a politically relevant and socially identified group.

The fact that group identities are constructed and therefore fluid does not mean that they are unreal or without meaning. Behavior and attitudes can be shaped by imagined ideas or concepts (Benhabib 2002, 7). Like Gutmann and Kymlicka, Benhabib suggests that the politics of ethnic or racial recognition can have an important place in democratic politics. Organizing around race or ethnicity,

> instead of leading to cultural separatism or balkanization, can initiate critical dialogue and reflection in public life about the very identity of the collectivity itself. Through such dialogue and reflection, the inevitable and problematical interdependence of images and conceptions of self and other are brought to light. Narratives of self and other are now rewoven together to take account of new contestations, retellings, and repositionings. The politics of complex cultural dialogue indeed involves the reconstitutions of the boundaries of the polity through the recognition of the claims of groups that have been wronged historically and whose very suffering and exclusion has, in some deep sense, been constitutive of the seemingly unitary identity of the "we" who constitutes the polity. . . . Such processes . . . offer a clear alternative to the politics of cultural enclavism in that they allow democratic dissent, debate, contestation, and challenge to be at the center of practices through which cultures are appropriated. (70–71)

Critics of ethnic organizations, then, wrongly assume that group membership is static and that boundaries of ethnic organizations are rigid and impermeable (Benhabib 2002). Contestation over group boundaries, inclusion, priorities, and mission is a common feature of ethnic organizations. Internal divisions and the resulting deliberation often lead to organizational change and renegotiation regarding group membership. The experience of Chinese Americans United for Self Empowerment (CAUSE) is a case in point. At its inception, CAUSE focused on empowering the Chinese American community in the West San Gabriel Valley in Los Angeles County, and its executive director was a man. Eventually,

CAUSE responded to claims outside the Chinese American community and to reflect its panethnic concerns changed its name to the Center for Asian Americans United for Self-Empowerment. Its second executive director was a Chinese American woman who employed several non-Chinese women as staff members. This radically transformed both the ethnic identity and gender dynamics of the organization. The mistaken assumption that ethnic boundaries are rigid underlies fears that ethnic organizations will contribute to the fragmentization of American society. Such assumptions deny contestations over difference taking place within organizations and with the larger political sphere on a day-to-day basis. A more complex view of identity would allow critics of ethnic organizations to see that balkanization is unlikely when the boundaries of groups are fluid and evolving.

The likelihood that political mobilization by ethnic-based community organizations will provoke ethnic divisiveness is also minimal given that some of these groups have forged multiethnic or multiracial alliances. Many ethnic organizations make substantive efforts to interact with a range of ethnic or racial communities. For example, New York's Chinese Staff and Workers' Association was founded as an independent union of Chinese restaurant workers. Today, however, it has Mexican members, and some of its Chinese American staff are multilingual, speaking English, Cantonese, and Spanish. The association is developing a campaign around worker's compensation issues and has been recruiting participants among both immigrants and U.S.-born whites and blacks. It also was the main force in creating the Latino Workers' Center, which is located in a predominantly Latino Lower East Side neighborhood. A more informal example can be found in a meeting that I attended in Los Angeles that included a multiethnic coalition of union leaders. Discussion revolved around issues of ethnic inclusion and diversity.

These are not merely ad hoc alliances, however. Umbrella groups have appeared that cover organizations serving Latino, Asian, African, Caribbean, and European communities. A notable case is the New York Immigration Coalition (NYIC), an "umbrella advocacy organization for approximately 200 groups in New York State that work with 'newcomers' to our country—immigrants, refugees, and asylees. . . . The NYIC's membership includes immigrant-rights advocates, immigrant community leaders and service providers, numerous community-based ethnic and non-profit human service organizations, and leaders from labor, academia, and the legal professions. Utilizing this multi-ethnic, multi-racial, and multi-sector base, the NYIC provides the opportunity for members to collaborate and implement strategies to address their common concerns" (New York Immigration Coalition n.d.). The coalition covers a broad range of immigrant-serving community organizations, including the American Association of Jews from the Former USSR (New York chapter), the Caribbean Women's Health Association, the National Coalition for Haitian Rights, the Chinese Progressive Association, the Latin American Integration Center, Alianza Dominicana, and Asian Americans for Equality, among others. Coalition building around multiple identities is a long-standing practice among advocacy groups. As Gutmann notes, "Many ascriptive groups, such as the NAACP and NOW, have never been only for themselves. Justice-friendly ascriptive groups often join coalitions for democratic justice" (2003, 129).

Interracial alliance building occurs in grassroots efforts as well as in the realm of electoral politics. Latinos, Asian Americans, whites, and blacks participated together in the Immigrant Workers Freedom Ride. Those groups have also worked together to strengthen minority political representation by, for example, supporting candidates and participating in the redistricting process (Wei 1993; Saito 1998; Saito and Park 2000; Lien 2001). These instances of multiracial coalition building belie the assumption that organizations with deep connections to a particular ethnic community will undermine core democratic values and promote racial separation or balkanization in the United States.

Labor as a Mobilizing Identity

When asked about their participation in politics, one of the most powerful identities invoked by immigrants was that of worker. In New York, I interviewed several Chinese garment workers who were active in their local unions, which had involved these women in politics by having them distribute political education flyers, help with the advertising of events, and participate in phone banks during elections. When asked about the most serious problems facing their communities, these women focused on labor-related issues, complaining of long hours and low wages and of work being sent overseas to foreign factories. One woman said, "If you leave early, the boss will yell at you. It's very difficult, hard work because they want both quality and quantity. They're very hard to please." A Mexican immigrant started volunteering with the Harlem-based Centro de la Comunidad Mexicana de Nueva York (CECOMEX), which works with Mexican immigrants, after learning about it from fellow restaurant workers.[3] CECOMEX, he said, "helps out Mexicans with problems with employers, helps them find jobs, and helps them open bank accounts." When asked about the most important issues facing Mexican immigrants in New York City, he listed the detainment of those without legal documents and worker exploitation, two issues that cut across racial and ethnic lines.

Gender as a Mobilizing Identity

Concerns arising from gender identity can provide a powerful catalyst for political involvement among immigrants. Peter Kwong (1996, 1997), who has studied the approximately five hundred garment factories that employ twenty thousand Chinese women in New York's Chinatown, recognizes that these low-paying, substandard factories are a potential site for political resistance and activism. Other scholars make similar observations. Miriam Ching Louie notes recent efforts by Asian Immigrant Women's Advocates to organize "immigrant women working in the garment, electronics, hotel, restaurant, nursing home, janitorial, and other low-wage industries in the San Francisco Bay Area and Santa Clara County's 'Silicon Valley'" (1997, 128).

Examining gender differences helps reveal how organizations adapt their mobilization strategies to meet a multiplicity of immigrant concerns. One Mexican immigrant in Queens who was very active in her church choir, the neighborhood association, and as a member of a *ballet folklórico* also joined the Queens Women's Network, an advocacy group dedicated to raising money for abused women. She got involved with the network because she wanted to see improvement in women's lives. A Mexican immigrant woman in Los Angeles echoed that concern when she noted that the community's most serious concerns include domestic violence and access to medical care for immigrant children. Asked if it was important for Chinese women to be active in U.S. politics, a Chinese immigrant woman in New York exclaimed, "Yes! You can't let men have all the power to do everything. We have home life and job, too. Women should be able to do it!"

Some organizations that work with immigrant communities explicitly mobilize them around gender-specific issues and concerns. Thousands of

United Farm Workers members and their sympathizers marched in Watsonville, California, in April 1997 to draw attention to organizing efforts among local strawberry workers. They protested not only poor pay but also the sexual harassment of women workers, submission to which was sometimes a condition of employment (Southwest Voter Registration and Education Project 1997, 3). Workers' Awaaz, which organizes South Asian low-wage workers in New York City, runs public campaigns around labor issues and educates live-in female South Asian domestic workers about labor and immigration laws. The organization also files legal cases against—and even demonstrates in front of the homes of—exploitative employers. To educate the public about their campaigns, it has run stories in feminist publications, such as *Ms. Magazine* (Workers' Awaaz, n.d.; Dalal 1998).

In addition to its multilingual outreach and education on the welfare system, employment discrimination, and the citizenship process, the NYIC engages in gender-related advocacy. In 2000, NYIC's Detention Working Group met with managers of the Varick Street Detention Center and district managers and staff of the Immigration and Naturalization Service to discuss ways to improve conditions in detention centers. This advocacy effort not only embraced a diversity of ethnic and racial groups but also focused on the plight of women asylum seekers: "Since the immigration law of 1996, asylum-seekers arriving at U.S. borders are sent back to their home countries, usually on the next plane, unless they can prove their fear of persecution upon return. Immigration officers often do not understand the language spoken by the asylum-seeker and ask flight attendants, who often work for the same government the asylum-seeker is fleeing, to translate. Women are often ashamed to tell a male translator or immigration officer stories of rape or abuse" (New York Immigration Coalition 2000, 4).

The Mothers of East Los Angeles was founded in 1986 to protest the building of a state prison in the community. This organization, which was led by East Los Angeles Latina women, ran a community education campaign, held weekly candlelight vigils, and lobbied in the state capitol. Many scholars, activists, and community members attribute the state's 1992 decision not to build the prison there to the group's actions (Pardo 1998). The organization has subsequently stood at the forefront of many fights against environmental racism in East Los Angeles. The Mothers of East Los Angeles, which emphasizes motherhood and the "mothering of the community," has utilized that particular gender identity as the foundation for community organizing (Medeiros 2004).

In the mid-1990s, the Chinese Staff and Workers' Association launched its Women's Empowerment Project and Occupational Health Committee. According to the association newsletter,

> Injured women built up this project through months of outreach in the sweatshops and on the streets, organizing educational workshops about occupational diseases, and finally forming a membership committee for injured workers. The project was built on the gains of the "enforce labor law" campaign, which exposed the sweatshop system to the public, won back pay for workers, and led to the arrest of certain bosses in minimum wage violations. Leaders of the project, all injured garment women, also began meeting with politicians to talk about their cases, about manufacturing accountability, and about sweatshop monitoring. (Chinese Staff and Workers' Association 1997, 1)

The workers met with members of the State Assembly Labor Committee as well as with city council members.

In 1997, the Women's Project also organized a New York City rally to protest gender discrimination at a sportswear corporation in Flushing, Queens. One garment worker involved with group described the project.

> Our Women's Project is structured in a way to provide opportunities for women to meet, get to know one another, and discuss collective ways to expose, challenge, or solve various problems. We need to break out of the trap set up for women, which embodies juggling different obligations including spending time with children, doing housework, and making a living. In the workplace, we are discriminated against and shut out from higher paying, more stable jobs; in the factories our labor is taken advantage of when bosses trick us out of our wages. Women are especially vulnerable to exploitation; many bosses think that they can control and bully women earlier. . . . I have seen that many women have already been coming forward to organize and fight for their rights. A group of women *dim sum* workers at the New Silver Palace [a large restaurant in New York City's Chinatown], who had endured hard work and sexism at the hands of their employer, is picketing four times a week to challenge their illegal firing. Their bosses tried to further humiliate them after firing them for their organizing activities by telling them that

they were "too old and too ugly" to work at the New Silver Palace. (quoted in Chinese Staff and Workers' Association 1999, 3).

In addition to picketing the restaurant, the Women's Empowerment Project and Occupational Health Committee attended congressional hearings on sweatshops in the United States and used that forum to call for employer accountability.[4]

Because the majority of recent immigrants to the United States are women, attention to their U.S. political participation is particularly important. I found that although most leadership positions in community organizations working with Chinese and Mexican immigrant communities were held by men, immigrant women also find opportunities to participate in U.S. politics. As mentioned earlier, although CAUSE's original executive director was a man, he was eventually replaced by an immigrant woman, Sandra Chen. Chen served in the position for several years and was replaced by another woman. In the Pilot Program on Immigrant-Led Hometown Associations, organized by the University of Southern California and the Los Angeles Immigrant Funders' Collaborative during 2003, women made up 35 percent of the attendees, who were leaders or were in line to become leaders of Mexican or Central American hometown and regional associations. One participant, Martha Jiménez, a leader of the Federation of Zacatecan Clubs of Southern California, noted that "in the future, it would be good to include a workshop on gender and leadership, that is, how to learn that both men and women want to work on a common agenda, and that there should be mutual respect within our organizations, which means that women should not be treated as if they were a big zero. . . . I liked what we did here because men and women have shown the same respect to each other when talking and doing everything, but we must see how we can bring that into our organizations" (Rivera-Salgado, Rodriguez, and Escala-Rabadan 2004, 23).

Immigrant women also occupy leadership positions in some union locals. In the late 1990s, Quyen Nguyen, a Vietnamese woman immigrant, worked as a key organizer for the United Food and Commercial Workers in Los Angeles. Fluent in Spanish and Vietnamese, she led many successful organizing campaigns for immigrant workers. In one instance, she helped to organize 1,000 workers, including 150 Chinese and Vietnamese, at the Farmer John meat processing facility in Los Angeles.

Changes in women's status following migration can create opportunities for women to take leadership even within such gendered institutions as the Catholic Church. One Mexican immigrant woman leader of the Asociación de Tepeyac explained that as part of the migration process, Mexican women with whom she works in New York often find their gender roles changing from primarily housework in Mexico to wage work in the United States. She contends that these transformations may be related to these women's political participation. That is, as their roles are transformed from housework to wage earner outside of the home, women may find themselves empowered not only economically but also politically as they gain independence and learn about opportunities to participate in politics. When asked whether Mexicans have more or fewer opportunities for participation in the United States or in Mexico, she responded, "The Mexican government doesn't help, doesn't let people do much of organized work. There's a lot of oppression, especially in the south. They don't have that much opportunity. But here, I think it's women who are working, and they feel like they have hope now. It changes little by little; it's not going to change one day to another. It's not now the women have that power, but it's changing, it's changing. They go to the demonstrations and every demonstration we do [in New York City], they feel stronger."

Internal Diversity and New Possibilities for Political Mobilization

Today, the internal diversity within an ethnic group shapes political mobilization. The variety and breadth of immigrant identities, which include but also go beyond ethnicity, are the nodes of connection between ethnic communities and community organizations. The type of political mobilization chosen by an organization reflects the diverse characteristics, needs, and resources of the immigrant community it serves. Strategy that responds to internal diversity encourages new possibilities for immigrant political mobilization that differ from those available to European immigrants of the past. As embodied in the experience of European immigrants, the traditional model of immigrant political incorporation proceeds in a linear fashion or as a series of steps (Dahl 1961). The model posits that as immigrants spend more time in the United States and move up the economic ladder, they are first organized around ethnic appeals. They next become citizens and then voters, and they eventually become indistinguishable from the mainstream population in terms of vote and candidate choice. However, for contemporary immigrants, this is not the pattern. The strategies and modes of mobilization undertaken by labor organizations, workers' centers, advocacy and social service organizations, ethnic voluntary associations, and religious institutions vary depending on the segment of a community that is targeted. Strategies can range from providing social services and citizenship classes to organizing demonstrations, mobilizing voters, and backing candidates. Moreover, not only do these various activities occur simultaneously, but no single activity is superior to or more important than another in terms of moving an immigrant toward full political participation. Thus, in contrast to the traditional model, an immigrant can experience several types of political mobilization simultaneously rather than moving through them as stages in a linear process.

The array of community organizations offers a range of activities in which immigrants can participate to become mobilized politically, among other things. Which activity appeals to which immigrant depends on his or her identity and concerns. These can include but are not limited to immigrant, ethnic, and racial status. Among other factors, an identity as a professional, a wage worker, a parent, or a member of a religious community can motivate an immigrant's involvement in politics. However, the pattern of contemporary immigrant mobilization is shaped not just by the nature of the community organization or by immigrant identity. The structures that are internal to specific immigrant communities also come into play. To uncover those structures, we need to ask what key dimensions define internal cleavages within a particular ethnic community.

Within the Chinese immigrant community, major divisions are based on language, class, region or country of origin, length of residence, and religion. The Mexican immigrant community has similar major divisions. For example, Mexicans may perceive distinctions based on whether an individual or a group speaks primarily English, Spanish, or one of many indigenous languages. Internal divisions often but not always coincide with settlement locality in the United States. Mexicans in New York differ from those in Los Angeles along dimensions of class, region of origin, and length of residence.

Even within the same city, differences in local settlement patterns occur. One leader of a nonprofit group points out that class, region of origin, and locality divide the Chinese community in Los Angeles: "There are many reasons why I think we're so scattered. Geographically, we live in different pockets, even though there are large populations in Monterey Park, there are a lot of people living in Rowland Heights, Walnut, and Hacienda Heights. And also, there's constantly new immigrants, and so we always have those differences—those that have been here, those that are just coming, those that are a little more economically challenged. So, then, there are all of these dynamics."

As the leader noted, location of residence divides Los Angeles's Chinese community. The major population centers are the downtown Chinatown and the various communities in the San Gabriel Valley. The Chinese who live in these geographically separate areas are socioeconomically distinct. Chinatown's population tends to have fewer resources than the population in the San Gabriel Valley. Whereas Chinatown's many residents tend to work in very small local businesses and the service industry, residents in the San Gabriel Valley are more likely to be entrepreneurs or involved in corporate or business ventures (Hum and Zonta 2000). These distinctions are related to the bifurcation by class background that was apparent among Chinese who arrived after the 1965 amendments to the Immigration and Nationality Act, which emphasized family reunification and gave preference to skilled or professionally trained immigrants. Thus, many poor, unskilled Chinese began joining their relatives, primarily laborers who had arrived in the United States before 1965. This group tended to settle, at least initially, in Chinatown. At the same time, wealthier Chinese with specialized professional and technical skills also began to arrive in substantial numbers, and they tended to bypass Chinatown, moving directly to the middle-class suburban communities (Li 1999). Chinatown's residents have gradually moved to the suburbs, but they often maintain connections with community organizations and downtown businesses.

Reflecting the needs of the local Chinese communities, the primary political institutions in each area are quite different as well. For example, the Chinatown Service Center, in operation for twenty-five years, provides social-adjustment counseling, employment training, job placement, and medical services to approximately twelve thousand people annually. Its staff also provides information about welfare legislation and assists with the citizenship-application process. In the San Gabriel Valley, the major political institutions include the CAUSE and the Taiwanese American Citizens League, both of which focus almost exclusively on electoral participation and voter education.

Despite the distinct missions of these organizations, one prominent activist named all three of them as being among "five groups you have to talk to to understand Chinese American politics in Los Angeles." Each organization uses different strategies and modes of mobilization—providing social services and citizenship classes, organizing demonstrations, mobilizing voters, and backing candidates. The types of political activity utilized reflect the local community's needs and resources rather than simply whether immigrants are newly arrived or more settled. A range of considerations come into play, including the class background and multiple identities of particular segments of the Chinese community. Thus, for the Los Angeles Chinese community, several types of political mobilization happen simultaneously in response to the concerns of particular subsets of Chinese immigrants. Community organizations capitalize on their knowledge of and familiarity with local immigrant communities' diverse elements. In contrast, political parties seem to pay very little attention to the features of local communities, which may pose a critical problem in terms of the ability to mobilize immigrants over the long term.

A similar set of processes occurs among institutions and different segments of the Mexican immigrant community. Although noticeable divisions exist within the Mexican communities in Los Angeles and in New York, it is also interesting to compare political mobilization among Mexican immigrants across the two metropolitan contexts. Like the Chinese community in the United States, the Mexican community is internally diverse. Because Mexican immigrants did not begin arriving in significant numbers in New York City until the mid-1980s, with most having migrated since 1995, many individuals of Mexican origin in New York are first-generation immigrants; fewer than half have legal documentation (Robert Smith 1996). Most come from south-central Mexico, and they are small in numbers compared to other Latino groups such as Dominicans and Puerto Ricans. In contrast, Los Angeles's historically well established Mexican community is the largest Latino group in the western United States, with members coming primarily from the central Mexican states of Guanajuato, Michoacán, México, and Jalisco.

These internal differences between the New York's and Los Angeles's Mexican immigrant populations shape the specific kinds of political mobilization in each locality. Because many Mexican immigrants in New York are not citizens, community leaders tend to focus on nonelectoral activities, such as protests, marches, and demonstrations. The Catholic-affiliated Asociación de Tepeyac has taken on most of the responsibility for political mobilizing in the Mexican community, and many of its political activities involve religious elements. The association lists among its goals certain political objectives, such as to "participate in the efforts of other organizations in demanding amnesty" and to "participate in struggles for just wages and demand a 40-hour work week," which appear alongside religious aims (to "continue home visits with our Lady of Guadalupe, and . . . have time for reflection and the rosary").

In Los Angeles, although the Catholic Church plays an important role in organizing immigrants, many other institutions mobilize them as well. For example, nearly thirty national organizations serving the Mexican community are based in Los Angeles, and there are hundreds of local organizations, ranging from legal aid or social service providers to business associations, cultural institutions, and hometown associations (Congressional Hispanic Caucus Institute 2001). Thus, compared to the political activities undertaken by Mexican immigrants in New York, activities that involve the community in Los Angeles are less likely to incorporate religious elements explicitly and are more likely to focus on other identities. A particularly salient example is region of origin, an identity around which 250 hometown associations have been created in Los Angeles.

Furthermore, the demographic dominance of Latinos and historical struggles for political empowerment in the Los Angeles region have led to significant gains in electoral representation at the local and state level. In 1991, Gloria Molina, the child of a Mexican immigrant mother and Mexican American father, was elected as one of five Los Angeles county supervisors, the most important political offices in Los Angeles. A Latino, Antonio Villaraigosa, representing Los Angeles's California Assembly District 45, held one of the state's most powerful positions, speaker of the house, and was elected mayor of the city of Los Angeles in 2005. Not surprisingly, although community organizations in Los Angeles are likely to organize marches and demonstrations and help Mexican immigrants to naturalize, they also mobilize the community around electoral activities, such as registering voters and supporting candidates sympathetic to Latino concerns.

These organizations do not follow the systematic pattern that was apparent in organizing European immigrants in the early twentieth century whereby civic institutions would first mobilize immigrants to attend a march or rally, then help them to learn English and naturalize, and finally get them to turn out to vote. Today, that array of activities can occur simultaneously rather than linearly or as steps on the road to political empowerment. An immigrant-rights organization that targets Mexicans in Los Angeles may organize workers to demonstrate for higher wages and fair treatment by employers. At the same time, a voting-rights organization is likely to be targeting the same population in an attempt to get them to naturalize and vote.

As is true in the Chinese community, the key for the Mexican community is that political mobilization is occurring as a set of simultaneous processes. That is, organizations in New York and Los Angeles are working with different segments of the Mexican immigrant community, thereby determining diverse and at times overlapping strategies for political mobilization. For example, the Asociación de Tepeyac organized an October 1999 trip to Washington, D.C., so that members could join a demonstration calling for general amnesty for undocumented workers. For months the group devoted time and resources to organizing the trip. A Los Angeles social service organization also sent staff to the Washington demonstration, but the majority of its regular efforts were concentrated on helping immigrants with the citizenship process. The variety of communities involved has elicited diverse and nuanced responses from community organizations, even drawing out some—like the Catholic Church—that normally are apolitical. Not surprisingly, immigrants, with their multiple self-identities—based on labor history, region of origin, religion, class, position in the life cycle, and numerous other things—interact with organizations in a multiplicity of political activities that occur simultaneously and often independently rather than as stages in a linear process. Community organizations recognize internal diversity within the Mexican communities and design their mobilization strategies accordingly. Political parties have not yet taken this crucial step, which may hinder their ability to mobilize immigrants.

Conclusion

Under the assumption that encouraging a recognition of ethnic identity discourages immigrant assimilation, some observers claim that ethnic organizations threaten to divide and balkanize American society. However, the long American tradition of ethnic-based political mobilization belies that assertion, as does the evidence that these organizations form cooperative alliances and coalitions that cross-cut immigrant identities in a variety of ways.

Not only do numerous internal distinctions within a particular ethnic community exist (in terms of class, citizenship status, gender, national origin, and language background, for example), but differences also exist between ethnic groups, such as Chinese and Mexican immigrants. As an aggregate group, Chinese immigrants are more educated and have a higher income than Mexican immigrants. They tend to exhibit higher rates of citizenship on average than their Mexican counterparts. Many Mexican immigrants live closer to their country of origin than do Chinese immigrants. Further, Chinese immigrants are characterized by greater language and religious diversity. Although both Chinese and Mexican immigrants are concentrated in big cities on coasts in nonswing states, Mexican immigrants also constitute a significant population in some swing states, including New Mexico, Colorado, and Arizona. There are also many more Mexican immigrants than Chinese immigrants. In the end, however, any attempt to evaluate immigrant mobilization should focus not simply on the specific differences between ethnic groups but also on how these differences and the identities associated with them become critical nodes around which civic institutions can mobilize.

In the absence of a consistent, committed effort by political parties, it appears that community organizations will play an important role in the political participation of contemporary immigrants. In their mobilization efforts, these organizations are utilizing issues of concern to immigrants. These issues may have their roots in racial or ethnic identity, but they also often transcend those identities. Recognizing that immigrant ethnic groups are not monolithic or homogenous, organizations respond to the significant internal diversity that exists within groups. Differences in religion, socioeconomic status, region, language, sexual orientation, and citizenship status offer many different axes around which to organize. Thus, just as community organizations shape the political participation of immigrants, the internal diversity within immigrant communities shapes the behavior of community organizations. Many organizations, including ethnic voluntary associations and advocacy and social service organizations, respond to local variations and patterns within immigrant communities they serve.

Immigrant political mobilization in the United States will be aided by community organizations willing to respond not just to the needs of specific immigrant, ethnic, or racial groups as blocs but also to the specific identities held by individual members of those groups and found within and across ethnic and racial communities.

6 *Mobilization of Latinos &*
Asian Americans
Evidence from Survey Data

*T*he qualitative evidence gathered in Mexican and Chinese communities in the United States suggests that community organizations play a significant role in the political mobilization of immigrant minorities. This is in surprising contrast to historic patterns, in which mainstream political parties were key to getting noncitizens to naturalize and vote. This qualitative evidence leads to two quantitatively testable hypotheses. The first is that Asian American and Latino immigrants do not view political parties as strong intermediaries representing their interests in the political arena. Instead, these immigrants are more likely to view community organizations as intermediaries representing their interests in the U.S. political system. The second is that when party organizations do choose to target minority immigrants, they are more likely to focus on voter mobilization than on other types of political activities, in contrast to community organizations, which are more likely to engage immigrants in a range of political activities other than voting, such as participation in demonstrations and petition drives.

The quantitative data used to test these two hypotheses come from the 2000–2001 Pilot National Asian American Political Survey (PNAAPS) (see Lien, Conway, and Wong 2004) and the 1989–90 Latino National Political Survey (LNPS) (see de la Garza et al. 1992). (For more information on these surveys, see the appendix, tables A1, A3.) The samples used include a large number of immigrants, many naturalized, who self-identify as either Asian American or Latino. Unless otherwise indicated, the label *immigrant* includes both nonnaturalized immigrants and naturalized citizens. For the analyses of voting, the sample includes only those who are eligible to vote—that is naturalized citizens who are registered to vote.

141

Party Activism in Latino Communities

Only the LNPS, which targeted members of Mexican, Puerto Rican,[1] and Cuban subgroups, included an adequate range of questions to address the first hypothesis, that political parties are less likely to be seen as intermediaries representing immigrant interests in the political system than are community organizations. Although the LNPS data have been available for sixteen years, other publicly available data on Latino political attitudes, such as the more recent 1999 *Washington Post*/Henry J. Kaiser Family Foundation/Harvard University National Survey on Latinos in America, do not contain questions that allow for testing this hypothesis.

The LNPS asked respondents, "Is there any group or organization that you think looks out for your concerns, even if you are not a member?" Twenty-four percent of Latino immigrants answered affirmatively, 57 percent answered negatively, and 19 percent responded, "Don't know" (n = 1808).[2] If respondents answered yes, they were then asked, "What group or organization is that?" The respondent could select from more than six hundred organizations, which later were categorized and coded into groups as (1) unions and professional organizations; (2) charity organizations; (3) religious groups; (4) traditional interest groups; (5) neighborhood, recreational, or school organizations; (6) Latino organizations or clubs; (7) government agencies; and (8) political parties and candidates.[3]

Consistent with the first hypothesis, Latino immigrant respondents who identified one of the six hundred organizations were more likely to name a community organization such as a religious group or Latino organization than a political party (table 1). Across all three Latino national-origin groups, the pattern is striking. Compared to their compatriots who named a political party or candidate, Mexican respondents were nine times more likely to name a religious group, Puerto Ricans were three times more likely to name a neighborhood organization, and Cuban respondents were fourteen times more likely to name a Latino organization.

Fifty-two percent of Latino immigrants answered "yes" when asked whether any organization looked after the concerns of their specific national-origin group. ("Thinking about Mexicans/Puerto Ricans/ Cubans, even if you are not a member [of the organization], is there any group or organization that you think looks out for Mexican/Puerto Rican/Cuban concerns?") Twenty percent answered "no," and 20 percent answered, "don't know." Those who answered "yes" were then asked a second question: "What group or organization was that?" They could identify up to three organizations. Among only those respondents to that second question who named a political party, labor or professional organization, religious group, neighborhood group, or Latino organization, very few responded by naming a party (table 2). Across the three ethnic groups, most of these respondents named a Latino organization. Notably, national origin affected the frequency to which a respondent named a particular type of organization as looking out for the concerns of his or her national-origin group. Mexican immigrants were much more likely than their Puerto Rican and especially Cuban counterparts to name a religious institution.

Thus, Latino immigrants in the LNPS show remarkable consistency in their perception that community organizations—especially ethnic voluntary associations and advocacy organizations and to some degree religious institutions—represent their interests. This is not to say that political parties never advocate on behalf of their Latino constituents. Indeed, in the Puerto Rican sample, the respondents who believed an organization advo-

TABLE 1. Latino Immigrants' Perceptions of Individual Representation by Various Organizations (in percentages)

	Mexican ($n = 113$)	Puerto Rican ($n = 68$)	Cuban ($n = 93$)
Union, labor, or professional organization	11	7	8
Neighborhood, recreational, or school organization	6	21	2
Religious group	28	27	10
Latino organization or group	28	25	43
Political party or candidate	3	7	3
Charity	14	6	24
Traditional interest group	4	0	7
Government agency	6	7	4

Source: LNPS.

Question: (1) "Is there any group or organization that you think looks out for your concerns, even if you are not a member?" (2) "What group or organization is that?" Cell entries reflect the percentage that mentioned each type of organization in the second part of the question. Those who answered "Don't know" or who declined to state a specific organization are not included. Note that the percentages do not total 100 percent due to rounding.

cated for their group's concerns were more likely to name a political party (6 percent) than they were to name a union (none). However, the data support the argument that Latino immigrants perceive that nonparty community organizations look out for their concerns and do not view political parties as doing so.

Some important caveats exist regarding these findings. First, the survey data represent a snapshot of Latino public opinion in 1989–90; attitudes may have shifted since that time (see chap. 3). Second, the survey question asks about advocacy, not mobilization, so although parties are not seen as advocates, they might still be mobilizing members of the Latino community. Third, most respondents in the LNPS answered "no" to the question of whether some sort of organization represented their individual concerns, and 28 percent answered "no" to the question of whether some type of organization represented their national-origin group. This is consistent with the argument that few organizations—parties or otherwise—engage in mass mobilization in immigrant communities. Yet it remains significant that those respondents who perceive that an organization represents their interests name community organizations but fail to name

TABLE 2. Latino Immigrants' Perceptions of Group Representation by Various Organizations (in percentages)

Percentage indicating:	Political party	Union, labor, or professional organization	Religious group	Neighborhood, recreational, or school organization	Latino organization
Mexican (*n* = 151)	6	11	23	5	63
Puerto Rican (*n* = 136)	6	0	13	7	80
Cuban (*n* = 237)	2	1	3	4	93

Source: LNPS.

Question: (1) "Thinking about Mexicans/Puerto Ricans/Cubans, even if you are not a member, is there any group or organization that you think looks out for Mexican/Puerto Rican/Cuban concerns?" (2) "What group or organization is that?" This data sample consists of *only* those respondents to the second question who named a party, labor organization or union, religious institution, Latino or Hispanic group, or community or neighborhood organization. Cell entries reflect the percentage of those respondents who named each type of organization. Note that the percentages do not total 100 percent because respondents could name up to three organizations.

political parties. This analysis certainly suggests that a range of community organizations constitute important vehicles for mobilizing Latino immigrants and the Latino community as a whole.

Another aspect of civic institutions' involvement in immigrant political mobilization—voter registration—was also analyzed (see table 3). Who encourages Latinos, especially Latino immigrants, to register to vote? For naturalized immigrants interviewed in the LNPS, 24 percent had been contacted about registering to vote, but fewer than 5 percent of that group had been contacted by a political party. Indeed, more respondents claimed that they had been contacted about registering to vote by an individual—for example, a family member, friend, or community member—than by a party. The survey did not ask did not ask about whether specific types of community organizations (such as labor organizations, workers' centers, social service organizations, advocacy organizations, ethnic voluntary associations, or religious institutions) had contacted respondents.

The LNPS reveals that regardless of ethnic origin, parties were not targeting large numbers of naturalized Latino immigrants to register to vote (table 3). Naturalized Mexicans clearly are much more likely to report contact by a family member, friend, or community member than by a political party. For those of Cuban origin, the difference is less dramatic. Strikingly, however, as U.S. citizens, all Puerto Ricans living in the United

TABLE 3.   Mobilization through Voter Registration among Latino Immigrants (in percentages)

Contacted to register by	Political party, candidate, or politician	Family member, friend, or individual in community
Mexican naturalized immigrant (n = 105)	8	20
Cuban naturalized immigrant (n = 234)	4	8
Puerto Rican immigrant (n = 429)	3	27

Source: LNPS.

Question: "Next, we would like to ask you about elections in the U.S. During 1988, did anyone talk to you about registering to vote? . . . Who spoke to you about registering to vote in the U.S.? (How do you know this person?)"

Note: Percentages in the first column were calculated by dividing the number of people reporting contact by a party, candidate, or politician by the total number of naturalized immigrants. Percentages in the second column were calculated similarly.

States are eligible to register to vote, but only 3 percent had been contacted by a political party, whereas 27 percent had been contacted by an individual. Overall, naturalized Latino immigrants interviewed in the LNPS were most likely to have been contacted by an individual, such as a family member, friend, or community member, than by a political party. The analysis supports the contention that parties are not perceived as an active force mobilizing minority immigrants to register to vote. Similar data are not available for Asian Americans because the questions asked about parties and mobilization in available surveys were too different to compare directly with the LNPS data.

Determinants of Asian American & Latino Political Participation

Does involvement with a community organization lead to participation in a wide array of political activities that may or may not include voting? To answer that hypothesis, we must examine the effects of affiliation with a community organization on political participation, manifested as (1) voting and as (2) taking part in a range of political activities other than voting, such as demonstrations and petition drives. The analyses used data from both the LNPS and the PNAAPS. In addition to questions about political contact, the LNPS includes questions about membership in or affiliation with Latino or Hispanic organizations and attendance at religious services (a measure of affiliation with a religious institution).[4] The PNAAPS included a comparable set of key variables, including whether respondents were members of an Asian American organization, attended religious services, or had been contacted by a political party or individual (via e-mail or letter or telephone call about a political campaign) in the past four years.

The association between a respondent having voted or having participated in political activities other than voting and his or her membership in an organization, attendance at religious services, or contact with a political party or individual concerning voter registration was analyzed (tables 4 and 5). The coefficients indicate whether any of three key independent variables (membership in an organization, contact by a party or individual, or attending religious services frequently) is associated with political participation, manifested as voting or as political activities other than voting. Other factors, including age, sex, education, family income, political engagement, English fluency, experience with discrimination, ethnic group, and length of residence, were controlled in the analyses.[5]

For the Latino sample, political participation other than voting was measured by a question asking respondents about participation in the past twelve months in a range of political activities, such as signing a petition, writing a letter to an editor or public official, attending a public meeting, or supporting a candidate for public office. Similarly, for the Asian American sample, participation other than voting was measured by a question asking, "During the past four years, have you participated in any of the following types of political activity in your community?" Respondents picked activities from a list that included, among other things, writing or phoning a government official, donating money to a campaign, signing a petition for a political cause, or taking part in a protest or demonstration. The Asian American and Latino data sets were analyzed separately. Again, for the analyses of voting, the sample includes only those who are eligible to vote—that is, naturalized citizens who had registered to vote.

For the first analysis, the dependent variable, voting in 1988 for Latino immigrants in the LNPS, was regressed on the key independent variables as well as on the set of control variables. (The full models appear in the appendix, tables A4, A5.) For Latino immigrants, being contacted by an individual and frequent attendance at religious services are associated strongly with voting in the 1988 election. Contrary to expectations, hav-

TABLE 4. Effect of Mobilization on Political Participation among Latino Immigrants by Source of Mobilization

	Member of a Latino or Hispanic organization	Contacted by political party, candidate, or politician	Contacted by family member, friend, or individual in community	Attends religious services frequently
Voted in 1988[a]	.63 (.59)	−.14 (.54)	.74*** (.30)	1.37*** (.35)
Participation other than voting[b]	.66** (.13)	−.12 (.21)	.30*** (.10)	.05** (.02)

Source: LNPS.

Note: Entries in parentheses are standard errors. Full equations are listed in appendix.

[a]Cell entries are coefficients from logistic equations. For voting analysis, the samples included only those who were eligible to vote—that is, citizens who were registered to vote.

[b]Cell entries are coefficients and standard errors from OLS equations. For the analysis of participation other than voting, the sample was not restricted by citizenship or registration.

$*p \le .10$ $**p \le .05$ $***p \le .01$

ing been contacted by a political party does not appear to be strongly associated with voter turnout in 1988. Thus, for Latino immigrants, nonpartisan contact and being active in a religious institution are closely associated with voting, but contact by a political party, candidate, or politician is not a major factor. The degree to which party contact affects voter turnout may have changed as the mainstream political parties more actively courted Latino registered voters, but even as late as 1988, that contact appeared to have had little effect on Latino mobilization.

The results for the analysis of immigrant political participation in activities other than voting show that being a member of a Hispanic organization, having been contacted by an individual, and attending religious services frequently are positive and statistically significant predictors for political participation in activities other than voting. In terms of magnitude, membership in a Latino or Hispanic organization is especially important. In sharp contrast, contact by a political party appears unrelated to participation in activities other than voting. Thus, analysis of the LNPS

TABLE 5. Effect of Mobilization on Political Participation among Asian American Immigrants by Source of Mobilization

	Member of Asian American organization	Contacted by political party	Contacted by individual in community	Attends religious services frequently
Voted in 2000[a]	.75	.75**	−.21	1.32**
	(.58)	(.36)	(.44)	(.55)
Voted consistently in 1998 and 2000[a]	−.12	.87***	.07	1.03***
	(.36)	(.30)	(.33)	(.39)
Participation other than voting[b]	.44***	.08	.57***	.03
	(.11)	(.09)	(.11)	(.03)

Source: PNAAPS.

Note: Voted consistently in 1998 and 2000 is coded as follows: 0 = did not vote in both 1998 and 2000, 1= voted in both 1998 and 2000. Entries in parentheses are standard errors. Full equations are listed in appendix.

[a]Cell entries are coefficients from logistic equations. For voting analysis, the samples included only citizens who were registered to vote (that is, only those individuals who were eligible to vote).

[b]Cell entries are coefficients and standard errors from OLS equations. For the analysis of participation other than voting, the sample was not restricted by citizenship or registration.

p ≤ .10   **p* ≤ .05   ***p* ≤ .01

data supports the hypothesis that involvement with a community organization—in this case measured by membership in a Hispanic organization or frequent attendance at church—is likely to lead to involvement in a range of political activities. Being contacted by an individual or frequently attending religious services increases the likelihood that immigrant Latinos will vote as well as take part in other types of political activities. This is consistent with past research showing a strong association between church attendance and political participation for the general population and minority groups as well (Harris 1994; Verba, Schlozman, and Brady 1995; Jones-Correa and Leal 2001). Membership in a Hispanic organization is associated with participation other than voting. This suggests that because community-based organizations are not in the business of winning elections, they are less likely to focus their mobilization efforts on voting alone, as political parties do. However, contact with a political party did not seem to increase likelihood of voting or participation in activities other than voting, after other variables were taken into account.

Uncertainty exists about the causal direction of the relationship between political contact and participation. Although contact may lead to more political participation, it is also probable that those who are most participatory are also the most likely to be targeted for contact by parties and other political groups (see Rosenstone and Hansen 1993; Verba, Schlozman, and Brady 1995; Leighley 2001). Thus, although a strong association between contact and participation exists, caution in interpreting the causal direction of that association is appropriate. Some evidence from field experiments indicates that contact precedes participation.[6]

To gain some understanding of the relative influence on voting of such factors as contact by a political party, membership in an organization, or attendance at religious services, voter turnout for Asian American immigrants was analyzed (see table 5). Of the different sources of mobilization, contact by a political party and frequent attendance at religious services was associated with voting in 2000. Consistency in voting (as measured by voter turnout in both 1998 and 2000) appears to be associated with either contact by a political party or attendance at religious service. In contrast, membership in an Asian American organization and having been contacted by an individual from the respondent's community did not appear to be associated with voter turnout. (For full model, see appendix, table A6.)

Similar to the findings for the LNPS analysis, for Asian American immigrants surveyed in the PNAAPS, membership in an Asian American organization emerges as one of the variables most closely associated with political activities other than voting (see table 5; for full model, see appendix, table A7). Those who belong to an Asian American organization are more likely to take part in a broad range of political activities, even when controlling for other factors such as socioeconomic status. For Asian American immigrants, contact by an individual in the community is also a very strong predictor of political participation other than voting. However, contact by a political party is not associated with participation in any activities beyond voting. These results seem to support the hypothesis that for immigrants, involvement with a community organization is likely to be related to greater participation in a range of political activities that may or may not include voting. The results reveal that for Asian American immigrants, there is no association between contact by a political party and participation in political activities other than voting. Although attendance at religious institutions was associated with both voting and participation other than voting for the Latino sample, for Asian Americans, frequent attendance at religious services appears to have no relationship to political participation other than voting, after other variables are taken into account.

Conclusions about Parties, Community Organizations, & Mobilization

The analysis of large-scale quantitative data using samples of Latino and Asian American immigrants has allowed us to test two hypotheses that emerged from qualitative research on Chinese and Mexican populations in New York and Los Angeles. The first is that immigrants do not view political parties as robust sources of political representation or mobilization and that community organizations play a role in fostering immigrants' political participation. The second is that when targeting immigrant communities, party organizations focus on voter mobilization, whereas community organizations are more likely to engage immigrants in a range of political activities other than voting. Thus, contact by a party may lead some immigrants to the polls, whereas membership in an Asian American or Latino organization or church is more likely to be associated with an immigrant taking part in an array of activities, such as signing a petition, writing a letter to the editor, attending a public meeting, or going to a rally.

Although the available surveys did not directly address the question of whether political parties and other nonparty organizations are mobilizing immigrants, the analysis corroborates the contention that parties do not have a strong presence in immigrant communities and that in contrast, community organizations are more involved in the representation and mobilization of immigrants. Among the Latino respondents who indicated that an organization watched out for their interests, many identified community organizations. These immigrants consistently asserted that community organizations were the groups most likely to represent their concerns. They did not make similar assertions about political parties.

The examination of mobilization as measured by voter registration showed that Latino immigrants report very low levels of contact by political parties. This is not to say that political parties never target immigrant communities: some respondents in both surveys reported being contacted by a political party. However, concerning registering to vote, Latino immigrants were more likely to be contacted by an individual than by a political party. This finding suggests that at least until very recently, parties have not been a robust force in the mobilization of Latino communities. Although political parties may now be making more of an effort to target Latinos, the analysis showed that in their minds, political parties must overcome a weak historical presence, even specifically in regard to voting-related activities.

As the second hypothesis predicted, the analysis showed that the effects of party outreach are generally distinct from the effects of mobilization involving community organizations. Efforts by a political party will affect primarily voter turnout, whereas community organizations are more likely to engage immigrants in a range of political activities other than voting. This finding is to be expected because community organizations have direct contact with many noncitizens (that is, people ineligible to vote) and because their organizational missions are rarely focused on election outcomes (especially in the case of nonprofit organizations, which are barred by law from electioneering). Thus, it is not surprising that these organizations would mobilize Asian Americans and Latinos, including immigrant members of these communities, to participate in a range of political activities.

Contact by a political party has an inconsistent effect on Latino and Asian American political participation. For Latino immigrants who took part in the LNPS, no association exists between party contact and any type of political activity, voting or otherwise, after other factors, such as socioeconomic status, political engagement, and other types of institutional connections are taken into account. For Asian American immigrants, being contacted by a political party is associated most strongly with consistent voting—that is, voting in both 1998 and 2000. Party contact was also associated with voter turnout for Asian American immigrants in 2000, but was not a consistent predictor of participation in political activities other than voting.

The analysis solidly supports the prediction that involvement with a community organization constitutes one of the strongest determinants of Latino and Asian American immigrant participation in political activities other than voting. For Latinos and Asian American immigrants in the samples, being a member of a community organization is always associated with participation in political activities other than voting, even when other possible determinants of participation are taken into account.

The findings presented here suggest that contemporary community organizations can play a vital role in mobilizing immigrants to engage in politics. Yet it is also true that neither parties nor community organizations have been engaging in mass mobilization of Asian American and Latino immigrants. One important question, then, is how both parties and other types of American civic institutions can become a stronger force in the political mobilization and incorporation of contemporary immigrants. The following chapters explore long-term mobilization strategies and building on immigrants' transnational attachments as two possible modes of attaining a more vital role for American civic institutions in immigrant political mobilization.

7 Revitalizing Civic Institutions in Immigrant Communities
Long-Term Strategies

Qualitative and quantitative evidence suggests that community organizations have assumed an important role in mobilizing Asian American and Latino immigrants. Contrary to historical patterns, political parties today are not engaging immigrants through mass-mobilization efforts and have been slow to develop a significant presence in immigrant communities. Parties are operating within a larger context of demographic change as immigrant groups from all over the world, especially Asia and Latin America, enter the United States in large numbers. Party behavior is influenced by the low rates of electoral participation that Asian Americans and Latinos exhibit relative to the rest of the population: parties consequently engage in selective mobilization, focusing their efforts on groups that vote at higher rates and on those Asian Americans and Latinos who are citizens and high-propensity voters. In contrast, community organizations, which through limited mobilization seek to reach beyond the most advantaged and civically engaged Asian Americans and Latinos, appear to be taking on some of the roles parties played in the past.

Demographic Features of Asian American & Latino Populations

Regardless of which set of institutions is most active in immigrant mobilization, both the Asian American and Latino communities present demographic characteristics that have affected their levels of political participation (table 6). Both groups represent a small percentage of the total U.S. population (Asian Americans are 4 percent and Latinos 13 percent, while the non-Latino white majority is 69 percent). Historically, small population size has contributed to the low rates of Latino and Asian American mobilization, but when the 2000 Census showed that Latinos for the first

153

time outnumbered African Americans, the two major parties took notice. The Census also revealed that although the Asian American population has been growing quickly, that group apparently still lacks a politically significant demographic presence in the United States. This situation has deterred party mobilization, although continuing growth may change that.

TABLE 6.   Demographic and Political Profile of Asian Americans and Latinos, 2000

	Asian Americans	Latinos
Percentage of U.S. population[a]	4	13
Percentage of growth 1990 to 2000[b]	72	58
Percentage of foreign-born	69	40
Percentage of noncitizens among adults	41	39
For those over twenty-five years old, percentage with a bachelor's degree[c]	44	10
Median per capita income	$22,352	$12,306
Median age	31 years	26 years
Percentage under eighteen years old	27	35
Registration rate among adults (%)	31	35
Registration rate among adult citizens (%)	52	57
Voting rate among adults (%)	25	28
Voting rate among adult citizens (%)	43	45
Voting rate among registered (%)	83	79
Percentage of voters in 2000 election[d]	2	5–7
Percentage increase in voters, 1996–2000	22	19
Percentage of population residing in battleground states, 2000[e]	20	20
Percentage of voters supporting Bush 2000	41	35
Percentage of voters supporting Gore 2000	55	62

Source: Myer 2001; U.S. Census Bureau 2001; CNN 2000; Jamieson, Shin, and Day 2002; Bauman and Graf 2003; Passell 2004; DeSipio and de la Garza 2005.

[a]Unless noted, statistics are based on those who reported that they were Asian alone or Asian in combination with another race. Those who reported that they were Asian alone in the 2000 Census accounted for 3.6 percent of the U.S. population.

[b]This calculation is based on the figures for race alone or in combination in the 2000 Census. If figures for race alone were used, the growth rate is 48 percent between 1990 and 2000.

[c]This calculation is based on the figure for those who identified as Asian alone.

[d]These figures are based on DeSipio and de la Garza 2005, table 1.9; Passell 2004. Estimates of the Latino vote vary from 4 percent to 7 percent (DeSipio and de la Garza 2005, table 1.9).

[e]Battleground states in 2000 included Arizona, Arkansas, Florida, Iowa, Maine, Michigan, Minnesota, Missouri, Nevada, New Hampshire, New Mexico, Ohio, Oregon, Pennsylvania, Tennessee, Washington, West Virginia, and Wisconsin.

Neither group has a share of the electorate that equates to its share of the overall U.S. population. Asian Americans comprised just 2 percent and Latinos just 5–7 percent of the voters in the 2000 presidential election (DeSipio and de la Garza 2005, 51; Passell 2004). In 2004, exit polls showed that Asian Americans constituted 2–3 percent of the electorate and Latinos 5–8 percent.[1]

Although they share some common demographic features that influence their participation in the political system, Asian Americans and Latinos differ in certain critical respects. One notable difference occurs in the area of socioeconomic status. Asian Americans as a whole exhibit the highest rates of educational achievement among the four major U.S. racial and ethnic groups. According to the 2000 Census, 44 percent of Asian Americans over age twenty-five held bachelor's degrees, compared to just 10 percent of Latinos in the same age group (table 6). The median per capita income in 2000 for Asian Americans ($22,325) eclipsed that of Latinos ($12,306).[2] Socioeconomic resources are one of the most consistent and powerful determinants of political participation, yet socioeconomic power has not translated into political power for Asian Americans. A primary reason is that a large number of foreign-born Asian American adults lack U.S. citizenship. About 40 percent of adult Asian Americans and Latinos were ineligible to vote in 2000 because they were not citizens. Having a large percentage of nonnaturalized individuals in their ranks continues to impede the participation of both Asian Americans and Latinos.

Latinos and Asian Americans also exhibit distinct patterns of naturalization. Immigrants from Asia tend to naturalize at higher rates than do those from other parts of the world, whereas immigrants from Latin America naturalize at lower rates (Portes and Rumbaut 1996). In 2000, according to Jeffrey Passell, only 30 percent of Latino immigrants with legal documents had naturalized, compared to 80 percent of immigrants from other parts of the world, and if Latino immigrants had naturalized at the same rate as other immigrants, an estimated seven hundred thousand additional Latinos would have been eligible to vote in 2000 (2004, 1). Changes in naturalization rates, especially those that result from efforts to streamline and accelerate the process, would likely result in higher rates of citizenship for both Latino and Asian American immigrants, inducing both Republicans and Democrats to pay greater attention to these newcomers.

Voter-registration rates for both Asian Americans and Latinos are also quite low. Only about one-third of adult Asian Americans and Latinos were registered to vote in 2000, but the registration rate climbs moderately for citizens in that group. For the registered voters, the turnout rates compare quite favorably with other groups—83 percent for Asian Americans and 79 percent for Latinos, compared to 86 percent for registered whites and 84 percent for registered blacks. Thus, racial and ethnic gaps in electoral participation shrink considerably after Asian Americans and Latinos register to vote but not when they merely meet the citizenship eligibility requirement for voting by naturalizing. Registration is clearly a key to increasing voting participation for both groups.

Citizenship status and registration are not the only demographic characteristics that affect electoral participation rates. Age also matters, since voters must be at least eighteen years old. In 2000, 27 percent of Asian Americans and 35 percent of Latinos were under eighteen, compared to 23 percent of white Americans. As Latino and Asian American young people come of political age, voting rates for both groups will no doubt increase. Until that time, however, lack of citizenship, low rates of registration, and a young population will continue to depress Asian American and Latino electoral participation.

Because members of these two groups do not vote at high rates, parties and candidates fail to target many in those groups for mass mobilization. The belief that, as groups, Asians and Latinos do not vote leads political strategists to ignore many immigrants, even though assistance with naturalization and particularly with registration could belie that assumption. The lack of interest in mobilizing Asian Americans and Latinos (at least those outside of the battleground states), whether newcomers or citizens, further depresses their rates of participation, creating a pattern of neglect by the mainstream parties. Parties may be overlooking an important trend, however. Recent years have seen a dramatic increase in the number of Asian American and Latino voters. From 1996 to 2000, the number of Latino voters increased 19 percent and that of Asian American voters increased 22 percent (table 6; see also Passell 2004). In contrast, the number of white voters increased just 4 percent.

In recent elections, mobilization by the two major parties has also depended on a group having a strong demographic presence in a battleground state. The vast majority of Asian Americans are concentrated on the East and West Coasts. In 2000, more than half of the Asian American population lived in just three states—California, New York, and Hawaii—

and Asian Americans accounted for more than 10 percent of the populations of California and Hawaii. However, only 20 percent of Asian Americans lived in battleground states, compared to 40 percent of non-Latino whites. Latinos are also regionally concentrated, with half living in just two states, California and Texas. However, although only 20 percent of all Latinos lived in battleground states in 2000, the Latino population was significant in certain ones. In particular, Latinos constitute a significant part of the population in Florida, Arizona, and New Mexico, critical states in close elections. Along with their larger demographic presence, Latinos' growing clout in battleground states partially accounts for why the two parties paid more attention to Latinos than to Asian Americans in 2000 and 2004.

In the 2000 election, exit polls showed that Latino and Asian American voters supported Al Gore at rates of 62 percent for Latinos and 55 percent for Asian Americans, while 35 percent of Latinos and 41 percent of Asian Americans voted for George W. Bush. In 2004, the Republican incumbent seemed to have made impressive gains among Latinos, gaining support from 44 percent of the members of that group, compared to 53 percent who backed his challenger, John Kerry (3 percent of the Latino electorate favored Ralph Nader or another candidate) (CNN 2004). Forty-four percent of Asian Americans voted for Bush, while 56 percent supported Kerry (CNN 2004). However, after the 2004 election, scholars and pundits argued that the exit poll data (based on polls sponsored by a consortium of media outlets, including NBC and CNN) relied on flawed sampling and weighting techniques that exaggerated Latino support for Bush (Fears 2004; Southwest Voter Registration and Education Project 2004). Regardless of the controversy over the validity of the exit poll results, most observers agreed that vote choice and partisan loyalties among Latinos remain "volatile" and were not solidified by the events of 2004 (Alonso-Zaldivar 2004). Similarly, although Asian Americans leaned toward the Democratic candidate in both races, their party loyalties are far from assured (Lien, Conway, and Wong 2004, 16). Although neither party has consolidated support among Asian Americans and Latinos, this fact manifests itself quite differently in terms of the parties' approach to each group. Both parties seem to believe that they can eventually win the support of Latinos with largely symbolic efforts. In contrast, the parties' appear to see Asian Americans not as potential swing voters but as a group that splits its vote and is therefore not worth mobilizing.

Despite its high level of educational attainment and economic power, parties are not likely to perceive Asian Americans as an important voting bloc because the group is relatively small and contains such a large proportion of nonnaturalized individuals and because those who are citizens exhibit low voter-registration rates. Low rates of voting contribute to a vicious cycle, as parties are reluctant to spend resources on those whom they view as being apathetic. Because the group is seen as having split partisan loyalties, neither party seems to view it as desirable to mobilize. Lack of party mobilization then further depresses participation. The concentration of the Asian American population outside the battleground states, the primary focus of recent presidential elections, has reinforced this pattern.

Latino demographics also exhibit traits that are associated with depressed political participation. Latinos are characterized by a high proportion of nonnaturalized individuals who are ineligible to vote and a high proportion of young people not yet of voting age (table 6). The low socioeconomic position of many Latinos constitutes another deterrent to their political participation. Despite their long history in the United States, Latinos have been slow to garner recognition from the two parties. However, the overall size of the Latino population in relation to other groups in the United States and the belief that their party loyalties can be won has now resulted in increasing attention, but it has been primarily symbolic and focused on registered Latino voters living in battleground states. As a consequence of these many factors, an increase in voter turnout has not developed despite the brisk growth rate for the Latino population.

Republican & Democratic Strategy: Short-Term or Shortsighted?

The parties' strategic targeting of high-propensity voters in battleground states may appear rational at first glance, but there are reasons to believe that this approach is shortsighted. As the largest minority population in the United States, Latinos have demographic strength. Asian Americans, the fastest-growing of the four major racial and ethnic groups during the 1990s, are not far behind. The U.S. Census Bureau projects that those identifying as "Asian alone" (not in combination with another race) will approach 10 percent of the U.S. population within the next four decades (U.S. Census Bureau 2004). Further, the numbers of Asian American and Latino voters are increasing at a much faster pace than the numbers for their white counterparts. Therefore, a longer-term approach to mobilizing Asian Americans and Latinos could have a dual benefit of speeding up participation rates for both groups and solidifying group loyalty to a given party.

At present, however, parties have not taken a long-term approach to mobilizing Asian Americans or Latinos, especially the immigrant members of these communities. In contrast to the past, parties have not been mobilizing immigrants on a mass level in the communities where they live. They primarily engage in selective mobilization of the most likely voters. Community organizations such as labor organizations, workers' centers, advocacy and social service organizations, ethnic voluntary associations, and religious institutions have stepped into the breach, but many of their efforts face significant challenges, such as lack of financial resources and competing priorities dictated by organizational mission. Thus, they engage in limited mobilization. Given that parties fail consistently to mobilize immigrants and that community organizations are limited in their ability or resources for a mass mobilization of immigrants, long-term, gradual political socialization over time may represent the only mechanism currently operating to increase the participation of large numbers of immigrants in the political system.

The Passage of Time as a Mechanism for Increasing Political Participation

A consistent theme during the interviews with Chinese and Mexican immigrants and community leaders was the importance of length of residence as an influence on contemporary immigrants' political participation in the United States. Those who work closely with immigrant communities often remarked on this relationship. One Mexican organizer in New York compared the political organization of Mexican communities in New York to those in Los Angeles and Chicago: "California was Mexico before, and Chicago is another place where Mexicans were there in the beginning of the century, so they have a lot of organizations—a lot. They have one organization for teachers, for students, for people who sell on the streets, for flower vendors—for everything, they have an organization. But they have been there for a hundred years." He emphasized that because the Mexican community in New York is relatively new, it will take time to establish an organizational infrastructure and develop leaders. Most community leaders mentioned that they expect to see more and varied political participation in their communities as individual members' duration of residence in the United States lengthens.

The director of a social-service center serving a mostly Chinese immigrant population in Sunset Park, New York, emphasized the political gains his community had gradually made: "We are seeing improvement. We saw that maybe five or six years ago—we were probably able to serve fifty or sixty people a day on Election Day. The last Election Day was about the local community school board, [and] we were able to mobilize a little over fifteen hundred Chinese to come out and vote. It's really amazing because that has never happened in the Brooklyn area." Interviews with immigrants themselves also show a consistent relationship between length of residence and political involvement. Chinese and Mexican respondents in the study indicated that they were more interested in U.S. politics at the time of the interview than when they had first arrived. When asked if she had become more interested in U.S. politics, one Chinese immigrant in Los Angeles responded, "When I first came, I didn't even want to bother listening. But now, after living here for so long, it's inevitable for me to become more interested than when I first was."

Length of Residence and Political Participation

Data from the Current Population Survey show a very strong association between length of residence and political participation across a representative sample of immigrant groups (Ramakrishnan and Espenshade 2001; Ramakrishnan 2003). For immigrant citizens from each of the four major U.S. racial and ethnic groups, voting participation increases dramatically with length of residence in the United States (see figure 1). Using the Current Population Survey 2002 Volunteer Supplement, a nationally representative sample that includes a large proportion of immigrants, S. Karthick Ramakrishnan (2003) found that long-term residents are more likely to work as volunteers than are new arrivals.[3] All four major U.S. racial groups demonstrated a strong relationship between length of residence and volunteering, although, across time, the relationship was most consistent for Asian American and Latino immigrants.

Alejandro Portes and Rubén Rumbaut (1996, 108), two prominent scholars of contemporary immigration, claim that not until after the passing of the first generation do subsequent generations of Latinos and Asian Americans turn their attention to U.S. politics. However, we should not dismiss the political participation of first-generation immigrants. Past studies of immigrant communities have emphasized that length of residence is an important determinant of civic participation for first-generation immigrants (Cain, Kiewiet, and Uhlaner 1991; Arvizu and Garcia 1996; Ong

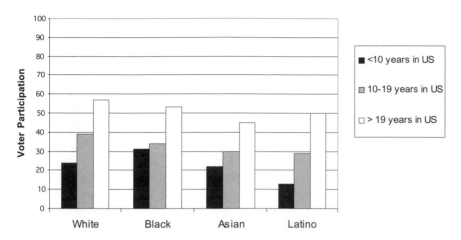

Fig. 1. Length of residence and voting participation among immigrants, midterm elections, 1994–98. (Data from Ramakrishnan and Espenshade 2001.)

and Nakanishi 1996; Jones-Correa 1998; Lien 2000; J. Wong 2001). These studies rely on data collected primarily in the late 1980s and early 1990s and, in some cases, data that are geographically limited to a particular state. More recent data from the 1999 *Washington Post*/Kaiser/Harvard University Survey of Latinos in America (LAT) and the 2000–2001 Pilot National Asian American Political Survey (PNAAPS) also show a positive association between length of residence and the political participation of contemporary Asian American and Latino immigrants. (For details on the LAT and PNAAPS, see appendix, tables A1, A2). In addition, these surveys include a wider range of questions than the Current Population Survey contains, allowing for a more in-depth analysis of that association.

The PNAAPS asked Asian Americans if they were registered to vote and if they had voted in 2000. A third question asked, "During the past four years, have you participated in any of the following types of political activity in your community?" Respondents picked activities from a list that included writing or phoning a government official, donating money to a campaign, signing a petition for a political cause, or taking part in a protest or demonstration. (For the exact wording of questions measuring participation in activities other than voting, see appendix, table A7.) Analysis excluded those who have lived in the United States for fewer than five years, the residency period required to naturalize and thus to register and to vote.[4]

For naturalized Asian Americans, registration rates increased with length of U.S. residence (see figure 2). Those who have lived in the United States for twenty-one years or longer are actually more likely to be registered voters (93 percent) than are U.S.-born Asian Americans (85 percent). A similar pattern holds for Asian American voter turnout in 2000. Of the Asian Americans who had lived in the United States for less than ten years, fewer than 30 percent indicated that they had voted, compared to more than 50 percent for those who had lived there for twenty-one years or more. Again, Asian immigrants who are long-term residents are even more likely to have voted in 2000 than are native-born Asian Americans. Answers to the third question also revealed that length of U.S. residence is a factor. For example, just 35 percent of those who have lived in the United States for less than a decade indicated that they had participated in a political activity other than voting during the four years prior to the survey, compared to 55 percent for those who have lived there for between twenty-one and twenty-five years. Interestingly, participation among the longest-term residents (twenty-six years or more) drops off slightly. Overall, however, participation in activities other than voting appears to increase with length of residence.

Using the LAT survey, voting participation was measured based on whether respondents voted in 1996 or 1998. (See appendix for details on the survey methodology.) Both election years are included in an attempt to capture consistent voting behavior. Turnout in a presidential election (1996) tends to be higher than turnout for a congressional election (1998), but people are more likely to recall whether they voted in the more recent election. Unlike the questions in the PNAAPS, the questions in the LAT measure participation in political activities other than voting by asking about whether respondents had worked or volunteered for a Latino political candidate; attended a public meeting or demonstration regarding Latino concerns; or contributed money to a Latino candidate or organization. The survey did not have a measure of general participation (that is, one that was not specifically related to supporting a Latino candidate or cause).

Like their Asian American counterparts, the Latino immigrants in the United States for the longest period of time are more likely to report that they had registered and voted than are more recent arrivals. Latinos who

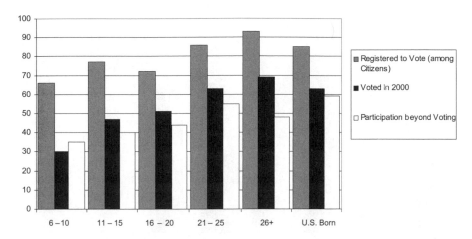

Fig. 2.   Political activity and years of U.S. residence: Asian Americans. (*Note:* Statistics on voting do not take into account eligibility. As shown, eligibility [registration] is also time dependent.) (Data from PNAAPS.)

have lived in the United States for twenty-six years or longer are just as likely to have registered and voted as are U.S.-born Latinos (figure 3). Participation in political activities other than voting is more consistent over time, although the newest residents are less likely to have participated (28 percent) than are residents who have lived in the United States for at least 26 years (35 percent).

Is it possible that these changes in political participation over time are simply a matter of increases in socioeconomic resources or age? In other words, might the basic socioeconomic model of political participation explain these trends? Using LAT data on voter registration and controlling for immigrant age and socioeconomic status, separate regression models tested for the effects of length of residence on voting in 1996 or 1998 and participation in political activities other than voting for Latinos (see table 7). Controlling in one equation for socioeconomic status (measured as education and income), age, and length of residence allows us to examine the separate effects of each variable on the type of political participation included in each model. The relationship between age and political participation is curvilinear for the Latino sample, indicating that Latino individ-

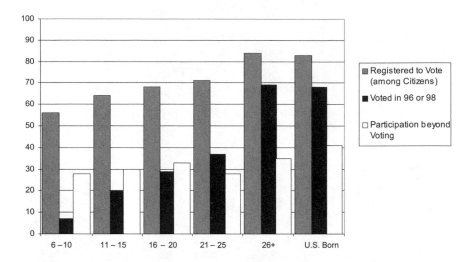

Fig. 3. Political activity and years of U.S. residence: Latinos. (*Note:* Statistics on voting do not take into account eligibility. As shown, eligibility [registration] is also time dependent.) (Data from LAT.)

TABLE 7. Political Participation and Length of Residence among Latinos

	Registered (among citizens)		Voted in 1996 or 1998 (among registered)		Participation in activities other than voting	
	b	SE	b	SE	b	SE
Education	.16***	.06	.36**	.09	.13***	.04
Household income	.04	.06	.00	.09	.05	.04
Age	.01	.00	.09**	.04	.06***	.02
Age squared	.01	.03	.00	.00	.00***	.00
Years in the United States	.03**	.01	.05*	.02	.02***	.01
Constant	−.78	.75	−3.33	1.01	−.27	.41
	−2 (Log-Likelihood) Initial = 663.74		−2 (Log-Likelihood) Initial = 393.36		−2 (Log-Likelihood) Initial = 1,647.18	
	−2 (Log-Likelihood) Convergence = 632.17		−2 (Log-Likelihood) Convergence = 338.87		−2 (Log-Likelihood) Convergence = 1,610.22	
	Chi-Square 31.58 (df 5)		Chi-Square 54.46 (df 5)		Chi-Square 36.96 (df 5)	
	$p < .00$		$p < .00$		$p < .00$	
	$N = 571$		$N = 418$		$N = 1,329$	

Source: LAT.

Note: Foreign-born sample only. Logistic regression used for all models.

$^*p \le .10$ $^{**}p \le .05$ $^{***}p \le .01$

uals are more likely to participate in politics as they grow older; among the very oldest, however, participation begins to drop off. Thus, a variable (age squared) that captures the curvilinear nature of the relationship is included. A similar set of analyses was conducted using the PNAAPS sample (see table 8). For both analyses, only those eligible to vote were included.

The most important result of these analyses is the consistently positive, statistically significant relationship between length of residence and the likelihood of Latino and Asian immigrants registering to vote, voting, and participating in political activities other than voting. And this holds true even after controlling for age, income, and education. With the exception of Asian-immigrant voter turnout in 2000, which shows a negative association between length of residence and participation, when one takes into account respondents' age, income, and education, length of residence exerts a positive influence on whether Asian American and Latino immigrants participate politically.

TABLE 8. Political Participation and Length of Residence among Asian Americans

	Registered (among citizens)		Voted in 2000 (among registered)		Participation in activities other than voting	
	b	SE	b	SE	b	SE
Education	.20**	.09	.45**	.12	.22***	.06
Household income	.10	.08	−.08	.10	.15***	.05
Age	.03***	.01	.04***	.01	.01	.01
Years in the United States	.04**	.02	−.06***	.02	.02*	.06
Constant	−1.65**	.55	−.49	.77	−2.39***	.36
	−2 (Log-Likelihood) Initial = 489.27 −2 (Log-Likelihood) Convergence = 451.39 Chi-Square 37.91(df 4) $p < .00$ N = 460		−2 (Log-Likelihood) Initial = 332.72 −2 (Log-Likelihood) Convergence = 300.46 Chi-Square 32.26 (df 4) $p < .00$ N = 357		−2 (Log-Likelihood) Initial = 1,041.92 −2 (Log-Likelihood) Convergence = 991.92 Chi-Square 50.00 (df 4) $p < .00$ N = 773	

Source: PNAAPS.

Note: Foreign-born sample only. Logistic regression used for all models.

$*p \leq .10$ $**p \leq .05$ $***p \leq .01$

Although for Asian immigrants, the relationship between length of residence and 2000 voter turnout is negative (b = −.06), an examination of consistency in voting (measured by voter behavior in 1998 and 2000) yields a positive and statistically significant relationship (b = .03, standard error = .01) (see tables 8 and 9). Length of residence is not a critical predictor of Asian-immigrant voter turnout in 2000, but a positive association exists between length of residence and turnout in the two consecutive elections. Thus, regardless of differences in age, income, and education, with each additional year of U.S. residence, Asian Americans can be expected to vote more consistently.

The effect of length of residence on Asian American and Latino political participation is highlighted by the following example.[5] The likelihood that a forty-five-year-old Mexican immigrant citizen with average education and income who has lived in the United States for just five years would be registered to vote is 64 percent, while that figure is 75 percent for an immigrant who has been in the United States for twenty years. Similarly, for a forty-seven-year-old Asian American immigrant citizen with average education and income who has lived in the United States for five years, the likelihood of being registered is 75 percent, versus 83 percent for an Asian American with the same characteristics who has lived in the United States for twenty years.

The findings also confirm that at the individual level, socioeconomic

TABLE 9.   Consistent Turnout among Asian Americans

	Turned out in 1998 and 2000	
Education	.19**	.09
Household income	−.13*	.08
Age	.02***	.01
Years in the United States	.03**	.01
Constant	−2.39***	.64

−2 (Log-Likelihood) Initial = 455.84
−2 (Log-Likelihood) Convergence = 432.89
Chi-Square 23.76 (df 4)
$p < .00$
$N = 357$

Source: PNAAPS.
Note: Foreign-born sample only. Logistic regression used for all models.
*$p \leq .10$ **$p \leq .05$ ***$p \leq .01$

status, especially education, is often a strong predictor of political participation among Asian American and Latino immigrants.[6] This conforms to
what we know about the positive relationship between education and
political involvement for European immigrants (an analysis of a European
immigrant sample is shown in appendix, table A8) and for the general
population in the United States (Verba and Nie 1972; Wolfinger and
Rosenstone 1980; Rosenstone and Hansen 1993; Verba, Schlozman, and
Brady 1995).[7] However, the results of the analyses of the LAT and
PNAAPS data show that even when socioeconomic status is taken into
account, length of residence is almost always key to the political participation of immigrants. We can conclude, then, that although socioeconomic
resources are important for immigrant participation, the passage of time
matters a great deal as well and exhibits an independent relationship with
participation.[8]

What types of acculturation processes explain why length of residence
matters for political participation? Additional multivariate analysis shows
that for Asian Americans, length of residence sometimes has an indirect
effect on political participation (J. Wong n.d.). That is, the effects of
length of residence can be explained by specific acculturation processes,
such as becoming more fluent in English, obtaining citizenship, or experiencing discrimination. For Latino immigrants, the direct effects of length
of residence on political participation persist, even when adaptive
processes are taken into account.

Contemporary Immigrants Are Similar to Earlier European Immigrants

Researchers who have compared earlier European immigrant groups to
contemporary Asian and Latin American immigrant groups generally
agree that the former were more active in politics than are the latter (see,
for example, DeSipio 2001; Sterne 2001; Waters 2001; Schier 2002).
How different are contemporary Asian American and Latino immigrants
from European immigrants of the past? Despite the low levels of political
participation among Asian American and Latino immigrants today, the
process of becoming politically involved over time, at least at the individual
level, does not appear to differ from that experienced by earlier European
immigrants.

It is especially useful to compare the experience of Irish immigrants to
that of contemporary nonwhite immigrants because the Irish constituted
"the first great ethnic minority in American cities" (Sowell 1986, 17). The

Irish represent a historical example of a "distinct and active ethnic group in American political life" (Cochran 1995, 590). For the Irish Americans who arrived during the 1800s, political success accumulated over several decades (Barone 2001). As one historian describes Irish Americans' political prospects over time, "The Irish began their political career in New York as the pawns of the Democratic machine. They exchanged their votes for unskilled jobs, petty licenses, and other relatively low-cost benefits. These 'crumbs' represented the absolute highest these impoverished newcomers expected. But as they grew in number, they became more American. . . . The crumbs grew into substantial slices, and by the 1860s, the time of [Boss] Tweed's hegemony, the Irish garnered the most jobs, the best patronage, and increasingly significant positions, even key leadership roles" (Diner quoted in Barone 2001, 52).

Kristi Andersen's (1979) case study of turnout in immigrant wards in Chicago also illustrates participation patterns among immigrants in the 1920s and 1930s. She finds that in the wards with the highest percentage of foreign-born residents from Europe, voter turnout increased dramatically over time. She estimates that in 1924, less than one-third of the potential electorate in immigrant neighborhoods voted, but by 1940, that figure rose to half. In a ward of mostly Czech and a few Russian immigrants, for example, turnout grew from 43 percent in 1924 to 75 percent in 1940 (109). Andersen attributes this surge primarily to mobilization of nonvoters by the Chicago Democratic machine, but it may also be traced in part to processes of acculturation that occurred over time as immigrants became more knowledgeable about and familiar with the political system, learned English, and acquired citizenship.[9] Thus, it seems European immigrants' political participation increased gradually along with length of residence.

Similarly, the passage of time (measured by length of residence) appears today to exert a powerful force on both Asian and Latino immigrant political participation. According to my statistical analysis, a potent association exists between length of residence and political participation for both groups, and the remarks made by immigrants during the interviews are quite consistent with these findings. A twenty-year-old Mexican immigrant living in Los Angeles for ten years said that he had become more interested in politics than when he first arrived in the United States because he could relate to more political issues and that some laws, such as Proposition 187 (a 1994 California ballot initiative that sought to limit social services for immigrants without documents), had affected him directly. A twenty-six-year-old Mexican immigrant living in New York for six years said that she had definitely become more interested in U.S. politics than when she first arrived; when she watched the news, it interested her because she knew it would affect her in one way or another. She had become "more conscious" of being in the United States.

Consequences of Long-Term Length of Residence on Aggregate Participation

Because California leads the nation in the percentage of foreign-born residents, the Golden State provides a good case for understanding the critical role that length of residence plays in terms of aggregate trends in political participation. According to Dowell Myers and John Pitkin, immigrants account for just over 10 percent of the total U.S. population but more than 25 percent of California's population. In comparison, 20 percent of New Yorkers and 18 percent of Floridians are immigrants (2001, 6). Not only has immigration driven demographic transformations in California, but the immigrant population is also changing. Significantly, more immigrants are becoming long-term residents (defined as someone who has lived in the United States for twenty-one or more years. Whereas long-term residents in California account for 21.9 percent of the current immigrant population, that figure is predicted to increase to 55 percent in twenty years (16). Based on their research using the Demographic Futures Database, Myers and Pitkin project that "over time, more immigrants remain in California, and as these immigrants age, the number of foreign-born residents who entered the United States more than twenty years ago is expected to soar by 364 percent from 1990 to 2020" (16). Consistent with these projections, recent arrivals (defined as those who have lived in the United States for ten or fewer years) are expected to constitute a much smaller share of the state's future population. By 2010, those who arrived during the peak periods of migration that characterized the 1980s and 1990s will have become long-term residents.[10]

In California and similar states, dramatic increases in the Asian American and Latino shares of the population are likely to lead to gains in political power for those groups. However, because long-term residents have a much higher propensity to vote than do recent arrivals, changes in the electorate's makeup are not likely to result simply from changes in the numbers of Asian Americans and Latinos in the state but also are likely to be the consequence of an increase in voting by the growing numbers of long-term immigrant residents. Thus, several processes are contributing to Asian Americans' and Latinos' growing political force in California and other high-immigration states. First is the increase in the two populations. More important, however, may be the increasing number of immigrants who are long-term residents—that is, those who are most likely to vote. Third, as they come of voting age, the children and grandchildren of immigrants will swell the ranks of eligible voters.

To understand Latino and Asian American political participation in the United States then, key comparisons should not be limited to differences between the first and second generations (Portes and Rumbaut 1996) but should also include distinctions between long-term residents and more recent arrivals. Further analysis suggests that voter turnout differences are, in many cases, larger between recent arrivals and long-term residents than between immigrants and the U.S.-born (J. Wong 2002). With steady population growth and the passage of time, Asian Americans and especially Latinos will inevitably become an increasingly important segment of the California electorate. It is also possible that for Asian and Latino immigrants, electoral power in a vote-rich state such as California will translate into increasing political clout at the national level as well.

Long-Term Strategies to Facilitate Immigrant Political Participation

Lack of mass mobilization by American civic institutions—either parties or community organizations—leaves the passage of time as the only consistent and powerful mechanism operating to increase the participation of large numbers of immigrants in the political system. As such, the current circumstances suggest that immigrant political participation rates will grow slowly and steadily rather than in dramatic surges.

Because the most pressing concern for the two major parties is the next immediate election, they often adopt very short-term mobilization strategies. For example, in the few weeks before an election, parties commonly spend most of their resources on direct mail, mass-media advertising, and phone contacts. When two strong candidates face off, campaign funds are likely to be spent both early and late in the season, and when a strong incumbent faces a weak challenger, the majority of campaign funds are especially likely to be spent late in the election season (Justin Fox and Indridason 2001). In the highly publicized 2003 California gubernatorial recall election, the embattled incumbent, Governor Gray Davis, as well as the major candidates vying to replace him deluged the airwaves with media spots and packed the mailboxes of registered voters with campaign flyers in the last week and a half before the election.

These approaches to mobilization are not only short term but also rely on strategic targeting of the most likely voters: registered citizens who vote regularly. A recent study of party strategy describes a campaign-management publication for Republican candidates that advises, "Ideally, you will only stop at the homes of registered voters. . . . In a large district, you may only want to stop at the homes of registered voters who have a history of voting in important elections" (cited in Leighley 2001, 59).

Given the short-term, targeted approach that the mainstream parties usually adopt, it should not be surprising that when asked about their affiliation, more than 20 percent of Asian American respondents in the PNAAPS reported that they do not think in terms of the traditional categories of Democrat, Republican, and independent. Nearly 10 percent of the immigrants polled indicated that they were not sure of their party affiliation. The 2001 *Washington Post*/Kaiser Family Foundation/Harvard University Survey on Race and Ethnicity asked a multiracial sample of respondents, "In politics today, do you consider yourself a Republican, a Democrat, an independent, or something else?" Asian Americans (19 percent) and Latinos (17 percent) were more likely to respond "something else," "nothing," or "don't know" to the question than were whites (9 percent) or blacks (12 percent). These statistics suggest that many groups with large immigrant populations lack a basic knowledge of the two major parties and the party system as a whole and are thus only weakly, if at all, connected to that system. Not only the two major parties but also third parties, such as the Green Party and the Labor Party, must establish meaningful relationships with immigrant voters to bring them into the parties' coalitions.

Parties that adopt short-term, targeted mobilization strategies are missing an important opportunity to build their voter base. Because many Asian American and Latino immigrants are noncitizens who demonstrate low rates of registration and who do not exhibit a long or consistent voting history, they are unlikely to be targeted by parties in the short period before an election takes place. Party strategies that neglect Asian American and Latino immigrants may not have a dramatic effect on party fortunes in the immediate future; however, as growing numbers of immigrants become long-term residents and citizens, they will certainly participate in politics at higher rates. Thus, parties will benefit in the long run if they direct some resources toward more long-term mobilization strategies directed at Asian American and Latino immigrants.

Political parties should consider the adoption of two long-term mobilization strategies if they want to build up their base in immigrant communities, especially in those communities that will someday be home to many long-term—and politically active—residents.

Mass Registration Drives.   Voter registration is the key to immigrant political participation. After registering, Asian American and Latino immigrants vote at rates comparable to the general population (Lien 2000; see also table 6). Parties currently do not use their resources to register newer immigrants; instead, they target those who are already registered and voting (Leighley 2001; DeSipio and de la Garza 2005). To accelerate immigrant political participation, parties should hold mass registration drives at regular intervals throughout the year, rather than only during the campaign season. These events should be held at citizenship ceremonies; at local immigrant community events, including holiday festivals, sporting events, and cultural celebrations; and at locations that immigrants frequent, such as grocery stores and parks.

Voter-Education Programs, Town Hall Meetings, and Workshops for Both Citizens and Noncitizens.   Parties should enhance immigrants' understanding of and familiarity with the political system to facilitate and accelerate political socialization. Pamphlets including short, accessible overviews of aspects of the political process, descriptions of the party's policy priorities, and explanations of the role that citizens can play in party organizations and in government should be widely distributed in immigrant communities. These materials should be prepared specifically with immigrants in mind and be made available in multilingual formats. Parties should introduce themselves to immigrant communities through town hall meetings that both are informational and solicit the opinions of immigrants and through workshops that aim to demystify local, state, and national politics. All these activities should also be maintained year-round and should also be offered at places and times that are easily accessible for immigrants.

These long-term strategies are likely to yield long-term gains for the parties. These strategies will create opportunities to attract new, loyal voters who could swell partisan ranks. Immigrants acquainted with the party system will be more likely to get involved in the political system, perhaps at a faster pace than is currently the case.

Civic Institutions Outside the Party System

Community organizations, such as labor organizations, workers' centers, advocacy and social service organizations, ethnic voluntary associations, and religious institutions, may be more likely than parties to invest in long-term mobilization of immigrants. Unlike parties, such groups are not tied to the election cycle; instead, they focus on increasing their political clout by building their membership base. An example is the National Association of Latino Elected Officials Education Fund (NALEO), an advocacy organization that was founded to respond to the lack of support for Latino candidates by the two major parties and that now declares itself the "leading national organization of Latino political empowerment."[11] It has taken an explicitly long-term approach to immigrant mobilization. In the spring and summer of 2004, NALEO, in cooperation with Univisión, a major Spanish-language television network, and *La Opinión,* a major Spanish-language newspaper, organized a "national listening tour," which held gatherings in town hall settings in Los Angeles, Houston, New York, Miami, and Chicago. The goal was to engage Latinos by soliciting their opinions on a range of political issues. The organizations recruited participants through leaflets sent in the mail and by running public service announcements. During the meetings, participants broke into discussion groups of fifteen to twenty people and were encouraged to talk about their perspectives on political participation and issues that they felt were relevant for the 2004 campaign.

Describing the effects of the forum, Erica Bernal, NALEO's director of communications, said, "It empowers people. Because all of a sudden they feel part of the process. . . . It triggers something in them, in feeling invited and part of the process. That what they're saying matters and is being heard." Bernal further discussed NALEO's goal of building a long-term relationship with Latinos and contrasted it to what she viewed as the goals of the mainstream parties:

Very simply put, the parties and the candidates are about winning elections, so they're about trying to appeal to their base and they're about trying to appeal to a small margin of voters who haven't made up their minds, and [the parties] try to bring them over to their side and mobilize them. NALEO is about expanding the Latino electorate. So there are very different strategies. . . . [W]e're talking to Latinos who are registered but have not had a history of participation, and we're trying to get them engaged, developing a long-term relationship with them cycle after cycle, so that they can become active, vote once, hopefully, vote again, and then get picked up by the parties and the candidates as high-propensity voters that are receiving information and mailers.

Because NALEO's focus is on "low-propensity, low-frequency voters," says Rosalind Gold, the organization's director of policy, research, and advocacy, "In our work, it is very difficult to see immediate results. Because these are people you have to keep contacting over and over and over again."

NALEO is clearly devoted to doing the difficult work of turning low-propensity voters into high-propensity voters over the course of many years. In this respect, the group is helping to lay the foundations of participation in the Latino community. Its members also constitute a critical bridge between the mainstream political system and Latinos and Latino immigrants. NALEO focuses on long-term engagement and specifically targets those individuals whom the parties tended to ignore. NALEO has raised sufficient resources to launch a large-scale mobilization effort. The group's *Ve y Vota* (Go Vote) voter-information hotline received thousands of calls during the 2004 presidential campaign, and NALEO targeted more than one hundred thousand individuals with its Get Out the Vote project, which included the country's largest phone bank aimed at mobilizing Latinos.

Community organizations with limited financial resources are impeded from adopting long-term voter mobilization strategies. However, labor organizations, workers' centers, advocacy and social service organizations, ethnic voluntary associations, and religious institutions may be resource rich in other ways. They are often staffed by individuals who are intimately familiar with the language, cultural traditions, and policy priorities of the community the organization serves. That knowledge, coupled with years of providing immigrants with services and information, can give an organization strong legitimacy that positions it to mobilize immigrants. Although most community organizations have nonpolitical missions and do not mobilize immigrants at a mass level, these groups are clearly help-ing to build the foundations of political participation in their communities through limited mobilization.

Conclusion

A strong, statistically significant positive relationship exists between length of U.S. residence and political participation for Asian American and Latino immigrants. One of the most important implications of this relationship is that increasing political participation for contemporary Asian American and Latino immigrants is likely to be slow and steady over time, just as it was in the past for European immigrant groups. Parties currently fail to mobilize immigrants on a mass level; when parties do attempt to reach out to these new arrivals, they engage in selective mobilization and do so using short-term strategies. Community organizations, which are otherwise well positioned to provide political socialization for immigrants, face restric-tions in terms of financial resources and time available for mass mobiliza-tion. Instead, they engage in limited mobilization. Given this situation, the simple passage of time appears to be the only consistent mechanism operating to increase the participation of large numbers of immigrants in the political system.

The evidence showing gradual increases in political participation for Asian American and Latino immigrants over time should be a signal to parties and other civic institutions. Short-term, get-out-the-vote mobiliza-tion strategies by political parties in the weeks before an election are not likely to be very effective at bringing new immigrants into the political sys-tem. Instead, parties should adopt a long-term approach to mobilizing Asian American and Latino immigrants, through regular mass voter-regis-tration drives, voter-education programs, and the establishment of a stronger presence in immigrant communities. By choosing to marginalize immigrants today, they are missing an important long-term opportunity. Despite institutional and political disincentives, parties should actively court Asian Americans and Latinos because the failure to do so will have consequences for party relevance in years to come. Further, long-term mobilization strategies can facilitate and accelerate immigrant political participation, contributing to a larger pool of high-propensity voters who would solidify and expand the parties' bases of supporters.

In contrast to parties, some community organizations engage in long-term mobilization strategies. Most, however, have nonpolitical missions and limited financial resources that prevent them from adopting long-term strategies for political mobilization of immigrants. Nevertheless, community organizations have other types of resources—in particular, sensitivity and understanding rooted in cultural, linguistic, and substantive knowledge of the local immigrant population, and legitimacy won through long service to that community. These attributes enable these groups to mobilize some Asian American and Latino immigrants, including those whom the parties do not traditionally target. This mobilization encompasses activities other than just voting and often cross-cuts ethnic and racial identity to leverage other immigrant identities. These efforts can provide a strong foundation for future participation and mass mobilization efforts.

8 Institutional Mobilization in a Transnational Context

Historically, U.S. immigrant communities have maintained strong connections with their countries of origin (Rosenblum 1973; W. Thomas and Znaniecki 1984; Jacobson 1995; Portes and Rumbaut 1996; Guarnizo and Smith 1998; Foner 2000). Immigration specialists underscore European immigrants' attachment to their countries of origin by documenting their remigration to their homelands.[1] During the first half of the twentieth century, fully one-third of all immigrants to the United States remigrated from the United States (Guarnizo and Smith 1998, 16; see also Morawska 2001; Wang 2001).

Non-European immigrants have also maintained ties with their countries of origin. As Madeline Hsu (2000) documents, Chinese migrants from Taishan (Toisan) County in Guandong, in southern China, who arrived in the United States at the beginning of the twentieth century helped to forge and sustain a transnational community through their "commitments to close relatives, such as wives, children, parents, and siblings" (5). For news and communication from their homeland, they relied on *quiakan*, Chinese magazines produced in Taishan and Hong Kong and distributed to the Taishan diaspora, and "Gold Mountain" firms were established to deliver remittances and letters between Taishanese migrants in the United States and people in Taishan.

Are contemporary Asian American and Latino immigrants who engage in transnational activities more or less likely to participate in U.S. politics than their counterparts who lack transnational connections? This remains an open question. One popular perspective asserts that immigrants who pursue transnational activities are too preoccupied with interests in their country of origin to pay attention to U.S. politics. A competing perspective suggests that immigrants in the U.S. may find themselves in a unique position that allows those who engage in transnational activity to take part simultaneously in their country of origin and in the U.S. political system.

Transnationalism

Transnationalism is defined as "the processes by which immigrants forge and sustain multi-stranded social relations that link together their societies of origin and settlement" (Basch, Schiller, and Blanc 1994, 7). Today, individuals who migrate to the United States have myriad ways to maintain connections to their country of origin. The very diverse ties that contemporary immigrants have to their homelands are often powerful. Immigrants maintain links to their country of origin by sending individual and collective financial remittances (Pessar 1987; Rogers 2000a; Georges 1990; Hamilton and Chinchilla 2002), investing in projects and property in their former hometowns (Robert Smith 1996, 1998), building cross-border social networks and communities (Basch, Schiller, and Blanc 1994; Robert Smith 1997; Smart and Smart 1998; Levitt 2001), communicating regularly with friends and relatives (Basch, Schiller, and Blanc 1994), making frequent trips back to the homeland (Rouse 1992), sharing, maintaining and creating popular culture (Iwabuchi 2002; Aparicio, Jáquez, and Cepeda 2003), and constructing multiple and overlapping identities and notions of citizenship (Jones-Correa 1998; Munch 2001, Verma 2002; Joppke and Morawska 2003). As has been well documented, immigrants continue to make economic contributions to their countries of origin long after migrating to the United States (Massey et al. 1987; Levitt 2001; Hamilton and Chinchilla 2002). Interwoven into these transnational activities, immigrants exhibit an interest in politics, in some cases related to the homeland, in others related to the United States, and on occasion explicitly related to the existence of a transnational community (Portes and Rumbaut 1996; Robert Smith 1996, 1997, 1998; Jones-Correa 1998; Karpathakis 1999; Hockenos 2003).

To help us understand the role of transnational attachments in the political lives of U.S. immigrants, we can turn to the body of literature on transnationalism, a topic that is receiving increasing scholarly and popular attention. Peggy Levitt's (2001) study of Dominican immigrants in Boston and their economic, social, political, and religious ties to their Dominican sending communities represents one of the most comprehensive among those that have emerged from various fields, including anthropology, sociology, and history. This body of work lets us examine how individuals maintain connections across national borders as well as their motivations for doing so (see, for example, Massey et al. 1987; Basch, Schiller, and Blanc 1994; Portes 1996; Robert Smith 1996, 1998; Guarnizo and M. Smith 1998; Hamilton and Chinchilla 2002; Espiritu 2003). Transnationalism has even merited popular attention, as evidenced by a series on transnational migration published in the *New York Times* on July 19–21, 1998.

The literature on transnationalism explicitly critiques the traditional immigration models that have posited a "straight-line" trajectory for assimilation, which starts with migration from the country of origin and ends with settlement in the destination country. In those models, when immigrants move from one place to another, they eventually shed their old identities and connections to the homeland and take on the traditions, identities, values, and practices of the new one (Handlin 1951). In contrast, researchers of transnationalism assert that migrants seldom sever connections with their countries of origin and that migration is often circular rather than linear (Grasmuck and Pessar 1991; Pessar 1997).

There is some debate in the literature over whether transnationalism is a phenomenon unique to the contemporary period (Foner 1997; Morawska 2001). Some scholars argue that circular migration and the forging of multiple connections to the homeland among present-day immigrants is quite different from the one-way migration of the past (Lie 1995). In particular, technological innovations such as air travel, electronic telecommunications, electronic funds transfers, and satellite television have enabled migrants to forge ties across national boundaries in ways that were not possible during the last great wave of migration. Others claim that transnational connections were a central feature of life for past waves of immigrants (Morawska 2001). Many European immigrants who initially arrived in the United States in the early 1900s exhibited circular migration patterns. Others, such as Italian migrants, sent money to their hometowns. Nevertheless, most scholars agree that some distinctions exist between the transnational lives of past and present immigrants. Notably, contemporary trasnationalism is facilitated by technological advances that "heighten the immediacy and frequency of migrants' contact with their sending communities and allow them to be actively involved in everyday life there in fundamentally different ways from the past" (Levitt 2001, 22).

Research on transnational attachments and political participation in the

United States among contemporary Asian and Latino immigrants has emerged only recently (see Basch, Schiller, and Blanc 1994; Ong and Nakanishi 1996, 289; Moreno 1997; Rogers 2000a and 2000b; Lien 2004; Lien 2005). Some scholars argue that strong ties to the homeland depress immigrants' participation in U.S. political life. Alejandro Portes and Rubén Rumbaut suggest that many European immigrants did not return to their countries of origin but nevertheless remained uninterested in American politics because they focused on the idea of returning: "Commitment to American political causes, especially those of a radical sort, was not particularly attractive to Hungarian, Italian, or Norwegian peasants whose goal was to save in order to buy land in their home villages" (1996, 101). And John C. Harles claims that immigrants generally direct their political interests exclusively toward the country of origin and that "ethnic reinforcement" in the form of media, communication, and cultural symbols supplied by the homeland depresses interest in American politics (1993, 111, 116).

In contrast to this body of work, the literature on transnationalism contends that transnational activity leads to additional political activity in the United States. Matthew Jacobson (1995) argues convincingly that an orientation toward the homeland can compel immigrants to become involved in American politics. He cites Stefan Barszczewski, a Polish immigrant activist, to illustrate how strong homeland ties informed Polish immigrants' political expression toward U.S. policies. According to Barszczewski, based on their own experiences in the homeland, Polish immigrants in the United States were compelled to speak out against American colonization of the Philippines and Cuba. Several researchers studying distinct populations in New York suggest that the most active participants in New York local politics are also the most active in organizational activities directed toward their countries of origin (Basch, Schiller, and Blanc 1994; Graham 1997; Robert Smith 1997). Linda Basch, Nina Glick Schiller, and Cristina Szanton Blanc report that transnational migrants from Grenada became involved in the U.S. political process to promote desired outcomes in Grenada. The immigrants they observed "had been in the United States a minimum of ten years and were as involved in the local politics of New York City as they were in the political life of Grenada" (1994, 226). Anna Karpathakis's description of Greek immigrants in New York City suggests that concern for homeland politics may lead to involvement in U.S. politics: "Greek immigrant community leaders began creating relations with American political institutions and mobilizing immigrant incorporation into the American polity with the aim and hope that the immigrants and their organizations would then act on behalf of the home society's territorial concerns" (1999, 64).

Transnationalism and Political Involvement

The 2000–2001 Pilot National Asian American Survey (PNAAPS), the 1999 *Washington Post*/Henry J. Kaiser Family Foundation/Harvard University National Survey on Latinos in America (LAT), and the 1989–1990 Latino National Political Survey (LNPS) show the degree to which some migrants maintain transnational ties. In general, both Latino and Asian American immigrants exhibit a high level of transnational activity. The LAT found that 59 percent of Latino immigrants regularly send money back to their homelands, including 44 percent of Mexican immigrants but only 21 percent of Cuban immigrants.[2]

The extent to which a particular national-origin group participates in homeland politics is likely to vary by the type of political regime that characterizes the country of origin (Lien 2004). The specific laws governing dual citizenship and presence or absence of mechanisms to facilitate voting by citizens living abroad are also undoubtedly influential. Excluding Cuban and "other Latino" immigrants, between 24 percent and 33 percent of those interviewed in the LAT reported having voted in their homeland since migrating to the United States (table 10). Cuba's lack of a democratic system and historical restrictions on travel to the island may account for the small percentage of people who say that they have voted in Cuba since migrating to the United States.

A number of structural factors not related to individual immigrants' level of interest in politics can shape their political involvement in homeland politics, including proximity to the homeland, whether it has a democratic government, specific electoral regulations and mechanisms for voting by nonresident citizens, the availability of dual citizenship, and the general openness of the homeland political regime to emigrants' political involvement. For example, the Mexican government's requirement that its citizens cast ballots in person in their Mexican place of residence on Election Day diminishes the possibility that immigrants can participate in homeland electoral politics.[3]

Asian Americans in the PNAAPS were not asked about remittances but were asked about how much contact they maintained with people in their home countries. Fully 44 percent of the immigrant respondents claimed to have contact at least once a month with someone in the country of origin. With the exception of the small number of Japanese immigrants in the sample who exhibited lower rates of contact, 40 percent or more of each national origin group kept in frequent contact with people in their homeland (table 10). In contrast, only 6 percent of all Asian American immigrants were active in homeland politics, although the proportion varied by national origin group (table 10). Because they are based on two different surveys using two distinct questions, Asian American and Latino immigrant participation in homeland politics cannot be compared directly.

The PNAAPS asked respondents specifically about their homeland-

TABLE 10. Transnational Activities among Asian American and Latino Immigrants

Latinos (N)	Regularly send money to homeland (%)	Voted in homeland since migrating to United States (%)
Puerto Rican (137)	29	29
Mexican (461)	44	24
Cuban (244)	21	12
Other Central or South American (500)	52	33
Other Latino (132)	65	17
Total Latino immigrants (1,477)	59	25

Asian Americans (N)	Homeland contact[a] (%)	Active in politics related to the homeland (%)
Chinese (279)	43	4
Korean (157)	45	5
Vietnamese (135)	41	10
Japanese (41)	32	7
Filipino (180)	42	6
South Asian (121)	44	7
Total Asian immigrants (913)	44	6

Source: PNAAPS, LAT.

Note: Statistics reported in each column are column percentages.

[a]Reported having contacted people in the homeland by phone, mail, or in person at least once a month during the twelve months prior to being interviewed.

related political activity ("After arriving in the United States, have you ever participated in any activity dealing with the politics of your home country?"). The LAT asked, "Since you have moved to the U.S., have you voted in country of origin/the country where you were born?" The LNPS included a question asking about concern for politics in the respondent's country of origin: "Some Mexicans/Puerto Ricans/Cubans are more concerned about government and politics in Mexico/Puerto Rico/Cuba than in the U.S. Others are more concerned about government and politics in the U.S. How about you?"[4] For all analyses of registration and voting, eligibility is taken into account (that is, those who are not eligible are excluded).

Asian American Immigrants and Transnational Politics

In the PNAAPS, 83 percent of citizens who were active and 77 percent of those citizens who were not active in homeland politics were registered to vote in the United States in 2000 (table 11). For turning out to vote in the 2000 presidential election, a similarly slim gap exists between those who were active in homeland politics and those who were not. The differences between registration and voting between the two groups (transnational and nontransnational) are not statistically significant, and involvement in homeland politics is not related to registration or voting, at least at the bivariate-level. (The small sample sizes prevent disaggregating the data on voter registration and voting by specific Asian American national-origin group.)

As noted, many researchers have assumed an inverse relationship between homeland political activism and U.S. political activism. Harles, for example, claims that, "For birds of passage, individuals whose orientation is consistently toward the country of origin, any sense of identification with, and thus inclination to participate in, American politics is extremely limited" (1993, 111). Yet the data analyzed here show that the relationship between activity in homeland politics and registration or voting in the United States is not negative but neutral—that is, no statistically significant differences exist (table 11). Those Asian Americans who are active in homeland politics are no less likely to register or vote in the United States than are those who are not active.

If one examines participation in political activities other than voting (writing or phoning a government official, donating money to a campaign, signing a petition for a political cause, taking part in a protest or demon-

TABLE 11. Transnational Political Orientations and Political Participation in the United States

Asian Americans (N)	Active in homeland politics	Not active in homeland politics
Percentage registered to vote		
(540)	83	77
Percentage who voted in 2000		
(417)	88	83
Percentage who participated in political activities other than voting		
Chinese (276)	75*	33
Korean (155)	83*	36
Vietnamese (128)	58*	31
Japanese (38)	33*	20
Filipino (173)	100*	45
South Asian (118)	100*	52

Latinos (N)	Voted in homeland since migrating to United States	Has not voted in homeland since migrating to United States
Percentage registered to vote		
(639)	72	73
Percentage who voted in 1996 or 1999 (466)	77	83
Percentage who participated in nonvoting activities (supporting a Latino candidate or cause)		
Puerto Rican (137)	39	37
Mexican (461)	27	28
Cuban (244)	29	32
Other Central or South American (503)	34	28
Other Latino (132)	39	28

Source: PNAAPS, LAT.
Row percentages *$p \leq .10$

stration, and other types of activities), the results are even more surprising.[5] Asian Americans who are active in homeland politics are more likely to be involved in nonvoting political activities than those who are not active in homeland politics. Further, the positive association is remarkably consistent across Asian American subgroups. (It is possible to examine specific subgroups in this case because the number of Asian American respondents included in the analysis of participation in activities other than voting is not restricted by citizenship or registration, as was the case for the voting and registration analyses.) The differences in participation in political activities other than voting between those who do and do not participate in homeland politics are statistically significant, except for Vietnamese immigrants. Additional multivariate analysis (appendix, table A7) confirms that activity related to politics in the country of origin is associated strongly with participation in political activities other than voting in the United States, even when other variables, such as socioeconomic status, political interest, and English language use, are taken into account.

The question that asked respondents if they had participated in political activities other than voting does not specify whether those activities involved political demands related to the United States or their country of origin. Thus, it may be that certain activities, such as contacting a U.S. government official or protesting in the United States, provide a vehicle for some immigrants to express political views related to their homelands. For example, immigrants might write letters to their congressional representatives about U.S. foreign policy toward their country of origin. However, even if that activity indicated an interest in homeland politics and a lack of interest in U.S. politics apart from issues relating specifically to the homeland, the act of contacting a U.S. representative may be related to one aspect of political socialization for immigrants. As they become more familiar with and experienced in interacting with U.S. government institutions, it is likely that they would also participate in activities aimed at influencing U.S. domestic politics.

Latino Immigrants and Transnational Politics

Is there an association between transnationalism and U.S. political participation among Latino immigrants? Portes and Rumbaut (1996, 95, 125) claim that immigrants are preoccupied with homeland politics, often at the expense of their U.S. political participation. Based on this argument, we could infer that those with strong ties to their homeland would be the least likely to participate in U.S. politics. Analysis of the LAT data does not support that assertion, however (table 11). Those who report voting in their country of origin after migrating to the United States are no less likely to register or to vote than are those who have never done so. Moreover, regardless of national-origin group, Latino immigrants who have voted in their homeland since coming to the United States participate in political activities other than voting at about the same rates as Latino immigrants who have not voted in their homelands. (The LAT defines "participation in political activities other than voting" as working or volunteering for a Latino political candidate, attending a public meeting or demonstration regarding Latino concerns, or contributing money to a Latino candidate or organization.) Multivariate analysis shows that these patterns remain true even after controlling for other factors such as socioeconomic status, political interest, and use of the English language (not shown in tables).

Voting in one's country of origin may be too limited a measure of transnational political participation to capture any association, either positive or negative, with U.S. political participation. In comparison to the LAT, the LNPS asked a more general question about respondents' interest in government and politics in both their homelands and the United States. Many LNPS respondents had an interest in U.S. politics. For example, 40 percent of Mexican immigrants reported that they were more concerned with U.S. than with Mexican politics, and 35 percent claimed that they were equally concerned with politics in both countries. Puerto Rican immigrants reported similar rates, while 55 percent of Cuban immigrants were more concerned with U.S. than with Cuban politics, and 27 percent were equally concerned with politics in both countries.

The LNPS measured participation in political activities other than voting by asking respondents if they had done any of seven possible activities within the past year: (1) signed a petition; (2) written a letter, telephoned, or sent a telegram to a newspaper editor or public official (3) attended a public meeting; (4) worn a campaign button, put a campaign sticker on the car, or placed a sign in the window or front yard; (5) attended any political meetings, rallies, speeches, or dinners in support of a particular candidate; (6) worked for pay or as a volunteer for a party or candidate; or (7) contributed money to an individual candidate, a political party, or some other political organization supporting a candidate or an issue in an election. The bivariate relationships suggest that those immigrants whose primary interest is in U.S. politics rather than homeland politics are more likely to participate in nonvoting political activities in the United States than are immigrants whose primary interest is homeland politics. Thirty-one percent of Mexican immigrants who claimed to be more concerned with U.S. than with Mexican politics had participated in U.S. political activities other than voting, compared to just 18 percent of those who were primarily concerned with Mexican politics. Similarly, 42 percent of Puerto Rican immigrants who said they were more concerned with U.S. than Puerto Rican politics participated in political activities other than voting in the United States, but only 24 percent of those who were primarily concerned with Puerto Rican politics took part in those activities. Finally, 27 percent of the Cuban immigrants who were primarily interested in U.S. politics participated in U.S. political activities other than voting, whereas 19 percent of those whose primary interest lay in Cuban politics were active in nonvoting political activities in the United States.

These bivariate relationships suggest that immigrants who are more interested in U.S. than homeland politics are also more likely to participate in U.S. political activities. However, multivariate analysis controlling for such factors as socioeconomic status, political engagement, and English-language dominance shows that for Latinos in the LNPS sample, the direction of the relationship between concern for homeland politics and participation in U.S. political activities varies by national-origin group. A dummy dependent variable was created from the seven questions about political activities other than voting, with respondents receiving either a score of 0 (participated in no activities) or 1 (participated in at least one of the seven activities).[6] When control variables are included, greater interest in homeland than U.S. politics is not strongly associated with activity in U.S. politics for Mexican immigrants (table 12). For Puerto Rican immigrants, after socioeconomic status and other variables likely to be related to political participation are accounted for, greater interest in homeland politics is negatively associated with U.S. political participation. For Cubans, the relationship runs in the opposite direction—being interested in Cuban politics is associated positively with activity in U.S. politics. Furthermore, the relationship is statistically significant. The relationship between the measures of transnational ties used here and political participation in the United States is both inconsistent across Latino groups and weak in some cases.

What might explain these differences in the relationship between inter-

TABLE 12.   Regression of Political Participation Other than Voting on Interest in Homeland Politics among Latino Immigrants

Independent variables	B	Standard error
Mexican Immigrants (*n* = 560)		
Age	−1.15	1.07
Education	1.87**	0.57
Income	−0.13	0.48
Female	0.20	0.24
Follow politics	0.74*	0.44
Strong partisan	−0.27	0.47
Ideology	−0.32	0.47
Member of Hispanic organization	1.83**	0.86
Party mobilization	1.69**	0.84
Individual mobilization	0.32	0.55
Religious attendance	0.67	0.45
Citizen	0.10	0.15
English language dominance	0.25	0.50
Experience with discrimination	0.49**	0.24
Years in the United States	0.03**	0.02
Interest in homeland politics	0.01	0.35
Constant	−3.98***	0.65

    −2 (Log-Likelihood) Initial = 565.95
    −2 (Log-Likelihood) Convergence = 497.55
    Chi-Square 68.40 (df 16)
    $p < .00$

Independent variables	B	Standard error
Puerto Rican Immigrants (*n* = 352)		
Age	−0.28	1.03
Education	2.20***	0.73
Income	0.37	0.58
Female	−0.28	0.29
Follow politics	0.72	0.50
Strong partisan	−0.13	0.28
Ideology	−0.17	0.46
Member of Hispanic organization	0.77	0.58
Party mobilization	0.79	0.96
Individual mobilization	0.62**	0.29
Religious attendance	0.21	0.41
English language dominance	1.07*	0.63
Experience with discrimination	0.34	0.30
Years in the United States	0.01	0.02
Interest in homeland politics	−0.69*	0.40
Constant	−3.33	0.75

TABLE 12.—*Continued*

Independent variables	B	Standard error
−2 (Log-Likelihood) Initial = 421.96		
−2 (Log-Likelihood) Convergence = 385.19		
Chi-Square 63.79 (df 15)		
$p < .00$		
Cuban Immigrants (n = 485)		
Age	−1.15	0.80
Education	−0.23	0.67
Income	1.39***	0.53
Female	0.15	0.27
Follow politics	1.10**	0.54
Strong partisan	−0.05	0.37
Ideology	0.65	0.48
Member of Hispanic organization	1.61***	0.41
Party mobilization	0.40	0.83
Individual mobilization	1.53**	0.64
Religious attendance	0.15	0.42
Citizen	0.33	0.19
English language dominance	1.54***	0.56
Experience with discrimination	0.12	0.36
Years in the United States	0.00	0.02
Interest in homeland politics	0.85**	0.43
Constant	−4.18	0.86
−2 (Log-Likelihood) Initial = 496.28		
−2 (Log-Likelihood) Convergence = 403.19		
Chi-Square 93.09 (df 16)		
$p < .00$		

Source: LNPS.
Dependent Variable: Dummy variable for political participation other than voting.
$*p \leq .10$ $**p \leq .05$ $***p \leq .01$

est in homeland politics and participation in U.S. politics? The analysis here accounts for individual factors, such as socioeconomic status, organizational membership, and length of residence. Factors that are not included in the analysis, such as U.S. foreign policy toward the homeland or whether homeland policies invite participation among emigrants, might help explain the distinctions among the national-origin groups. For example, some Puerto Rican immigrants interested in homeland politics may disapprove of U.S. policies toward the island, feel negatively toward the U.S. government, and consequently choose not to participate in U.S. politics as much as do those who are uninterested in Puerto Rican politics. Refugees who have fled the Cuban communist regime but remain interested in Cuban politics might also take part in U.S. politics to help shape policies toward the Cuban government. These observations are speculative, but they reveal the necessity of additional research on how transnational attitudes and behaviors affect immigrants' political participation (Pantoja 2005).

The LAT and LNPS survey data suggest that, contrary to popular rhetoric and some academic claims, having an interest in homeland politics generally does not make an immigrant less likely to participate in U.S. political activities than an immigrant who lacks that interest. Instead, among Latino immigrants, little association exists between U.S. political participation and involvement in homeland politics (defined as voting in homeland elections). In terms of attitudes toward involvement in homeland politics, measured by having a greater interest in homeland than in U.S. politics, the association with participation in U.S. politics is inconsistent and varies by national origin.

Transnational Political Participation: Qualitative Data

Because the quantitative data from the three surveys allow us to examine only a limited range of transnational attachments, it is especially important to consider other data as well. The qualitative information collected for this book sheds additional light on the relationship between transnationalism and U.S. political participation. All of the immigrants interviewed during the research for the book were asked about their transnational activities and attachments. Almost all Chinese and Mexican immigrants maintained some kind of contact with their homelands, especially staying in touch with friends or relatives and sending them gifts and money. Respondents also regularly followed the news in their countries of origin. In addition, many reported that after moving to the United States, it was still "easy" to stay current on homeland issues because of new communication technologies, such as the Internet and television.

Many of the immigrants felt that their ability to participate in U.S. politics was limited by their lack of understanding of the political system, the time it took out of their daily schedules to get involved, lack of mobilization and other barriers. However, a preoccupation with life and politics in their countries of origin did not seem to be one of the factors that limited participation in U.S. politics. One Mexican immigrant woman who had lived in Los Angeles for twenty-two years said that she maintained strong ties to Mexico, following Mexican political and social issues, visiting Mexico at least once a year, and keeping in touch with and sending money and gifts to friends and relatives. Furthermore, she said she would be interested in pursuing dual nationality. Yet she also claimed to be more interested in U.S. than Mexican politics because "U.S. political issues are important" and they affect her life and decisions. She felt that it was "important to get involved, but obstacles, such as language barriers, ma[d]e it difficult."

A Chinese woman who had immigrated to New York City in 1969 also exhibited strong transnational ties. She had made several trips back to Hong Kong and kept in touch with friends and relatives living there. She also followed major news from her homeland, having found that it was easy to get information through the Internet. However, these ties to Hong Kong did not inhibit her interest in U.S. politics. She was involved in a Chinese American community organization because "in order for other people to learn about the Chinese people, you need to get out there and participate so they can get past stereotypes." Furthermore, she reported, "I am registered to vote and read the newspapers, watch TV, and read magazines to get information about United States politics because it is my responsibility to know what is going on before I vote."

These examples and the survey data discussed earlier show that immigrants maintain a variety of strong ties with their countries of origin. However, transnational ties do not necessarily mean that immigrants are preoccupied with their homelands and therefore uninterested in the U.S. political system. Some U.S. community organizations, including the Asian Immigrant Women's Advocates and a growing number of hometown associations, have embraced their immigrant members' transnational concerns. These organizations help to facilitate transnational political involvement by organizing such things as fund-raisers in the United States for hometown projects and by bringing workers together across borders to fight exploitation, for example. The skills and experience these organizations provide to their members can then be transferred to their U.S. political participation, enhancing their ability to take part.

Dual Citizenship & Transnational Government Structures

Opportunities for immigrants in the United States to participate in politics in their homelands are expanding. One of the ways that immigrants can maintain links with their country of origin is through dual nationality. Taiwan recognizes dual nationality in many cases, but the People's Republic of China does not. In March 1998, Mexico's consulates in the United States began to allow Mexican immigrants and their children to apply for dual nationality, meaning that people could retain or regain their legal rights in Mexico while simultaneously holding U.S. citizenship. Because foreigners have been able only to lease rather than buy land in Mexico, dual citizenship was very important in terms of property ownership and investments. Mexican immigrants interviewed in Los Angeles seemed much more enthusiastic about opportunities for dual nationality than those interviewed in New York. When asked if they were taking advantage of this opportunity, none of the immigrants in New York responded positively, although several of the Los Angeles respondents indicated that they were definitely planning to apply for dual nationality. This suggests that because Mexican immigrants in Los Angeles are more likely than those in New York to be legal U.S. residents or citizens, travel back and forth regularly between the two countries, and own property in both—that they were more likely to see dual nationality under Mexican law as a real advantage, preventing them from having to choose between U.S. citizenship and rights granted only to Mexican citizens. For immigrants who were not legal residents, however, the dual-nationality option was a moot point because they would have to take steps to regularize their status so that they could apply to undergo the U.S. naturalization process before the issue of dual nationality would come into play. A thirty-three-year-old immigrant man without legal documents who was interviewed in New York responded that the Mexican dual-nationality law "doesn't affect me because it doesn't help with my stay here in the U.S." In contrast, a naturalized Mexican immigrant who came to Los Angeles as a child in 1983 said that he would apply because it would allow him to have "equal rights in both countries." A naturalized Mexican woman who had immigrated to Los Angeles in 1982 claimed that she would be interested in holding dual nationality because she wished to legalize her property ownings in Mexico. It is likely that the differences between Los Angeles's and New York's proximity to Mexico also account for the level of interest among Mexicans in the two localities.

Another development in Mexican politics that likely affects that country's immigrant population is the possibility that Mexican migrants to the United States and other countries will be allowed to vote in the 2006 Mexican presidential election. Enrico Marcelli and Wayne Cornelius (2005, 433) estimate that by 2006, expatriates will make up about 14 percent of the Mexican electorate, giving them significant influence over the election outcome. Vicente Fox, whose election to the presidency of Mexico broke the Partido Revolucionario Institucional's seventy-year hegemony, has long supported giving immigrants in the United States the right to take part in Mexican elections. Although Mexican expatriates currently have the right to vote in Mexican elections, no mechanism exists to allow them to exercise that right. Instead, expatriates must register to vote several months before an election and return to Mexico to cast their votes. Proposals have been put forth to allow Mexican citizens in the United States to vote at consulates or over the Internet, but both ideas have been rejected because of concerns relating to staffing and fraud.

The Mexican state of Zacatecas has led the country in encouraging transnational political participation. In August 2003, the state legislature unanimously approved a state constitutional amendment allowing Zacatecan expatriates to vote in state and municipal elections. Moreover, the legislation allows for campaigning in the United States and for emigrants and their children (even those not born in Zacatecas) to run for office. The Zacatecan population in the United States is about 1.5 million, equal to state's current resident population. In 2004, Andrés Bermúdez, a native of Zacatecas who had emigrated to California and become a successful businessman, won election as mayor of his native town, Jerez. Two other U.S. residents won seats in the Zacatecas legislature reserved for overseas citizens.

Furthermore, Fox's 2000 campaign was truly transnational in scope. He campaigned in several U.S. cities, urging Mexican immigrants to help persuade friends and family back home to vote for him: "We come to recommend that the best way to participate at this time is to phone your friends and family, to write letters" (quoted in Anderson 2000, A-20). During his visit to Los Angeles, he said he would consider allowing Mexican immigrants in the United States to cast absentee ballots in Mexican elections.

California has a population of at least 3 million Mexican immigrants, and the Los Angeles metropolitan area alone is home to the largest concentration of Mexicans outside of Mexico City (Dillon 2003, A-12).[7] If Mexican immigrants were fully to exercise that right, California could become one of the most significant blocs of voters in Mexican elections.

Implications for American Civic Institutions

Immigration scholars often assume that first-generation immigrants are uninterested in U.S. politics because they are preoccupied with life in their countries of origin (Harles 1993). Portes and Rumbaut's influential review of contemporary immigration embraces that assumption: "For the most part, the politics of the first generation—to the extent that such politics have existed—have been characterized by an overriding preoccupation with the old country" (1996, 95). They go on to suggest that the "early political concerns of the foreign born today seldom have to do with matters American. Instead, they tend to center on issues and problems back home" (108). Not until the second generation comes of age does this orientation change, as "time and the passing of the first generation inexorably turn immigrant communities toward American concerns" (124).

Better measures of transnational activities and attachments are needed to understand fully their effects on political participation in the United States. The findings in this chapter, which draws on both quantitative and qualitative methods, compel one to question the popular assumption that immigrants' interest in or concerns related to their homelands imply their indifference toward U.S. political life. By assuming that immigrants are concerned primarily with homeland politics, the standard models too easily dismiss first-generation immigrants' political participation. The data do not support the widespread belief that immigrants focus solely on homeland issues at the expense of interest in American politics.

To maximize their appeal to the growing numbers of immigrants living in the United States, civic institutions should adopt a more transnational view of immigrant political mobilization. This might mean learning more about immigrants' homeland concerns and helping immigrants to communicate with the public and to organize around those concerns. Such an approach would help to build immigrants' communication and organizational skills, thereby, in turn, helping to facilitate their participation in

U.S. politics. Systematic analysis of survey data reveals little evidence to support the notion that immigrants are preoccupied with homeland politics at the expense of involvement in American politics. Rather, for immigrants from Mexico, Puerto Rico, and Cuba, active involvement or interest in homeland politics exists completely independently of their level of U.S. political participation. Furthermore, for some immigrant groups, including Asian Americans and most Asian American subgroups, those who are active in homeland politics tend also to be the most active in U.S. politics.

Some community organizations such as workers' centers, advocacy organizations, ethnic voluntary associations, and religious institutions incorporate immigrants' transnational orientations into strategies for organizing. For example, approximately seven hundred Mexican hometown and migrant associations operate in the United States (Jonathan Fox and Rivera-Salgado 2004). These organizations, based on social networks forged among migrants from the same village or town, work explicitly to strengthen their ties to the community living abroad with the goal of improving social, economic, and political conditions for all members of the transnational community—that is, the population living in the American as well as the Mexican communities. Mexican hometown associations (a form of ethnic voluntary association) and U.S.-based local and national ethnic advocacy organizations are only beginning to collaborate, but signs indicate that the two types of organizations are working together on behalf of U.S. immigration policy reforms and on specific political issues for immigrants, such as access to driver's licenses for those without legal residency. The League of United Latin American Citizens, a national-level advocacy organization, is forging closer ties with local hometown associations in regard to shared policy concerns (Americas Program, Interhemispheric Resource Center 2003). In their study of organizational strategies used by indigenous and mestizo Mexican immigrants living in Los Angeles, Jonathan Fox and Gaspar Rivera-Salgado predict that as groups of hometown associations increasingly organize into formal federations, they will become "the political intermediaries between the migrants, the Mexican government, and varied political actors in the United States (from local, state, and federal politicians to unions, NGOs, and academic researchers)" (2004, 1).

Political parties, especially local party organizations, may benefit if they can reach out to immigrants by paying more attention to their transnational concerns. Local party organizations could staff and sponsor information booths at the many festivals and celebrations sponsored by hometown associations in the United States. They could also develop internal educational programs that would help to inform party activists about the transnational concerns that are part of the daily lives of the immigrant members of their communities. For example, local party organization leaders in New York City might meet with Fujianese immigrants in Chinatown to discuss conditions and political issues in the sending communities and how these conditions are shaping political commitments and divisions within the Fujianese community in New York City.

These recommendations do not imply an oversimplified or utopian view of transnational politics. In his book on the homeland political activism of immigrants from the former Yugoslavia, Paul Hockenos (2003) points out that although many observers might assume that transnational politics contributes to the eradication of national borders and traditional conceptions of the nation-state, those involved in transnational politics often engage in political agendas promoting nationalism. Transnational communities tend to be ethnically homogenous, and in some cases, he claims, powerful members of the community may react with hostility to attempts to integrate the homeland or promote more ethnic inclusion.

Nevertheless, the findings presented in this chapter suggest that participation in transnational politics may actually lead some immigrants to participate more fully in American politics. Although participation in transnational politics has little impact on whether an immigrant votes in U.S. elections, that participation may contribute to greater involvement in other types of political activities in the United States and to more engagement in civic life generally. Thus, actors in American civic institutions could strengthen their ties with Asian American and Latino immigrants if those institutions would foster rather than dismiss participation in homeland politics by U.S. immigrants.

9 Conclusion

American Civic Institutions and Immigrant Mobilization at the Dawn of the Twenty-first Century

*I*mmigrants arriving in America today encounter an institutional landscape that differs dramatically from that encountered by European immigrants of the past. Political parties no longer have a strong presence at the neighborhood level, nor do they work hand in hand with community institutions to mobilize immigrants. In the absence of intense, consistent, and committed local efforts by parties to mobilize Asian American and Latino immigrants, community organizations—labor organizations, workers' centers, social service organizations, advocacy organizations, ethnic voluntary associations, and religious institutions—may represent the brightest prospect for fostering immigrant involvement in the U.S. political system.

The fact that American civic institutions matter for the political mobilization of immigrants should not come as a surprise. The importance of institutions for participatory democracy and mobilization is well established. In their extensive study of civic voluntarism in the United States, Sidney Verba, Kay Lehman Schlozman, and Henry E. Brady argue that community institutions are the "backbone of civil society," serving as sites of recruitment to political activities and places where civic skills are fostered (1995, 369). Robert Putnam (2000, 339) has praised civic institutions for their role in creating social capital. Community institutions bring people together, build trust between individuals, allow people to share information, and instill citizens with democratic habits. Building on these studies, this book focuses on the extent to which American civic institutions are fulfilling the promise of democratic inclusion for contemporary immigrants, offering concrete examples of institutions that have effectively mobilized immigrants politically. The volume examines the incentives influencing civic institutions in their behavior toward immigrants as a means of understanding why mainstream political parties are largely absent in minority communities and why community organizations have succeeded in mobilizing immigrants.

Most U.S. immigrants today come from Asia and Latin America. Largely because of that immigration, the Asian American and Latino populations are growing at a phenomenal rate. Yet the political strength of these groups does not match their demographic strength. The immigrant members of these communities, in particular, turn out to vote at very low rates. Observers too often mistakenly attribute this phenomenon to immigrants' political apathy arising from cultural norms or an orientation toward the homeland. This book shows that it is necessary to look beyond the immigrants themselves to American civic institutions to understand the impediments to immigrant political mobilization that exist today.

In contrast to the past, when parties were central to political mobilization, community organizations—labor organizations, workers' centers, advocacy and social service organizations, ethnic voluntary associations, and religious institutions—are now helping to bring immigrants into the political system to a greater extent than ever before. These organizations provide immigrants with opportunities to participate in an array of political activities that includes but is not limited to registration and voting. Immigrants are marching for amnesty, organizing against anti-immigrant voter propositions, demonstrating for workers' rights, taking part in political theater groups, and petitioning local governments to reform workers' compensation programs. Surprisingly, many immigrants who participate in such activities are those who lack citizenship or legal residency, who have limited English skills, and who live on poverty wages. According to traditional socioeconomic theories of political participation, these individuals should be among the least likely to be politically active.

For the most part, political participation does not take place overnight. Many immigrants' first experiences with the political system come through what has been described here as limited mobilization. Yet there may be ways for American civic institutions—both community organizations and political parties—to speed up that process by expanding their involvement in limited mobilization and by supporting programs for civic education. These institutions can induce immigrants to become involved in politics through positive encouragement and incentives and by providing opportunities for immigrants to learn about and take part in the political system. Furthermore, political parties, which were integral to immigrants' political mobilization in the past, may be able to better position themselves to expand their constituency in immigrant communities and their relevance in the immigrants' everyday lives.

Political Parties & Immigrant Communities

By 1965, when Asians and Latin Americans began arriving in the United States in unprecedented numbers, the political landscape was already undergoing major transformations. Coupled with a generalized weakening of the party system (Wattenberg 1996), the appearance in the past twenty-five years of media-driven, candidate-centered campaigns has led to a major diminishment of neighborhood-level party activity (Conway 2001). The current failure of American political parties to bring a broad range of immigrant ethnic-minority communities into the political system can be attributed to: (1) a weakened local party structure and changing campaign tactics, (2) selective mobilization strategies and maintenance of existing party coalitions, and (3) assumptions about immigrants' and median voters' political attitudes. These factors explain why parties no longer have a strong presence in the mobilization of immigrant communities. Nevertheless, parties are the key institution responsible for linking a nation's people to its government; thus, they play a critical role in the democratic process (Schattschneider 1942; Dahl 1967; Eldersveld and Walton 2000). In a healthy democracy, the parties bear responsibility for providing representation in government for all people, including immigrants, rather than for only society's most advantaged groups.

Are the country's immigrants likely to be the targets of greater party interest in the coming years? Will parties again work with community organizations to build the kind of mutually reinforcing relationships that helped bring earlier waves of Irish, Jewish, and Italian immigrants into the American political system (Sterne 2001)? Some scholars and popular press accounts suggest that parties have gradually begun to turn their attention to immigrants (see, for example, Uhlaner and García 1998; Riley 2004). However, recent history does not suggest that we will see a dramatic end to immigrant exclusion by the two major parties. During the 2004 election, the Democratic and Republican Parties reached out to Latinos more than ever before, yet their efforts were mainly symbolic and selective and did not include mass mobilization, the normative strategy for political incorporation in the first half of the twentieth century. In addition, parties continue to target a specific subset of the Latino community—that is, registered voters in battleground states. Many immigrant Latinos are never targeted for mobilization because they do not live in those areas. Others are not targeted because party leaders assume that Latinos are unlikely voters based on a demographic profile marked by a lack of financial resources, education, and citizenship. The parties have also overlooked those non-Latino ethnic groups that include a large proportion of immigrants, particularly Asian Americans, the fastest-growing racial group in the United States and one that has a higher proportion of immigrants than Latinos.

Despite the three disincentives that parties face, they could again become a force for the political socialization of immigrants. To do so, the parties will need to take a more active role in immigrant communities by participating in community events, offering naturalization and voter-education workshops, regularly registering immigrants to vote (rather than only during political campaign season), and maintaining a high profile in places frequented by immigrant populations. These mobilization strategies would help to engage immigrants in the political system over the long term rather than merely aiming to turn them out to vote on Election Day. Parties need to overcome the phobia about disrupting existing coalitions by recognizing that courting other constituencies could have a high payoff in terms of votes. They also need to overcome misperceptions about immigrant and minority-group apathy by recognizing that lack of education and poverty, as blocks to voter turnout, could be offset by party mobilization efforts. Taking these steps would not only increase the parties' relevance in immigrant communities but also bring them long-term gains by expanding their constituencies and solidifying future partisan loyalties.

Community Organizations & Immigrant Communities

In contrast to parties, community organizations have already shown great potential for mobilizing immigrants. Several characteristics position community organizations for success in politically mobilizing minority immigrant groups. First, as they did with European immigrants, community organizations are providing valuable social services and representation, which can attract and hold an immigrant constituency. Motivated by a desire for organizational maintenance, these organizations willingly reach out to immigrants. Second, the organizations are led and staffed by people with strong connections to the immigrant and existing expertise vis-à-vis the immigrant group. The presence of first- or second-generation immigrants in positions of leadership provides important human capital. These individuals are fluent in the ethnic language and sensitive to the community's cultural traditions and policy priorities. These characteristics, often coupled with many years of service to the community, endow organizations with significant legitimacy in eyes of their constituencies. Third, an organization with transnational connections has opportunities to build coalitions and to politically engage the constituency. Through its community outreach efforts, the seemingly narrow hometown association opens pathways for its immigrant members to interact and become familiar with their U.S. community. In so doing, their regional (and ethnic or racial) identity broadens to include an identity as members of a new community in the United States. Hometown associations actively maintain ties with the country of origin, yet rather than diverting the attention of immigrants away from an involvement in U.S. politics, transnational activities can heighten interest in politics generally, thereby helping to draw newcomers into the American political system. Although they do not always engage in active or direct political participation, community organizations provide an institutional setting in which immigrants learn communication and organizational skills that can be easily transferred to the political sphere (Verba, Schlozman, and Brady 1995). Community organizations also act as advocates for immigrants, helping to offset racial and ethnic discrimination. As such, such groups can empower immigrants to challenge stereotypes and become more involved in the political system.

The grassroots nature of many community organizations places them in a web of relations with the members of the communities they serve. That web is the source of information and cultural understanding that directs the efforts of these organizations, strengthening their bases and enabling them to engage in activities and endeavors that forward the political representation, mobilization, and participation of immigrants in the United States. The limited but vital role that community organizations play in immigrants' political mobilization, socialization, and participation is likely to continue as parties continue their shift toward more national-level, media-driven tactics. In the absence of a strong party presence at the local level, community organizations are among the only civic institutions mobilizing immigrants in their local communities.

When it comes to political mobilization of their constituencies, community organizations engage in a range of activities. Some are aimed directly at electoral participation—voter registration drives, get-out-the-vote campaigns, lobbying, and citizenship classes. Others are nonelectoral in nature, such as petition drives, demonstrations, marches, and protests. Because these activities are not mass forms of mobilization, their political effectiveness may be limited in terms of direct electoral effects. However, from the perspective of the immigrant, these activities provide an institutional bridge to the larger community, civic education required for naturalization and hence for voting, and a sense of empowerment and political socialization.

Although many community organizations' efforts are not aimed at turning out the vote, they do foster action and involvement that has visible consequences for the political system and policy making. New York City's Chinese Staff and Workers' Association has sent immigrant women working in garment factories to testify before Congress for antisweatshop laws. The Asociación de Tepeyac has organized Mexican immigrants to protest outside of Manhattan restaurants to challenge exploitative employers. The Brooklyn Chinese American Association provides social services to immigrants but also helps Chinese immigrants register to vote. One-Stop Immigration, a social service provider mainly for Latino immigrants in Los Angeles, has sent immigrants to Washington, D.C., to march for amnesty legislation. The Center for Asian Americans United for Self-Empowerment registers Asian American immigrant voters in Los Angeles. A New York City runners' club for Mexican immigrants is a focal point for intraethnic socializing but has also created opportunities for members to learn how to negotiate the city bureaucracy. Local unions nationwide organized the Immigrant Workers Freedom Ride, which toured the country and culminated with demonstrations in Washington, D.C.

This array of actions on the part of a range of community organizations merits support and encouragement because it provides mechanisms so that ethnic minorities can become familiar and comfortable with participation in the U.S. political system. Political parties, nongovernment organizations, and government agencies, among others, should consider how to reinforce such efforts to better serve immigrant communities as they move toward fuller political incorporation into U.S. society.

However, because of the constraints on these organizations, they engage primarily in limited mobilization. For most of these groups, the primary mission is not political mobilization but instead providing much-needed social services, networking, labor advocacy, or even spiritual ministering. Consequently, most organizations cannot engage full time or consistently in political activities. In addition, most confront serious limitations in financial resources that place mass mobilization efforts out of reach. Nevertheless, as noted earlier, labor organizations, workers' centers, advocacy and social service organizations, ethnic voluntary associations, and religious institutions are often rich in human capital and legitimacy, unique resources that help them to mobilize immigrants. Although most of these groups do not mobilize immigrants at a mass level, they are clearly laying the groundwork for political participation. New technologies, such as electronic communication, may help some organizations, even those that are underfunded, reach larger numbers of people. However, it will take more financial resources to increase the face-to-face contact with community members, which is at the heart of immigrant mobilization.

Despite their limitations, some community organizations have even mobilized some of the least advantaged segments of the immigrant community, such as day laborers, garment workers, and undocumented immigrants. These are often individuals with few resources who do not speak English and who are not citizens—those whom parties tend to shun under the assumption that they are unlikely to participate politically. Understanding the characteristics that have enabled community organizations to mobilize this segment of the population can provide important lessons about how civic institutions might mobilize immigrants more generally. The strengths that community organizations bring to immigrant mobilization provide a model for other civic organizations to follow.

Do Group Differences Matter for Mobilization?

This book focused on two panethnic groups, Asian Americans and Latinos. They can be compared along several dimensions. Both have had a long U.S. presence marked by racial discrimination. Consequently, unlike earlier waves of European immigrants, the white majority has never fully accepted Asians and Latinos. Today, the ongoing arrival of new immigrants from Asia and Latin America continues to shape both communities, creating fractures along a multitude of ethnic, national, generational, class, religious, and linguistic lines. Another similarity is that majorities of both groups are concentrated in large metropolitan areas in the coastal states.

The two groups also exhibit differences. Latinos are a much larger population than Asian Americans, but Asian Americans are better educated, earn more, and have higher citizenship rates. Latinos tend to live much closer to their homelands than do Asian Americans and consequently exhibit a propensity for circular- or return-migration patterns. In addition, Latinos, unlike Asian Americans, are also a growing presence in some key battleground states, including New Mexico, Colorado, and Arizona.

These characteristics affect the extent to which the groups are mobilized, especially by the political parties. Until recently, the major parties ignored both populations because they were characterized as "low-propensity voters," owing to their high proportion of noncitizens and low rates of turnout. Racial stereotypes also reinforced party leaders' view that both groups were politically apathetic and therefore not worth mobilizing. Internal diversity in terms of class, length of residence, and ethnicity presents challenges for mobilization as well. Parties have been slow to recognize the specific needs and interests of the diverse elements within each group, thereby hampering their ability to mobilize Asian Americans and Latinos. Yet in the last two presidential elections, the two parties devoted more attention than ever before to Latinos, especially those registered to vote in the battleground states. Asian Americans have received less attention than their Latino counterparts have received from the two parties. One reason is that Asian Americans constitute a smaller proportion of the population and have been underrepresented in battleground states in recent elections.

When it comes to mobilization and the role of community organizations in that process, ethnic group similarities and differences are less critical than might be expected. What matters for community organizations are several features shared by both communities, and the most successful organizations recognize these features in their attempts to mobilize immigrants. First, as two of the fastest-growing groups in the United States, Asian Americans and Latinos will in the future certainly become a significant group of voters. As such, they should not be treated as politically marginal. Second, each group comprises multiple and cross-cutting identities. Ethnicity and racial background are key components of those identities, but not to the exclusion of other identities based on occupation, class status, region of origin, gender, and even length of residence, among other things. Community organizations mobilize immigrants more effectively if they take these multiple and intersecting identities into account. Third, coalitions are being built across communities based on shared identities and interests. Community organizations unite diverse groups of immigrants around common concerns, such as immigrant rights, worker rights, language issues, women's issues, and environmental concerns. Fourth, organizing around multiple identities and the potential for coalition building does not have to come at the expense of ethnic-group recognition. Race and ethnicity may be socially constructed, but they remain politically relevant categories in the United States. Community organizations have been successful in large part because they foster a positive ethnic identity for immigrants that helps them to combat negative stereotypes. A strong ethnic identity can also empower disadvantaged individuals to take part in political life.

Community organizations' strategies for mobilizing immigrants depend to some degree on the specific features of each ethnic group. Latino community organizations utilize different cultural symbols when reaching out to Latinos than Asian American organizations employ when reaching out to their constituencies. In some cases, Latino and Asian American organizations mobilize around different policy priorities. Latino organizations have been more active regarding calls for amnesty for undocumented workers, while Asian American organizations have been more involved in fighting for harsher penalties for people who commit hate crimes. But common ground exists as well. Both types of organizations have been strong advocates for antisweatshop legislation and streamlining the naturalization process.

This book has found striking similarities between groups in terms of the roles, strategies, and limitations of both parties and community organizations in mobilizing Latino and Asian American immigrants. The political participation of both groups is negatively impacted by the nationalization of the two parties and their heavy reliance on selective recruitment strategies and media outreach. For both groups, community organizations play a vital role in political mobilization, and the activities of labor organizations, workers' centers, social service organizations, advocacy organizations, ethnic voluntary associations, and religious institutions provide key examples of that mobilization. This common institutional context is relevant for understanding the participation of both Asian American and Latino immigrants, despite the important differences between the two groups.

Racial Balkanization: Myth or Reality?

Because social service, advocacy, and ethnic voluntary associations tend to work with specific ethnic communities, some academics and pundits have charged that a strong orientation based on race and ethnicity might serve to encourage an unhealthy degree of ethnic identity that would divide and balkanize American society. Are we likely to see such a development? The answer is no. Ethnic organizations have existed throughout American history, and they tend to reflect rather than define society's already existing broader racial hierarchies and divisions. In the vast majority of cases, ethnic organizations emerge in reaction to racial and ethnic discrimination to make claims for inclusion in the larger society. Two ethnic organizations discussed in this volume, Los Angeles's Asian Pacific American Legal Center and the Latino Workers' Center on the Lower East Side of Manhattan, arose in reaction to social, economic, and political exclusion based on race. Their goal is to promote democratic inclusion, not racial exclusion. Although most of the organizations discussed in this volume work with particular ethnic communities, they often mobilize constituents around multiple and intersecting identities, and when necessary, they work to build coalitions with other organizations that have similar goals. For example, when the Chinese Staff and Workers Association undertakes a campaign against a local sweatshop, it activates Asian American women's identities as immigrant Asian women and as garment workers. A Mexican hometown association representing indigenous migrants mobilizes members based on their intersecting ethnic, immigrant, and regional identities. The intersection of these identities based on ethnicity, gender, religious affiliation, occupation, and regional origin plays an important role in shaping immigrant political mobilization, even within ethnic organizations. Moreover, the existence of the New York Immigration Coalition and other such groups that bring together immigrants of multiple ethnic backgrounds and identities undermines claims that ethnic organizations threaten Anglo-Protestant American culture by promoting a separatist identity (Huntington 2004).

Revitalizing Political Parties in Local Communities

Contemporary immigration has transformed the U.S. population, cities, and culture. How can political parties remain relevant in an increasingly diverse nation? How can they become a positive force in the political lives of people in the United States, both members of the country's growing immigrant population and the population more generally?

For Asian American and Latino immigrants, participation in electoral and nonelectoral politics increases steadily with length of residence in the United States. As was the case with earlier groups of immigrants, high rates of political participation do not occur immediately but usually increase gradually over a long period. Given that U.S. civic institutions are either unwilling or unable to engage in mobilization efforts, it is clear that political socialization over time represents the only consistent mechanism for bringing a large number of immigrants into the political system. Even though community organizations engage primarily in limited mobilization, they have been more effective than parties in mobilizing immigrants because these groups constitute a consistent and trusted presence in immigrant communities. Mobilization efforts that are not connected to a community institution are not likely to succeed. Immigrants, like the rest of the population, are much more likely to take part in a political activity when the request comes from someone they trust who is part of everyday life, such as a social service provider, a church leader, or a union organizer. In contrast, immigrants are less likely to respond to requests from strangers knocking on their doors or calling them before an election, even if that call is in their native language. The usual political-party tactic of mobilizing a select group of citizens who are most likely to vote and getting out the vote in the short period immediately before an election does not seem likely to elicit the intended results or to build an engaged constituency among immigrants.

Most importantly, parties should focus on strategies that will help immigrants to become more knowledgeable, familiar, and engaged with the U.S. political system. Why reach out to noncitizens when they cannot vote? Because today's noncitizens are tomorrow's citizens. By reaching out to immigrants when they first arrive in the United States, parties can broaden their future political base. Consistently and year-round, not just during key moments in the election cycle, parties should sponsor voter-education programs and workshops for both citizens and noncitizens and mass voter registration drives at citizenship ceremonies. Parties should also host town hall meetings where immigrants can ask questions and get information about party platforms and policy priorities. Parties should also make a point of having a presence at community events, such as ethnic celebrations, and in such places as ethnic grocery stores. If parties interact with immigrant communities on a regular, sustained basis, that continuity will create trust and familiarity and build long-term relationships. Parties too often constitute only a fleeting presence in immigrant communities, seeking votes with the least amount of effort and offering little in return.

Parties and other actors in the civic sphere need to reconceive of how they view immigrants' involvement in homeland politics as well as their transnational connections. Rather than discouraging transnational contacts, they quite possibly should be encouraged. Observers often assume that immigrants pursue homeland interests at the expense of U.S. political participation; however, this perspective ignores the complex relationship between transnational attachments and political involvement. In this book, the analysis of surveys and qualitative interviews suggest that although Latino and Asian American immigrants maintain strong connections to their countries of origin, their transnational orientations do not lead to a preoccupation with homeland affairs at the expense of U.S. political participation. For some groups, such as Asian American immigrants, transnationalism is associated with more U.S. political participation in activities other than voting. This finding should lead U.S. civic institutions to regard transnational activists as a potential source of mobilization and participatory political leadership rather than to dismiss them as disloyal to or uninterested in the American political system.

For their part, community organizations must continue to build on their established strengths. They should mobilize around ethnicity while continuing to recognize the multiplicity of identities that individual immigrants exhibit. These groups should focus their efforts on a range of political activities outside of voting but also devote additional resources to immigrant naturalization and voter registration as well as to voter education. This approach would lay the foundation for political action and increased influence across the democratic arena. Finally, community organizations should acknowledge the individual limits of their particular group, with the understanding that if each organization does a small part, their collective efforts can have an enormous impact on immigrant communities.

Political parties' future role in mobilizing immigrants remains unclear. During the 2000 and 2004 presidential elections, the Republican and Democratic Parties strove to portray themselves as inclusive of ethnic and racial minorities and explicitly attempted to reach out to Latinos. Perhaps these recent campaigns signaled a new willingness to court minorities, including ethnic immigrant communities. Yet the parties' commitment to bringing Asian American and Latino immigrants into the political system is far from assured. Partisan attempts at greater inclusion of immigrants have been limited primarily to symbolic gestures. Mass mobilization strategies directed at immigrants remain largely absent from the parties' agendas. Even when they do reach out to Asian Americans and Latinos, Republicans and Democrats focus on those individuals with a strong propensity to vote (registered citizens) and on those whose votes count most from a partisan perspective (voters living in battleground states). The focus on the battleground states has led to racial disparities in mobilization, since non-Latino white voters are twice as likely as Latinos and Asian Americans to live in those places. Selective mobilization remains the norm.

The scope of contemporary party outreach efforts toward immigrants remains limited. This means that most Asian Americans and Latinos—but especially immigrants—are relegated to the margins of the political system. The parties may view Latinos as potential future partners but have yet to turn their attention toward other immigrant groups. Asian Americans, a population dominated by the foreign-born, remain largely unrecognized by the major parties. Community organizations' successes should not lead parties to shirk the responsibility for mobilizing immigrants and other people of color. Community organizations alone should not have to take on the task of immigrant political mobilization.

Political parties are among the most powerful institutions in the nation and have the resources and mandate to expand their circle of inclusion. Ironically, as their resources have increased, political parties seem less and less able directly to touch people's lives. This is true not just for immigrants but for the American population more generally. The parties' national-level strategies, their reliance on media outreach and direct mail at the expense of face-to-face contact, and the reduction in the number of truly competitive seats in federal and state races have led to a failure to mobilize people locally around the specific issues that touch their lives most deeply. Parties appear to be unmotivated not just to mobilize immigrants but also to mobilize other segments of the U.S. population, including people who live outside battleground states.

In the 2004 presidential election, the number of voters reached record heights. With nearly 60 percent of eligible voters going to the polls, turnout in that year was the highest, as a proportion of the overall eligible population, since 1968. A study by the Shorenstein Center on the Press, Politics and Public Policy at Harvard University (Patterson 2004) showed that election-year issues provided most first-time voters with their motivation to go to the polls. In addition, a large proportion voted because they disliked one of the candidates, George W. Bush or John Kerry. Mobilization also contributed to the high turnout. Strikingly, many more first-time voters (61 percent) compared to repeat voters (21 percent) claimed that they voted because a family member or friend encouraged them to vote. Similarly, more first-time voters (14 percent) than repeat voters (4 percent) said that they voted because a group or organization helped them to register. Indeed, election observers attributed the high turnout rates to "massive get-out-the-vote efforts" (Rainey 2004, A-31).

The huge voter turnout in 2004 shows that people can be mobilized to participate in politics, but it remains unclear whether the parties were responsible for this mobilization. The Republicans relied primarily on unpaid volunteers for their get-out-the-vote programs. For the most part, Republicans turned out their base—who were already mobilized, high-propensity voters—including many right-leaning Christian conservatives. Turnout in Florida and five other southern states with large populations who identify as members of the Christian Right was the highest since Reconstruction (Rainey 2004, 31). In contrast, the Democrats relied on tax-exempt political advocacy organizations (known as 527 committees after the section of the tax code that created them), such as America Coming Together, MoveOn.org, and America Votes. Many of these committees are tied to community organizations. For example, America Votes is an alliance of nonprofit advocacy groups and labor organizations, including the AFL-CIO, the NAACP National Voter Fund, and the Sierra Club. Thus, the Republicans relied on their base of high-propensity voters, including many community organizations, while the Democrats relied on other groups to reach out to new voters. The problem of lack of party mobilization is particularly acute for immigrants but is a feature of the American political system that affects other members of the population as well. Thus, the 2004 election both illustrates the power of political mobilization to expand political participation and calls into question how involved political parties were in that process.

This is not to suggest that a return to the political machines of old, which were often associated with corruption and cronyism, is the appropriate remedy for lack of immigrant mobilization by major political parties. However, although Progressive Era municipal reforms contributed to the decline of machine power by attacking corruption and political favoritism, those reforms did not include mechanisms for mobilizing minority communities (Fraga 1988). Harold A. Stone, Don K. Price, and Kathryn H. Stone (1939, 79) described how municipal reformers in Dallas drew support from "the middle- and upper-class areas" while neglecting the "Negro sections." Luis Fraga (1988) notes that municipal reforms, including the institutionalization of city-manager-type governments, at-large nonpartisan elections, and slating groups (lists of candidates endorsed or put forward by reformers), solidified the power of the reform movement's white, probusiness base and thereby ensured that the most privileged members of the community would dominate politically in cities such as Los Angeles where minorities, including minority immigrants, were becoming a major demographic presence.

There are several ways to increase mobilization in the United States more generally. Parties could foster a greater presence at the local level and become more involved in the local issues and concerns that bring people together across American neighborhoods. Parties could also shift some resources from national-level media outreach to face-to-face contact as a means of building the networks of trust that could lead to more participation. The U.S. government could also set aside resources for community organizations to develop programs dedicated to helping people become more involved in the political system. Linking mobilization efforts to trusted community institutions is critical for increasing U.S. political participation. Finally, it is important to recognize that American civic institutions exist within a larger political context that may require reform if immigrants are going to be mobilized en masse. For example, reforms that encourage political competition would also increase institutional incentives to mobilize people. Current redistricting practices encourage partisan gerrymandering, which favors incumbents at the expense of creating competitive seats and thus depresses political mobilization.[1] Taking redistricting out of the hands of incumbents and parties and placing it in the hands of independent nonpartisan commissions would likely increase electoral competition and mobilization. Reforms to the electoral college and campaign finance systems that would create competitive conditions across the country, not just in a handful of battleground states, would also increase electoral competition and encourage candidates and parties to mobilize more people.

In the absence of large-scale political reforms, parties and community organizations should do their part to maintain a healthy democracy by helping more people to have a voice in the political system. True political equality in this country will be achieved only when American civic institutions reach out to all who contribute to American life.

Appendix
Methodology and Data Sources

The research on which this book is based used multiple methods, including both quantitative survey data and qualitative in-depth interviews, to examine American civic institutions and their role in mobilizing Latino and Asian American immigrants. I compared those populations—in particular, Chinese and Mexican immigrant subgroups—in two metropolitan areas, New York and Los Angeles.

Statistical analysis of quantitative data allowed for a broad, systematic, individual-level analysis of political attitudes and participation across these groups. A main advantage of survey data is that they permit researchers to isolate the particular effects of a variable on individual attitudes and behavior. In many cases, quantitative data also make it possible to generalize those relationships to the larger population and to make predictions about attitudes and behavior with some degree of accuracy. However, surveys are limited in some important respects. They capture a single moment in time—a snapshot of individual attitudes and behavior—but do not provide a process-oriented view. The predetermined categories for the survey questions allow little room for nuance or explanation in individuals' answers. Most importantly, surveys do not permit researchers to consider in-depth the role of social, geographic, and institutional contexts as influences on attitudes and behavior. In contrast, qualitative methods facilitate investigation of how and why people exhibit the behaviors they do because interactions are less structured and allow for open-ended responses. Using qualitative methods, researchers explicitly take into account the role of social, geographic, and political context. This project built on the strengths of both methods.

Comparing two ethnic groups of different social, historical, and political backgrounds allowed me to explore critical issues suggested by the survey data: How do previous political involvement and experiences with a particular political regime affect political participation in the United States? What types of challenges to political involvement exist? Do these change over time? And how does being a member of a racial or ethnic minority group affect the way that immigrants feel about becoming involved in the American system? Comparing immigrants in Los Angeles and New York also allowed me to consider geographic context to understand better how locality affects immigrant political involvement (Mahler 1996). Both cities have large Latino and Asian American communities, but the political environment is different with regard to immigration politics, the relationship of each group to other ethnic groups, and immigrant mobilization.

Quantitative Survey Data

The majority of the quantitative data for this study come from the 2000–2001 Pilot National Asian American Survey (PNAAPS), the 1989–1990 Latino National Political Survey (LNPS) (see de la Garza et al. 1992), and the 1999 *Washington Post/*Henry J. Kaiser Family Foundation/Harvard University National Survey on Latinos in America (LAT). The PNAAPS included 1,218 adults of Asian American descent (308 Chinese, 168 Korean, 137 Vietnamese, 198 Japanese, 266 Filipino, and 141 South Asian). The major Asian American population centers in the United States—Los Angeles, New York, Honolulu, San Francisco, and Chicago—were included in the survey. The telephone survey took place between November 16, 2000, and January 28, 2001. Respondents were randomly selected using random-digit dialing at targeted Asian zip code densities and listed-surname frames. Selection probability for each ethnic sample was approximate to the size of the 1990 Census figures for the ethnic population in each metropolitan area. When possible, the respondents were interviewed in their preferred language (English, Mandarin Chinese, Cantonese, Korean, or Vietnamese). Respondents of Japanese, Filipino, and South Asian descent were interviewed in English. Pei-te Lien, M. Margaret Conway, and Janelle Wong (2004) provide baseline survey results for each Asian ethnic group included in the study. (For details on the methodology used and the limitations of the survey, see Lien, Conway, and Wong 2004.)

The LAT was conducted by telephone between June 30 and August 30,

1999. The study included a nationally representative, randomly selected sample of 4,614 adults, eighteen years of age and older, including 2,417 Latinos and 2,197 non-Latinos. According to the survey documentation, the margins of sampling error for each group are ± 2 percent for total respondents and ± 2 percent for Latinos. Respondents are coded as Latino if they answered affirmatively to the question, "Are you, yourself, of Hispanic or Latin origin or descent, such as Mexican, Puerto Rican, Cuban, or some other Latin background?" Respondents were interviewed in English or Spanish. Fifty-three percent of the Latino interviews were conducted predominantly in Spanish. The final sample included 818 Mexicans, 318 Puerto Ricans, 312 Cubans, 593 Central or South Americans, and 340 other Latinos.[1]

The LNPS used a multistage probability sample based on 1980 census data. The survey specifically targeted members of the Mexican, Puerto Rican, and Cuban Latino subgroups living in the United States for face-to-face interviews with bilingual interviewers in the language the respondent felt most comfortable using (English or Spanish). Interviews were conducted with people over eighteen years of age. A total of 2,817 interviews with U.S. residents of Latino descent were conducted, 1,546 with persons of Mexican ancestry, 589 with persons of Puerto Rican ancestry, and 682 with persons Cuban ancestry. In addition, 598 interviews with "non-Latinos" were completed. The sample is representative of 91 percent of the Mexican, Puerto Rican, and Cuban populations in the United States. The overall response rate among Latinos was 74 percent. Data collection took place primarily between July 1989 and March 1990. Based on the original screening identification question, respondents were assigned to a national-origin group (Mexican, Puerto Rican, or Cuban origin).[2] Responses to a question asking for the respondent's country of birth were used to determine immigrant status.[3] (Descriptive statistics of the three survey samples are contained in tables A1, A2, and A3.) I conducted a series of multivariate analyses to distinguish between distinct influences on political participation, such as mobilization by a party or community-based organization and socioeconomic status.

Qualitative Data

I did fieldwork in New York and Los Angeles in 1999 and 2000. This fieldwork consisted of participant observation, extensive note taking, gathering materials from community organizations, and interviews with key informants. In both cities, I attended meetings and events hosted by Chinese and Mexican community organizations, and I worked on voter registration drives, helped conduct exit polls in immigrant communities, and attended marches and demonstrations for immigrant rights. I lived in New York from 1997 to 2000 and during that time volunteered regularly with community organizations working with immigrants in the city.

The qualitative component of the study is based in part on that field research and on forty interviews conducted with Mexican and Chinese immigrants in the two cities. These two subgroups were compared along important dimensions, including their relative population size, length of residence, settlement histories, proximity to countries of origin, socioeconomic resources, and electoral representation.

I also conducted interviews with forty individuals affiliated with organizations providing social, legal, political, or issue-oriented services for Chinese or Mexican immigrants in New York or Los Angeles. These included One-Stop Immigration, the Asian Pacific American Labor Association, the Coalition for Humane Immigrant Rights, and the Asian Pacific American Legal Center in Los Angeles, and the Chinese Staff and Workers Association, the Catholic Archdiocese, and the Asociación Tepeyac in New York. I was interested in interviewing organizational activists who work with Mexican and Chinese immigrant communities as well as rank-and-file (nonelite) members of each community. Activists provide a broad overview of community dynamics, organizational setting, institutional context, and participation patterns.[4] I asked activists about their personal backgrounds, the development and history of their organizations, political participation in their communities, the larger political and institutional context, and coalition building.

Bilingual research assistants helped conduct interviews with nonelite immigrants in New York City and Los Angeles. The research assistants were selected for their skills in conducting interviews and because they had contacts within the local immigrant communities. Two research assistants, one who had grown up in a Chinese immigrant community and one who was raised in a Mexican community in New York City, conducted the interviews with non-English-speaking immigrants in New York. Similarly, two research assistants, one from a Mexican community and the other from a Chinese community in Los Angeles, conducted the interviews with non-English-speakers in that city. When possible, I accompanied the research assistants during the interviews. Having grown up in immigrant communities themselves, all four of these research assistants were insiders, familiar with the communities in which they were working and sharing a similar ethnic, language, and immigrant background with those being interviewed (Fahim 1977; Aguilar 1981; Bennoune 1985; Kanuha 2000).

The sample of nonelite immigrants was generated through recruitment by the research assistants and through my social and academic network.[5] A similar technique has been used by past researchers who have targeted immigrant-dominant communities (Espiritu 2001). One reason I used this sampling method is that my target population sample consists of immigrants. Immigrants, especially those without documents, are a hard-to-reach population. I determined that a targeted sample was the best method to use since I lacked the resources to randomly canvass a large group of immigrants. A targeted sample, recruited by the research assistants and through my existing social and academic network, enabled us to establish trust between the interviewee and the interviewer as well gain access more easily to potential interviewees (Kanuha 2000). The existing relationship between the interviewees and interviewers was critical in terms of getting immigrants to participate in the study.

The research assistants received several hours of training before conducting the interviews. Interviews with immigrants were done mostly in person, with a few conducted over the phone. Interviews occurred primarily in Cantonese or Spanish, although some of the respondents opted to be interviewed in English.[6] Interview guides were used that included questions about each interviewee's immigration and settlement history, transnational activities, political participation in their countries of origin and in the United States, contact with other minorities, racial identity, and experiences with racial discrimination. The data from interviews and fieldwork are used primarily to gather information on institutional and community context, to provide descriptive information about immigrants' political involvement, and to illustrate trends found in the quantitative data.

Because of the small sample sizes and sampling methods, the qualitative data are not representative of the general population. Conversely, qualitative interviews provide a more personal, descriptive, and process-oriented view of the ways that Chinese and Mexican immigrants and community leaders come to understand politics in their everyday lives and communities.

TABLE A1.   Descriptive Statistics of the Pilot National Asian American Political
Survey Sample

	Total (N = 1,218)	Chinese (N = 308)	Korean (N = 168)	Vietnamese (N = 137)	Japanese (N = 198)	Filipino (N = 266)	South Asian (N = 141)
Foreign born	75%	91%	94%	99%	21%	68%	86%
Citizens (among foreign born)	59%	60%	53%	67%	37%	73%	43%
Planning to become citizen (among noncitizens)	70%	63%	77%	91%	27%	81%	63%
Median education	College	College	College	High school	Some college	Some college	College
Mean age in years	44 (17.4)	47 (17.8)	47 (17.4)	44 (14.1)	49 (19.7)	40 (16.6)	36 (13.4)
Mean years in U.S. among immigrants	13.1 (9.1)	12.07 (8.7)	14.8 (8.6)	12.3 (7.0)	16.6 (14.8)	14.7 (9.6)	10.7 (8.8)
Median family or household income	$30–39K	$30–39K	$30–39K	$30–39K	$30–39K	$40–59K	$40–59K

Source: 2000–2001 PNAAPS.

Note: Standard deviations are in parentheses.

TABLE A2. **Descriptive Statistics of the National Survey on Latinos in America Sample**

	Total (N = 2,412)	Puerto Rican (N = 318)	Mexican (N = 818)	Cuban (N = 312)	Central and S. American (N = 593)	Other Latino (N = 340)
Foreign born	61%	43%	56%	78%	85%	40%
Citizens (among foreign born)	44%	NA	28%	63%	32%	51%
Planning to become citizen (among noncitizens)	84%	NA	80%	91%	87%	84%
Median education	High school	High school	High school	Business, tech./ vocational beyond high school	High school	Some college
Mean age in years	39 (15.6)	39 (15.6)	35 (13.3)	46 (18.5)	37 (14.9)	38 (15.6)
Mean years in U.S. among immigrants	17 (11.9)	25 (14.7)	14 (10.1)	23 (13.3)	14 (9.4)	17 (12.3)
Median family or household income	$20– 29,999K	$20– 29,999K	Less than $20K	$20– 29,999K	$20– 29,999K	$25– 35,000K

Source: 1999 LAT.

Note: Standard deviations are in parentheses.

TABLE A3.   Descriptive Statistics of the Latino National Political Survey Sample

	Total sample (N = 3,412)	Mexican (N = 1,545)	Puerto Rican (N = 589)	Cuban (N = 680)
Immigrants	55%	50%	73%	90%
Citizens (among foreign born)	28%	14%	NA	38%
Applying for/planning to apply for citizenship (among noncitizens)	75%	77%	NA	74%
Median education (years in school)	11	10	10	11
Mean age in years	42	37.7	39.9	50.6
	(17.1)	(13.9)	(15.8)	(17.8)
Mean years in U.S. among immigrants	19.5	16.7	24.2	19.7
	(12.8)	(13.5)	(13.3)	(10.1)
Median family or household income	$17–19,999K	$17–19,999K	$11–12,999K	$17–19,999K

Source: 1989–90 LNPS.
Note: Standard deviations are in parentheses.

TABLE A4. Voting Participation among Eligible Latino Immigrants

Independent variables	Logistic analysis of vote turnout in 1988 (N = 528)	
	B	Std. Err.
Socioeconomic status		
Age	2.24***	0.67
Female	0.25	0.24
Education	0.81	0.62
Family income	0.25	0.48
Political engagement		
Follow politics	1.42***	0.42
Strong partisan	0.73***	0.24
Strong ideology	0.08	0.42
Organizational affiliation and mobilization		
Member of Hispanic organization	0.63	0.59
Mobilized by party	−0.14	0.54
Mobilized by individual	0.74***	0.30
Religious attendance	1.37***	0.35
Minority group status and language		
English language use	0.11	0.45
Personal discrimination	0.51*	0.28
Ethnic group (comparison group is Cuban)		
Mexican origin	−0.62	0.40
Puerto Rican origin	−0.55	0.31
Constant	−2.70***	0.77

-2 (LL^a) Initial = 577.94
-2 (LL) Converg = 496.25
Chi-Square 81.70 (df 15)
$p < .00$

Source: LNPS.

Logistic analysis of voter turnout in 1988: 1 = Voted in 1988, 0 = Registered but did not vote in 1988.

Note: Including controls for length of residence or political participation in homeland politics does not change the results.

^{a}LL = Log-Likelihood.

*p ≤ .10   **p ≤ .05   ***p ≤ .01

TABLE A5. Participation in Activities Other than Voting among Latino Immigrants

Variable	Participation in activities other than voting (N = 1,394)	
	B	Std. Error
Socioeconomic status		
Age	0.00	0.00
Female	0.03	0.06
Education	0.04***	0.01
Family income	0.03***	0.01
Political engagement		
Citizenship status	0.06*	0.04
Follow politics	0.08***	0.02
Strong partisan	−0.08	0.08
Ideology	0.01	0.02
Organizational affiliation and mobilization		
Member of Hispanic organization	0.66***	0.13
Mobilized by a party	−0.12	0.21
Mobilized by individual	0.30***	0.10
Religious attendance	0.05**	0.02
Minority group status and language		
English language use	0.08***	0.03
Personal discrimination	0.18***	0.07
Ethnic group (comparison group is Cuban)		
Mexican origin	0.10	0.08
Puerto Rican origin	0.09	0.09
Migration-related variables		
Years in the United States	0.01***	0.00
Active in homeland politics	0.03	0.08
Constant	−1.21	0.22
	Adjusted R-Square = .15	

Source: LNPS.

Note: OLS Regression, Dependent Variable = Index of Participation beyond Voting; "We would like to find out about some of the things people in the U.S. do to make their views known. Which of the activities listed on this card, if any, have you done in the past twelve months? (1) Signed a petition regarding an issue or problem that concerns you? (2) Written a letter, telephoned or sent a telegram to an editor or public official regarding issues that concern you? (3) Attend a public meeting? (4) Worn a campaign button, put a campaign sticker on your car, or placed a sign in your window or in front of your house? (5) Gone to any political meetings, rallies, speeches, or dinner in support of a particular candidate? (6) Worked either for pay or on a volunteer basis for a party or a candidate running for office? (7) Contributed money to an individual candidate, a political party, or some other political organization supporting a candidate or an issue in an election?"

*$p \leq .10$ **$p \leq .05$ ***$p \leq .01$

TABLE A6. Voting Participation among Eligible Asian American Immigrants

Independent variables	Logistic analysis of voter turnout in 2000 ($N = 336$)		Logistic analysis of consistent vote turnout (1998 and 2000) ($N = 336$)	
	B	Std. Err.	B	Std. Err.
Socioeconomic status				
Education	2.43**	0.78	1.25**	0.55
Family income	−0.43	0.76	−1.40***	0.56
Age	2.55**	1.13	2.71***	0.87
Female	0.12	0.36	−0.12	0.27
Political engagement				
Political interest	0.45	0.53	0.32	0.41
Strong partisanship	0.95**	0.48	0.46	0.35
Ideology (Conservative)	1.49**	0.72	−0.50	0.53
Organizational affiliation and mobilization				
Member of Asian American organization	0.75	0.58	−0.12	0.36
Mobilized by political party	0.75**	0.36	0.87***	0.30
Mobilized by individual	−0.21	0.44	0.07	0.33
Religious attendance	1.32**	0.55	1.03***	0.39
Minority group status and language				
English language use	−0.23	0.97	−1.18	0.78
Experience with discrimination	0.03	0.52	0.21	0.39
Migration-related variables				
Percentage of life in United States	−2.54***	1.02	0.88	0.85
Educated outside of the United States	−0.14	0.44	−0.48	0.34
Active in homeland politics	−0.65	0.85	0.43	0.59
National origin group (comparison category is Japanese)				
Chinese	−0.14	1.10	−1.76*	0.95
Korean	−2.56**	1.11	−2.50***	0.96
Vietnamese	0.64	1.15	−1.16	0.94
Filipino	−1.46	1.02	−1.43	0.89
Indian	−0.87	1.15	−1.90**	0.95
Constant	−0.51	1.47	−0.68	1.21

−2 (LL[a]) Initial = 318.35   −2 (LL) Initial = 424.91
−2 (LL) Convergence = 244.24   −2 (LL) Convergence = 365.32
Chi-Square 74.11 (df 21)   Chi-Square 59.59 (df 21)
$p < .00$ $p < .00$

Source: PNAPPS.

Logistic analysis of voter turnout in 2000: 1 = Voted in 2000, 0 = Registered but did not vote in 2000. Logistic analysis of voter turnout in 1998 and 2000: 1 = Voted in 1998 and 2000, 0 = Registered but did not vote in 1998 and 2000.

[a]LL = Log-Likelihood.

*$p \leq .10$ **$p \leq .05$ ***$p \leq .01$

TABLE A7. Participation in Activities Other than Voting among Asian American Immigrants

Variable	Immigrant sample (N = 727)	
	B	Std. Error
Socioeconomic status		
Education	.04	.03
Family income	.08***	.02
Age	.00	.00
Female	−.12*	.08
Political engagement		
Political interest	.21***	.04
Strong partisanship	.04*	.02
Ideology (Conservative)	.01	.03
Citizen	.03	.09
Organizational affiliation and mobilization		
Member of Asian American organization	.44***	.11
Mobilized by political party	.08	.09
Mobilized by individual	.57***	.11
Religious attendance	.03	.03
Minority group status and language		
English language use	−.01	.07
Experience with discrimination	.21*	.11
Migration-related variables		
Percentage of life in United States	.13	.24
Educated outside of the United States	−.23**	.10
Active in homeland politics	1.27***	.16
National origin group (comparison category is Japanese)		
Chinese	.39*	.21
Korean	.31	.21
Vietnamese	.59***	.21
Filipino	.44**	.20
Indian	.68***	.21
Constant	−1.17***	.30
Adjusted R-Square = .31		

Source: PNAAPS.

Note: OLS Regression, Dependent Variable is Index of Participation beyond Voting; "During the past four years, have you participated in any of the following types of political activity in your community? (ACCEPT MULTIPLE ANSWERS)" 1 = written or phoned a government official, 2 = contacted an editor of a newspaper, magazine, or TV station, 3 = donated money to a political campaign, 4 = attended a public meeting, political rally, or fund-raiser, 5 = worked with others in your community to solve a problem, 6 = signed a petition for a political cause, 7 = taken part in a protest or demonstration (7-point index). Control variables included in model but not shown in table are age, female, and length of time at current residence. The coefficient for age is positive and statistically significant only for the foreign-born, and that for length of residence at current address is positive and significant only for the full sample.

*p ≤ .10   **p ≤ .05   ***p ≤ .01

TABLE A8. Logistic Regression of Education on Political Activity among pre-1965 European Immigrant Sample (*N* = 401)

Independent variables	B	Standard error
Age	.143*	.071
Age-squared	−.001*	.001
Education (0 = < H.S, 1 = H.S. +)	.549*	.200
Grew up outside of U.S.	.084	.241
Constant	−5.330	2.100

Initial −2 Log-Likelihood = 445.874
−2 Log-Likelihood at Convergence = 439.263

Source: NES Cumulative File for 1952–65.

Dependent Variable: Participation in a Political Activity (talking to someone to influence their vote, attending a political meeting or rally, working for a party or candidate, wearing a button, giving money to a campaign, or writing to a public official); 0 = participated in at least one activity; 1= did not participate in a political activity.

*p ≤ .10

Notes

Chapter 1

1. I use the term *community organization* in this book to refer to organizations that serve a particular community—that is, immigrants—rather than to suggest that an organization serves a specific geographic locale.

2. The wave of immigration that the United States is experiencing today parallels the mass migration that occurred one hundred years ago. U.S. immigration peaked from 1900 to 1910 and then decreased after the 1920s as a result of immigration policies and a declining economy. During the 1960s, restrictive and discriminatory immigration laws were liberalized, and immigration began to increase dramatically. Although only 3 million immigrants arrived in the United States in the 1960s, nearly 8 million immigrants entered the country in the 1990s (Shinagawa 1996; Lollock 2001; Westphal 2001).

3. The Current Population Survey (CPS) defines the foreign-born population as those civilian persons currently living in noninstitutional housing who entered the United States with immigrant visas or as spouses or children of immigrants; who were admitted in a refugee status; who entered with student visas and overstayed; or who entered the United States without documents. The CPS may underestimate the U.S. foreign-born population by failing to account fully for the undocumented population. According to a recent news report by Cindy Rodriguez (2001), the 2000 Census showed a higher than expected number of Asians and Latinos, which is most likely attributable to undocumented immigrants. She reported that the number of undocumented immigrants in the United States may be 11 million, 5 million more than the U.S. Immigration and Naturalization Service had estimated.

4. *Latino* refers to residents of the United States who trace their ancestry to Latin America or the Spanish-speaking countries of the Caribbean. I use the term *Asian* or *Asian American* interchangeably to refer to those U.S. residents who trace their ancestry to Asia, Southeast Asia, the Indian subcontinent, or the Pacific Islands. Some scholars also use the term *Asian American* to refer only to those of Asian ancestry who are U.S. citizens by birth or naturalization. However, many immigrants from Asia who are not citizens plan eventually to make the United States their permanent home and contribute to American life. In many cases, I use

227

the term *Asian American* rather than *Asian* to refer to people of Asian descent living permanently in the United States regardless of their place of birth or citizenship status. Although scholars often use the term *Asian* to refer to people of Asian origin in the United States, that term fails to distinguish people in Asia from those in the United States and can contribute to the stereotype that people of Asian ancestry in the United States are perpetual foreigners. I use *Mexican* and *Mexican American* interchangeably to refer to someone of Mexican origin living in the United States. Similarly, I use the terms *Chinese* and *Chinese American* interchangeably to refer to someone of Chinese origin living in the United States.

5. The trend in California illustrates the effect of immigration compared to the effect of birthrate. The population in California has been growing steadily since the 1960s. However, unlike the past, the current growth is occurring in the proportion of foreign-born *newcomers* to the state, and this will remain true in the future. In 1970, immigrants constituted less than 10 percent of the state's population; by 1990, they comprised more than 20 percent. In absolute numbers, the immigrant population in California doubled between 1980 and 1990 (Myers and Pitkin 2001).

6. For example, according to data from the 2000 Census, more than 10 percent of California's population (including approximately 30 percent in San Francisco County and 12 percent in Los Angeles County) is Asian American. In Queens County, New York, 18 percent of the residents are Asian American. The statistics on the Asian American population included in this section are taken from www.census.gov/population/www/documentation/twps0029/tab08.htm; www.census.gov/population/cen2000/phc-t1/tab01.txt; www.factfinder.census.gov/home/en/pldata.html (Census 2000 Redistricting Summary File).

7. In New Mexico, California, and Texas, for example, Latinos account for at least 30 percent of the state's population. Latinos are the dominant ethnic group in some localities. In multiethnic Los Angeles County, Latinos comprise approximately 45 percent of the population, followed by whites (35 percent), Asian Americans (12 percent), and blacks (10 percent). The statistics on the Latino population included in this section are taken from www.census.gov/population/cen2000/phc-t1/tab01.txt and www.factfinder.census.gov/home/en/pldata.html (Census 2000 Redistricting Summary File).

8. For a good discussion of how researchers have gauged the extent of a group's substantive participation and incorporation into the political system, see Browning, Marshall, and Tabb 1984; Davidson and Grofman 1994.

9. For studies of vote choice among Latinos, see J. Garcia and Arce 1988; de la Garza et al. 1992; Barreto and Woods 2000. For research on electoral turnout among Latinos, see Arvizu and Garcia 1996; DeSipio 1996; Shaw, de la Garza, and Lee 2000; Pantoja, Ramirez, and Segura 2001. For examinations of political participation among Latinos, see de la Garza et al. 1992; Verba, Schlozman, and Brady 1995; Hero and Campbell 1996; F. Garcia 1997; Jones-Correa 1998. For research on Asian American political attitudes and behavior, see Cain 1988; Nakanishi 1991; Kwoh and Hui 1993; Tam 1995; Ong and Nakanishi 1996; Lien 1997, 2001; Lien, Conway, and Wong 2004). For information on internal diver-

sity in political attitudes and behavior within those communities, see de la Garza et al. 1992; Tam 1995; F. Garcia 1997; Lien 2001; Lien, Conway, and Wong 2003. For comparisons of Latino and Asian American political attitudes and behavior, see Cain, Kiewiet, and Uhlaner 1991; Uhlaner 1991; Lien 1994, 1997; Saito 1998; Cho 1999.

10. For research on political participation among Asian Americans and Latinos, see de la Garza and DeSipio 1997; Jones-Correa 1998; DeSipio, de la Garza, and Setzler 1999; Lien 2001; Lien, Conway, and Wong 2004.

11. Political activity can be construed as system-challenging and radical in that it defies the existing governmental system in an attempt to alter it dramatically or replace it altogether. Political activity may also be seen as normal, seeking to create changes within the framework of the current system. Although some studies link immigrant groups to radical politics (Rosenblum 1973; Portes and Rumbaut 1996), the activities that I most often encountered can appropriately be categorized as normal politics. I am indebted to Gaspar Rivera-Salgado for helping me to think through these distinctions as they relate to immigrants in particular.

12. In some cases, the gap in participation rates between new arrivals and first-generation immigrants who have resided for long periods in the United States is greater than the gap in participation rates when comparing first-generation immigrants as a whole with native-born (second- or subsequent-generation-) immigrants.

Chapter 2

1. Omi and Winant define racial formation as "the socio-historical process by which racial categories are created, inhabited, transformed, and destroyed" (1994, 55). For studies of racial formation among Asian Americans and Latinos, see Espiritu 1992; Sanchez 1993; Takaki 1993; Almaguer 1994; Omi and Winant 1994; Haney-Lopez 1996; Lowe 1996; Rogers Smith 1997; Jacobson 1998; Perea et al. 2000; C. Kim 2000; Nobles 2000.

2. Haney-Lopez (1996, 38) estimates that as many as half a million people were "repatriated" to Mexico.

3. Historian Matthew Frye Jacobson (1998) argues that although immigrants from Europe were considered white, a meaningful hierarchy based in part on phenotype and ethnic stereotypes existed within that broad category, which thus included several "white races."

4. New York City includes fifty-nine community districts, geographic areas established by local law in 1975. They range in area from less than nine hundred acres to almost fifteen thousand acres and in population from fewer than thirty-five thousand residents to more than two hundred thousand (New York City Department of Planning 2001b).

5. The 2000 Census showed more than 3 million people of Mexican origin living in Los Angeles County, approximately 50 percent of them immigrants (Allen and Turner 2002).

6. Sanchez (1993) observes that it is likely that the organization also used the Independence Day events to advertise its life insurance services.

7. James Lai examines the relationship between elected representation and mobilization of the Asian American community. He finds a strong relationship between Asian American elected officials and community organizations, which suggests that "politically-active community-based organizations play both *support-ive* and *proactive* roles in the recruitment of future Asian Pacific American elected officials" (2000, 7).

8. Despite these similarities to the U.S. system, there is widespread dispute over designation of Mexico as a democracy, since the executive exercises a dominant role over the judiciary and legislature, the government is highly centralized, and the country had one-party rule for more than seventy years (1929–2000).

Chapter 3

1. James Q. Wilson (1995, 96–97) distinguishes between "party organizations" and "political machines." A party organization is "a group of persons who consciously coordinate their activities so as to influence the choice of candidates for elective office," whereas a political machine is "a party organization relying chiefly on the attraction of material rewards."

2. Steven Erie (1988, 2) writes that although they had their roots in the Jacksonian period (1820s and 1830s), full-fledged urban machines emerged only in the late 1800s.

3. I am indebted to Michael Jones-Correa and Ann Crigler for sharing these important observations with me.

4. Turnout in the 2004 presidential election spiked to the highest levels since 1968, with the increase attributed to a unique set of factors, including voters' strong feelings about the Iraq war, the polarizing effects of the Bush presidency, and a close race that led to strong voter-mobilization efforts (in the battleground states where Asian Americans and Latinos are underrepresented) by the parties and other groups. Because of these unique circumstances, it is difficult to conclude whether the election changed overall trends in turnout or represents a special circumstance.

5. Noncitizens could participate in many elections until the 1920s but today are barred from voting in federal and most state and local elections. Exceptions include New York and Chicago school board elections and local offices in several municipalities in Maryland and Massachusetts (Hayduk 2002).

6. Furthermore, intraminority racial stereotypes are quite prevalent (Johnson, Farrell, and Guinn 1997).

7. I am indebted to Efrain Escobedo, with whom I worked during his tenure as a McNair Research Scholar at the University of Southern California, for his synthesis and analysis of Latino outreach efforts.

8. Although Latinos did not uniformly oppose such anti-immigrant initiatives as California's Proposition 187, exit polls clearly show that the majority of the Latino community, including those who were born in the United States, opposed the initiative. Latinos were by far the most opposed to the initiative, although a majority of blacks and Asian Americans also voted against the measure. Less than 20 percent of Latino voters supported Proposition 187, as did 63 percent of white

voters. Latino Voter Forums conducted by the National Association of Latino Elected Officials demonstrated that although nonimmigrant Latinos often opposed illegal immigration, few supported Proposition 187 or other such policies, viewing them as not just anti-immigrant but anti-Latino.

9. The Web site was available in English and Spanish only. See http://www .democrats.org/ (accessed December 5, 2003).

10. Battleground states included Arizona, Arkansas, Florida, Iowa, Maine, Michigan, Minnesota, Missouri, Nevada, New Hampshire, New Mexico, Ohio, Oregon, Pennsylvania, Tennessee, Washington, West Virginia, and Wisconsin.

11. Gold also mentioned that the candidates had failed to include Latinos in their inner circle of advisers.

12. Bloomberg, a lifelong Democrat, ran for mayor as a Republican.

13. On party clubs in New York City, see also Peel 1968; Adler and Blank 1975.

14. This observation conforms to Mollenkopf's analysis showing that in 1988, three out of four of the party organizations in Latino assembly districts were noncompetitive (1992, table 4.1).

15. Philip Kasinitz (1992) argues that Afro-Caribbeans were overrepresented in New York City politics between 1935 and 1965. These political leaders tended to deemphasize their Afro-Caribbean ethnic origins in public life, although they maintained a strong sense of ethnic identity in their personal lives (55).

Chapter 4

1. On noncitizen voting rights, see chap. 3, n. 5.

2. Because I did not interview a representative sample of community leaders or conduct a survey of a scientific sample of national organizations, caution should be used when applying these observations more generally.

3. This book places national labor unions and their local affiliates under the category labor organizations and distinguishes them from independent worker centers and independent unions. The latter deal with labor issues, but the focus is often less on union organizing than on advocacy on behalf of workers. Although the AFL-CIO is a national organization, it sponsors local, face-to-face activities with immigrants—for example, the Immigrant Workers' Freedom Ride, which was organized in different localities. Thus, for the purposes of this work, the AFL-CIO is counted among the community organizations.

4. As discussed earlier, California's Proposition 187 was a 1994 ballot measure that sought to deny benefits to immigrants without legal documents. Proposition 209 was an anti-affirmative-action measure that passed in 1996 in California.

5. I am indebted to Eric Oliver for sharing this observation.

6. I have grouped workers' centers with labor organizations because both are active primarily around worker issues and worker rights. However, some workers' centers were started because workers and community leaders felt that unions were not doing a good job of representing or protecting workers.

7. Because the Democratic Party is no longer mobilizing at the neighborhood level, it must now rely heavily on unions to turn out support for candidates. This

reinforces the claim that unions and other local community organizations bear the primary responsibility for direct mobilization of immigrants.

8. In 2002, the 1.4 million-member Teamsters Union and New York City's 200,000-member health-care-workers union endorsed Governor George Pataki, a Republican, for reelection, and Andy Stern, Service Employees International Union president, worked with Tom DeLay, the House Republican whip, on federal policies affecting airport security screeners. A senior official in the Bush White House claimed in May 2002 that the "level of union support for Republicans in the House and Senate has jumped from 6 percent to nearly 20 percent, and I think it will go even higher before the election season is over" (quoted in Lambro 2002, A-19).

9. Unions have developed get-out-the-vote and political education programs that are separate from any candidate campaign as a way of maintaining independence from the Democratic Party (Greenhouse 1998a). In 1998, the director of the AFL-CIO announced a commitment to an explicitly grassroots campaign around the congressional elections rather than engaging in the more common practice of making large campaign contributions (Dark 2000). In the weeks leading up to the November election, the AFL-CIO registered half a million new voters (AFL-CIO 1998) by going door to door, passing out leaflets, and organizing local rallies and corporate campaigns (Seelye 1998). During the 2000 presidential campaign, AFL-CIO leaders went on a People Power 2000 tour, and union members handed out 14 million leaflets at work sites and focused on one-on-one neighborhood canvassing (Chang 2001).

10. Is it appropriate to group these different types of nonprofit community-based organizations together under one category? Such lumping may obscure differences in funding sources, the historical context that has shaped their development, and whether their origins are linked to local movements or government programs. However, community-based nonprofit status represents one key way that the organizations described in this section are similar, and that is why I have chosen to categorize them as such.

11. J. Lin (1998) notes that since the 1970s, pro-Beijing supporters have challenged the dominance of Nationalist Party (KMT) loyalists within the CCBA.

12. Jones-Correa was referring to immigrant men in particular in this case, but I suspect that the example applies to immigrants of both genders.

13. Although more than 75 percent of Latinos report that they are Roman Catholic, Latino converts are becoming a significant presence within the Protestant Pentecostal movement. For example, Los Angeles is home to about one thousand Latino Pentecostal churches (Orr 1999).

14. See Dahl 1961; Wolfinger and Rosenstone 1980; Conway 1991; Verba, Schlozman, and Brady 1995. Scholars who study participation among groups made up of a large proportion of immigrants criticize these socioeconomic theories because they fail to consider migration-related variables such as language proficiency, minority status, experience in the country of origin, and length of residence (Cain, Kiewiet, and Uhlaner 1991; Uhlaner and Garcia 1998; Cho 1999; Junn 1999; J. Wong 2000). For example, a number of scholars have questioned

the applicability of the socioeconomic model for Asian Americans, who, on average, demonstrate high levels of education along with low levels of political activity (Tam 1995; Lien 1997; Cho 1999; Junn 1999).

Chapter 5

1. For potential inegalitarian responses by ethnic organizations to cleavages within groups, see Cohen 1999; Strolovitch 2002; D. Warren 2003.

2. For a quantitative study supporting this point, see T. Lee 2004.

3. According to the organization's Web site, "CECOMEX es una institución no lucrativa que activamente trabaja para mejorar la imagen y el bienestar de la Comunidad Mexicana de Nueva York. CECOMEX tiene sus puertas abiertas a todas las comunidades sin importar raza, color, nacionalidad, credo, posicion socio-economica, estatus legal u orientación sexual. Estamos localizados en el corazón de Harlem Hispano donde hay 63 negocios Mexicanos que orgullosamente representamos. Ademas, se estima que mas de 16,000 residentes Mexicanos habitan en esta area. CECOMEX labora en los cinco condados del area metropolitana y algunas partes de Nueva Jersey. Nuestra organizacion se enfoca en lidiar con la problemática socio-política y económica que afecta a nuestra comunidad que se estima esta compuesta de mas de 250,000 personas sólo en el area metropolitana, según el Censo de 1990, pero hoy en día se calcula a 850,000 en la Ciudad de Nueva York [CECOMEX is a nonprofit organization that actively works to improve the image and well-being of the Mexican community in New York. CECOMEX opens its doors to all communities, without regard to race, color, nationality, religion, socioeconomic position, legal status, or sexual orientation. We are located in the heart of Spanish Harlem, where there are 63 Mexican businesses that we proudly represent. Moreover, an estimated 16,000 Mexican residents live there. CECOMEX works in five counties in the metropolitan region and in some parts of New Jersey. Our organization focuses on combating sociopolitical and economic problems that affect our community, which the 1990 Census estimated at more than 250,000 people in the metropolitan area alone but which today is calculated at more than 850,000 in New York City]."

4. A body of research on the relationships among gender, migration, and political participation is slowly emerging, and it suggests that gender is likely to play an especially important role in the political involvement of immigrants. Michael Jones-Correa claims that working outside of the home for pay gives Latin American immigrant women in the United States more economic independence than they would have in their countries of origin and that they are more likely than Latin American immigrant men to "find reasons for adapting to their stay in United States" (1998, 345). He concludes that because women are more likely than men to remain in the United States, women are also more likely to naturalize and participate in American politics.

Chapter 6

1. Many studies that focus on immigrant populations include Puerto Ricans while noting differences in citizenship status and travel restrictions between them

and other immigrant groups (Marshall 1987; Acosta-Belen 1988; C. Davis, Haub, and Willette 1988; Jennings 1988; Safa 1988; de la Garza et al. 1992). Puerto Rico became a U.S. colonial territory in 1898, and because Puerto Ricans have been U.S. citizens at birth since 1917, they may travel without restriction between the United States and Puerto Rico. Puerto Rico has its own political parties, representative government, and separate laws. Puerto Ricans living on the island choose delegates for the Republican and Democratic National Conventions but cannot vote in U.S. presidential elections. However, Puerto Ricans who have immigrated to the United States can vote after registering in one of the fifty states or Washington, D.C. Most studies that include Puerto Ricans tend to refer to individuals who move from Puerto Rico to the continental U.S. as either Puerto Rican immigrants or Puerto Rican migrants. In this discussion, *Puerto Rican* refers to people of Puerto Rican origin whether born in the United States or on the island. *Puerto Rican immigrant* refers only to individuals born on the island but who have since migrated to the United States.

2. When respondents indicated that they preferred to use Spanish, they were asked: "¿Piensa que hay algún grupo u organización que se preocupa por sus intereses, aunque no sea usted miembro?"

3. Those individuals who answered "Don't know" or who declined to state a specific organization are not included in these categories.

4. The LNPS question about membership in an organization asked, "Some of these questions will refer to [your national-origin group]. By [national-origin group], I mean all people born in the U.S. who are of [that country's] ancestry, as well as people born in [that country] who now live here. Please tell me the names of any organizations or associations that you belong to or have given money or goods to in the past twelve months that are . . ." One category was "General Latino, Hispanic organizations/Mexican American organizations/Cuban American organizations and Puerto Rican organizations." That category included ninety-seven possible responses, among them the National Association of Latino Elected Officials; the League of United Latin American Citizens; the National Council of La Raza; Aspira (National Associations of Chicago, Florida, New Jersey, New York, and Puerto Rico); the Cuban American Committee; and Mexican American, Cuban American, or Puerto Rican American community centers and neighborhood organizations.

5. See appendix tables A4–7 for full models. In the LNPS, political engagement was measured by questions asking about the extent to which respondents followed politics, their strength of partisanship, and their strength of ideology (strong liberal or strong conservative). For analyses of participation in activities outside of voting, citizenship status was also used as a measure of political engagement. Experience with discrimination was measured by a question asking respondents, "Because you are a Mexican/Puerto Rican/Cuban, have you ever been turned down as renter or buyer of a home, or been treated rudely in a restaurant, been denied a job, or experienced other important types of discrimination?" In the PNAAPS, questions about the degree of interest in politics, partisanship, and ideology were used to measure political engagement. Again, citizenship was included

as a variable for analysis of participation outside of voting. Experience with discrimination was measured by the question, "Have you ever personally experienced discrimination in the United States?" A follow-up question asked whether respondents had been discriminated against based on race or ethnicity.

6. Scholars have recently attempted to address this causality issue by conducting field experiments that compare a randomly selected treatment group of individuals who are contacted to a randomly selected control group who are not contacted. The results of the studies show some evidence that contacting leads to more participation (D. Green and Gerber 2002; R. Ramirez forthcoming; J. Wong 2004). However, results of mobilization through contact vary according to type of contact and sample.

Chapter 7

1. The CNN exit poll (2004), based on a sample of 13,660 respondents interviewed immediately after leaving the polling place, estimated that Asian Americans comprised 2 percent of the electorate and Latinos 8 percent. Based on a sample of 5,154 voters, the *Los Angeles Times* (2004) estimated that Latinos represented 5 percent of the electorate and Asian Americans 3 percent. Most of those respondents were Californians, but the *Times* conducted the survey in 136 polling places nationwide.

2. Asian American socioeconomic resources vary greatly by national-origin group. Japanese Americans have among the highest incomes in the United States, whereas Vietnamese and Hmong Americans have among the lowest.

3. The 2002 Current Population Survey Volunteer Supplement includes valid responses from 2,769 white, 682 black, 4,293 Latino, and 2,360 Asian American immigrants (Ramakrishnan 2003). Not all volunteer activities are political in nature, but the survey does show organizational affiliation, which is often associated with political participation.

4. In this chapter, Latino and Asian American participation in activities other than voting is measured by a dummy variable. Those who indicate that they took part in any activity other than voting are assigned a value of 1, and those who did not take part in any activity are assigned a value of 0. Thus, the variable simply measures whether one took part in any activity. In the preceding chapter, participation in activities beyond voting was measured by an index of participation that better captured participation across a range of activities.

5. The example provided was generated by converting the coefficients generated by the regressions to odds ratios.

6. What is true at the individual level may not be the case at the aggregate level. Even though individual Asian Americans with more socioeconomic resources participate at higher levels than those with fewer resources, higher average socioeconomic status for Asian Americans as a group has not translated into high average voting rates for the group.

7. The data on earlier European immigrants do not contain enough detail about length of residence to conduct a comparative analysis.

8. Further correlation analysis suggested a positive association between length

of residence and political participation for several Latino subgroups (the LAT distinguished among Puerto Ricans, Mexicans, Cubans, other Central and South Americans, and other Latinos) and several Asian American subgroups (Chinese, Koreans, Vietnamese, Japanese, Filipinos, and South Asians). Those who had not met the five-year residency requirement and Puerto Ricans, who are already U.S. citizens, were not included in the analysis of the relationship between length of residence and citizenship. Unfortunately, small sample sizes for specific ethnic groups prevent multivariate analyses (see appendix, tables A1 and A2 for number of respondents).

9. Although immigration rates were highest in the first and second decades of the twentieth century, naturalization rates crested in the four years before 1928, very likely initiating the upward trend in turnout among immigrants that Andersen (1979) documents.

10. These figures assume that the most recent immigration trends will continue with immigration rates stabilizing.

11. This description is taken from the National Association of Latino Elected Officials' Web site: http://www.naleo.org/membership.htm (accessed December 11, 2004).

Chapter 8

1. I use the term *homeland* to refer to a migrant's country of origin. I do not intend to imply that the United States or receiving community is any less a real home to migrants than the country of origin, nor do I mean to suggest that immigrants are more loyal to one country than another.

2. Given that since the early 1960s, the United States has limited the amount of remittances that can be sent to the island, Cuban immigrants exhibit lower remittance rates. What is surprising is that despite the restrictions, one in five Cubans regularly sends money to the island. In recent years, the U.S. government has increased the upper limit for cash remittances.

3. In 1996, the Mexican congress voted to allow Mexican citizens living abroad to vote in Mexican elections without having to return to Mexico, but the major Mexican parties disagreed about how to implement specific voting mechanisms.

4. About 14 percent of Latino immigrants in the LNPS indicated that they were more concerned with politics in the homeland, 46 percent said that they were more concerned with politics in the United States, 32 percent claimed that they were concerned with both, and 8 percent didn't know or had no opinion.

5. Some of these activities, such as donating to a political campaign, may require immigrants to be permanent residents.

6. The dependent variable for this analysis is a dummy variable for participation in activities other than voting. This variable measures whether an individual took part in any political activity. In contrast, the variable used to measure participation other than voting in the analysis using the LNPS data in chapter 6 was based on an index created from the seven questions about political activities other than voting. That variable allows for analysis of whether an individual participated

in a range of political activities. One question asked in chapter 6 was whether involvement with a community organization was associated with political participation in a range of activities; thus, the index of participation was the appropriate measure of participation.

7. This estimate of California's Mexican immigrant population is very likely low because it does not take into account those men and women who entered the United States without documents.

Chapter 9

1. I am indebted to Michael-Jones Correa for his insights regarding the larger political system's importance in structuring mobilization in the United States.

Appendix

1. See *Washington Post*/Kaiser Family Foundation/Harvard University National Survey on Latinos in America, available at http://www.kff.org/kaiser-polls/3023-index.cfm (accessed January 7, 2004).

2. The screening question was used primarily to simplify analyses. Respondents were also asked to self-identify both ethnically and racially. For example, 0.3 percent of the Mexican respondents, 5.1 percent of the Puerto Rican respondents, and 2.6 percent of the Cuban respondents self-identified as black. A majority in each of these groups self-identified as white.

3. Puerto Rico was one of the response categories for this question, and 73 percent of those who were screened into the study as being of Puerto Rican origin indicated Puerto Rico when asked their country of birth.

4. I defined activists as individuals who (1) consider themselves to be actively involved with either the Chinese or the Mexican community (including immigrants); (2) are considered to be involved with that community by at least two other individuals; and (3) are affiliated with an organization or office that provides social, legal, political, or issue-oriented services to or advocacy for Chinese or Mexican immigrants in New York or Los Angeles. I identified the leaders of well-known immigrant-serving institutions and advocacy groups by attending local community events, such as the Asian Pacific American Heritage Festival in New York City, and through directories of community organizations. The interviewees provided some additional contacts. I conducted interviews between June and November 1999 using both a sample based on the national and local reputation of the organizations and a snowball sampling method. Although most organizational leaders with whom I spoke were bilingual, interviews were conducted in English.

5. The research assistants were not community activists.

6. Although I would have liked to include Mandarin Chinese speakers in the study, I lacked the resources to conduct interviews with Chinese immigrants in three languages. A follow-up study that includes Mandarin speakers is planned.

References

Abcarian, Robin. 1996. "They're Ready for Action; Protests: It Seems as If Every Group with a Burning Issue Has Come to the GOP Convention." *Los Angeles Times,* August 14, A-1.

Abu-Lughod, Janet. 1999. *New York, Chicago, Los Angeles: America's Global Cities.* Minneapolis: University of Minnesota Press.

Acosta, Teresa. 2002. *Alianza Hispano-Americana* Handbook of Texas Online. Available at http://www.tsha.utexas.edu/handbook/online/articles/view/AA/vna2.html. Accessed January 18, 2004.

Acosta-Belen, Edna. 1988. "From Settlers to Newcomers: The Hispanic Legacy in the United States." In *The Hispanic Experience in the United States,* edited by Edna Acosta-Belen and Barbara R. Sjostrom. Westport, CT: Praeger.

Acuna, Rodolfo. 1988. *Occupied America: A History of Chicanos.* 3d ed. New York: Harper Collins.

Acuna, Rodolfo. 1996. *Anything but Mexican: Chicanos in Contemporary Los Angeles.* New York: Verso.

Adler, Norman, and Blanche Blank. 1975. *Political Clubs in New York.* New York: Praeger.

AFL-CIO. 1998. *Working Families Vote!* Available at http://www.aflcio.org/labor98. Accessed June 12, 2000.

Aguilar, John. 1981. "Insider Research: An Ethnography of a Debate." In *Anthropologists at Home in North America: Methods and Issues in the Study of One's Own Society,* edited by D. A. Messerschmidt. New York: Cambridge University Press.

Alarcón, Norma. 1998. "Chicana Feminism: In the Tracks of 'the' Native Woman." In *Living Chicana Theory,* edited by Carla Trujillo. Berkeley: Third Woman Press.

Alarcón, Norma, Ana Castillo, and Cherríe Moraga, eds. 1993. *The Sexuality of Latinas.* Berkeley: Third Woman Press.

Alba, Richard D., and Victor Nee. 1997. "Rethinking Assimilation Theory for a New Era of Immigrants." *International Migration Review* 31:826–75.

Alex-Assensoh, Yvette, and A. B. Assensoh. 2001. "Inner-City Contexts, Church Attendance, and African-American Political Participation." *Journal of Politics* 63:886–901.

Allen, James, and Eugene Turner. 2002. *Changing Faces, Changing Places: Mapping Southern Californians.* Northridge: Center for Geographical Studies, California State University, Northridge.

Almaguer, Tomas. 1994. *Racial Fault Lines: The Historical Origins of White Supremacy in California.* Berkeley: University of California Press.

Almond, Gabriel, and Sidney Verba. 1965. *The Civic Culture: Political Attitudes and Democracy in Five Nations.* New York: Little, Brown.

Alonso-Zaldivar, Ricardo. 1999. "Big Apple Takes on the Flavor of Mexico." *Los Angeles Times,* February 19, A-1.

Alonso-Zaldivar, Ricardo. 2004. "Bush Snags Much More of the Latino Vote, Exit Polls Show; His 7 Percentage-Point Gain in Support over 2000 Is a Strategic Political Win. But the Constituency's Support Is Considered 'Volatile.'" *Los Angeles Times,* November 4, A-30.

American Association for the Advancement of Science. 2000. "Letter to Attorney General Janet Reno (concerning the matter of the continued denial of bail and the conditions of pre-trial incarceration of Dr. Wen Ho Lee)." Federation of American Scientists. Available at http://www.fas.org/sgp/news/2000/03/aaaslet.html. Accessed June 15, 2005.

Americas Program, Interhemispheric Resource Center. 2003. "Mexican Hometown Associations." *Citizen Action in the Americas* 5:1–8. Available at http://americas.irc-online.org/pdf/series/05.hta.pdf. Accessed June 20, 2005.

Andersen, Kristi. 1979. *The Creation of a Democratic Majority, 1928–1936.* Chicago: University of Chicago Press.

Andersen, Kristi, and Elizabeth Cohen. 2003. *Political Institutions and the Incorporation of Immigrants.* Available at http://www.nd.edu/~amdemoc/Andersen&Cohen.pdf. Accessed January 18, 2004.

Anderson, John Ward. 2000. "Politicians without Borders; Mexico's Candidates Court Support of Migrants in U.S." *Washington Post,* May 8, 20.

Aparicio, Frances R., and Cándida F. Jáquez, with María Elena Cepeda. 2003. *Musical Migrations: Transnationalism and Cultural Hybridity in Latin/o America.* New York: Palgrave Macmillan.

Appadurai, Arjun. 1996. *Modernity at Large: Cultural Dimensions of Globalization.* Minneapolis: University of Minnesota Press.

Arax, Mark. 1987. "Monterey Park: Nation's 1st Suburban Chinatown." *Los Angeles Times,* April 6, 1.

Archdeacon, Thomas J. 1983. *Becoming American: An Ethnic History.* New York: Free Press.

Arian, Asher, Arthur S. Goldberg, John Mollenkopf, and Edward T. Rogowsky. 1991. *Changing New York City Politics.* New York: Routledge.

Armas, Genaro. 2004. *Asian Population Lacks Political Clout.* Lexis-Nexis Academic Universe, 2004 (July 19). Available at http://web.lexis-nexis.com/universe/document?_m=9c2bc3835cb576aaeff46082f378ae00&_docnum=1&wchp=dGLbVtz-zSkVb&_md5=c81a43ae96fdae3d77ff4e25ad478100. Accessed October 11, 2004.

Aronowitz, Stanley. 1998. *From the Ashes of the Old: American Labor and America's Future*. Boston: Houghton Mifflin.

Arvizu, John R., and F. Chris Garcia. 1996. "Latino Voting Participation: Explaining and Differentiating Latino Voting Turnout." *Hispanic Journal of Behavioral Sciences* 18:104–28.

Asian Pacific American Legal Center. 1998. *November 1998 Southern California Voter Survey Report*. Los Angeles: Asian Pacific American Legal Center.

Ayon, David. 2000. "Latinos: Once Wooed, Now Nearly Forgotten." *Los Angeles Times*, October 29, B-1.

Banfield, Edward C., and James Q. Wilson. 1963. *City Politics*. Cambridge: Harvard University Press.

Barnes, Jessica S., and Claudette Bennett. 2002. *The Asian Population: 2000*. Washington, DC: U.S. Department of Commerce, Bureau of the Census.

Barone, Michael. 2001. *The New Americans*. Washington, DC: Regnery.

Barreto, Matt, and Nathan Woods. 2000. *Voting Patterns and Dramatic Growth of the Latino Electorate in Los Angeles County, 1994–1998*. Claremont, CA: Tomas Rivera Policy Institute.

Basch, Linda, Nina Glick Schiller, and Cristina Szanton Blanc. 1994. *Nations Unbound: Transnational Projects, Postcolonial Predicaments, and Deterritorialized Nation-States*. Langhorne, PA: Gordon and Breach.

Bauman, Kurt, and Nikki Graf. 2003. "Educational Attainment: 2000." *Census 2000 Brief, C2KBR-24*. Washington, DC: U.S. Census Bureau.

Becker, Maki. 2001. "Board Seeks Minority Voices but the Struggle Persists to Find Interested Latinos." *New York Daily News*, April 9, 2.

Bedolla, Lisa Garcia. 2005. *Fluid Borders: Latino Power, Identity, and Politics in Los Angeles*. Berkeley: University of California.

Benhabib, Seyla. 2002. *The Claims of Culture: Equality and Diversity in the Global Era*. Princeton: Princeton University Press.

Bennoune, Mahfoud. 1985. "What Does It Mean to Be a Third World Anthropologist?" *Dialectical Anthropology* 9:357–64.

Berry, Jeffrey. 1997. *The Interest Group Society*. 3d ed. New York: Longman.

Bonacich, Edna. 1999. "Latino Immigrant Workers in the Los Angeles Apparel Industry." In *Latino Social Movements*, edited by Rodolfo D. Torres and George Katsiaficas. New York: Routledge.

Brooklyn AIDS Task Force. 2003. 2003 Sunset Park HIV/AIDS and Health Profile. Available at http://www.nyaidscoalition.org/binary-data/NYAC_PDF/pdf/24-1.pdf#search='Sunset%20Park%20Brooklyn%20Asian%20population. Accessed June 14, 2005.

Browning, Rufus P., Dale Rogers Marshall, and David H. Tabb. 1984. *Protest Is Not Enough*. Berkeley: University of California Press.

Burns, Peter, and James G. Gimpel. 2000. "Economic Insecurity, Prejudicial Stereotypes, and Public Opinion on Immigration Policy." *Political Science Quarterly* 115:201–26.

Cain, Bruce E. 1988. "Asian Electoral Power: Imminent or Illusory?" *Election Politics* 5:27–30.

Cain, Bruce E., D. Roderick Kiewiet, and Carole J. Uhlaner. 1991. "The Acquisition of Partisanship by Latinos and Asian Americans." *American Journal of Political Science* 35:390–422.

Cain, Bruce E., and Ken McCue. 1985. "The Efficacy of Registration Drives." *Journal of Politics* 47:1221–30.

Calhoun-Brown, Allison. 1996. "African American Churches and Political Mobilization: The Psychological Impact of Organizational Resources." *Journal of Politics* 58:935–53.

Ceaser, James. 1978. "Political Parties and Presidential Ambition." *Journal of Politics* 40:708–39.

CECOMEX. 2004. Home page. Available at http://www.cecomex.com/. Accessed February 13, 2004.

Center for the Study of Los Angeles at Loyola Marymount University. 2005. 2005 Los Angeles Mayoral Election Exit Poll Results. Available at http://www.lmu.edu/csla/press/releases_2005/Files/May17_by_Race.pdf. Accessed June 20, 2005.

Chan, Sucheng. 1991a. *Asian Americans: An Interpretive History*. Boston: Twayne.

Chan, Sucheng, ed. 1991b. *Entry Denied: Exclusion and the Chinese Community in America, 1882–1943*. Philadelphia: Temple University Press.

Chang, Tracy F. 2001. "The Labour Vote in the U.S. National Elections, 1948–2000." *Political Quarterly* 72:375–85.

Chavez, Linda. 1991. *Out of the Barrio: Toward a New Politics of Hispanic Assimilation*. New York: Basic Books.

Chen, Carolyn. 2001. "The Religious Varieties of Ethnic Presence: A Comparison between a Taiwanese Immigrant Buddhist Temple and an Evangelical Christian Church." Unpublished manuscript.

Chen, Hsiang-Shui. 1992. *Chinatown No More: Taiwan Immigrants in Contemporary New York*. Ithaca: Cornell University Press.

Chen, May, and Kent Wong. 1998. "The Challenge of Diversity and Inclusion in the AFL-CIO." In *A New Labor Movement for a New Century*, edited by Gregory Mantsios. New York: Garland.

Cheng, Lucie, and Philip Yang. 1996. "The 'Model Minority' Deconstructed." In *Ethnic Los Angeles*, edited by Roger Waldinger and Mehdi Bozorgmehr. New York: Russell Sage.

Chinea, Jorge L. 1996. "Ethnic Prejudice and Anti-Immigration Policies in Times of Economic Stress: Mexican Repatriation from the United States, 1929–1939." *EastWind/West Wind* (winter): 9–13.

Chinese Staff and Workers' Association. 1997. "Garment Women Organize against Deadly Hours of Overwork." *CSWA News: The Voice of the Chinese American Worker* (fall): 1–6.

Chinese Staff and Workers' Association. 1999. "Women Workers Should Stand Up." *CSWA News: The Voice of the Chinese American Worker* (summer): 1–4.

Cho, Wendy K. Tam. 1999. "Naturalization, Socialization, Participation: Immigrants and (Non-) Voting." *Journal of Politics* 61:1140–55.

Christian, Nichole M. 2000. "Detroit Journal: Mexican Immigrants Lead a Revival." *New York Times,* May 21, sec. 1, p. 20.

Cigler, Allan J. 1985. "Special Interests and the Policy Process." *Policy Studies Journal* 14:318–25.

Citrin, Jack, and Benjamin Highton. 2002. *How Race, Ethnicity, and Immigration Shape the California Electorate.* San Francisco: Public Policy Institute of California.

Claffey, Mike, Tom Raftery, and Don Singleton. 1998. "Mexicans Celebrate Holy Patron." *New York Daily News,* December 13, 6.

Cleeland, Nancy. 2000. "Union Ranks up in '99, Led by California." *Los Angeles Times,* January 20, A-1.

CNN. 2000. *2000 Presidential Election National Exit Poll.* Available at http://www.cnn.com/ELECTION/2000/results/index.epolls.html. Accessed November 5, 2004.

CNN. 2004. *2004 Presidential Election National Exit Poll.* Available at http://www.cnn.com/ELECTION/2004/pages/results/states/US/P/00/epolls.0.html. Accessed November 5, 2004.

Cochran, David. 1995. "Ethnic Diversity and Democratic Stability: The Case of the Irish Americans." *Political Science Quarterly* 110:587–605.

Cohen, Cathy. 1999. *The Boundaries of Blackness: AIDS and the Breakdown of Black Politics.* Chicago: University of Chicago Press.

Committee of 100 with the Anti-Defamation League. 2001. *American Attitudes towards Chinese Americans and Asian Americans.* Survey Conducted by Marttila Communications Group and Yankelovich Partners. Available at http://www.committee100.org/Published/C100survey.pdf. Accessed February 6, 2004.

Congressional Hispanic Caucus Institute. 2001. *National Directory of Hispanic Organizations, 2000–2001.* Washington, DC: Congressional Hispanic Caucus Institute.

Connerly, Ward. 2003. "We Are Multi-Racial—But We Should Be Colour-Blind; Californian Voters Have the Chance to Ban Racial Categorization." *Daily Telegraph (London),* October 2, 26.

Conway, M. Margaret. 1991. *Political Participation in the United States.* 2d ed. Washington, DC: Congressional Quarterly Press.

Conway, M. Margaret. 2001. "Political Participation in American Elections: Who Decides What." In *America's Choice,* edited by William J. Crotty. New York: Westview.

Cordero-Guzmán, Héctor R., Robert C. Smith, and Ramón Grosfoguel, eds. 2001. *Migration, Transnationalization, and Race in a Changing New York.* Philadelphia: Temple University Press.

Cornwell, Elmer E. 1960. "Party Absorption of Ethnic Groups: The Case of Providence, Rhode Island." *Social Forces* 38:205–10.

Cunningham, Hilary. 1998. "Sanctuary and Sovereignty: Church and State along the U.S.-Mexico Border." *Journal of Church and State* 40:370–86.

Dahl, Robert A. 1961. *Who Governs? Democracy and Power in an American City.* New Haven: Yale University Press.

Dahl, Robert A. 1967. *Pluralist Democracy in the United States: Conflict and Consent.* Chicago: Rand McNally.

Dahl, Robert. 1998. *On Democracy.* New Haven: Yale University Press.

Dalal, Anaga. 1998. "Cleaning Up Exploitation." *Ms. Magazine,* March/April, 12.

Dark, Taylor E., III. 2000. "Labor and the Democratic Party: A Report on the 1998 Elections." *Journal of Labor Research* 21:627–40.

Dart, John. 1996. "Religion: Church Acknowledges Close Ties to the Christian Coalition." *Los Angeles Times,* March 23, B-9.

Davidson, Chandler, and Bernard Grofman. 1994. "Editor's Introduction." In *Quiet Revolution in the South: The Impact of the Voting Rights Act 1965–1990,* edited by Chandler Davidson and Bernard Grofman. Princeton: Princeton University Press.

Davis, Cary, Carl Haub, and JoAnne L. Willette. 1988. "U.S. Hispanics: Changing the Face of America." In *The Hispanic Experience in the United States: Contemporary Issues and Perspectives,* edited by Edna Acosta-Belen and Barbara R. Sjostrom. Westport, CT: Praeger.

Davis, Mike. 1992. *City of Quartz: Excavating the Future in Los Angeles.* New York: Vintage.

de la Garza, Rodolfo, and Louis DeSipio. 1996. "Latinos and the 1992 Elections: A National Perspective." In *Ethnic Ironies: Latino Politics in the 1992 Elections,* edited by Rodolfo de la Garza and Louis DeSipio. Boulder, CO: Westview.

de la Garza, Rodolfo O., and Louis DeSipio. 1997. "Save the Baby, Change the Bathwater, and Scrub the Tub: Latino Electoral Participation after Twenty Years of Voting Rights Act Coverage." In *Pursuing Power: Latinos and the Political System,* edited by F. Chris Garcia. Notre Dame: Notre Dame University Press.

de la Garza, Rodolfo O., Louis DeSipio, F. Chris Garcia, John Garcia, and Angelo Falcon. 1992. *Latino Voices: Mexican, Puerto Rican, and Cuban Perspectives on American Politics.* Boulder, CO: Westview.

de la Garza, Rodolfo, Martha Menchaca, and Louis DeSipio. 1994. *Barrio Ballots: Latino Politics in the 1990 Elections.* Boulder, CO: Westview.

del Olmo, Frank. 2000. "Democrats May Have Lost Latinos." *Los Angeles Times,* August 20, M-5.

DeSipio, Louis. 1996. *Counting on the Latino Vote.* Charlottesville: University Press of Virginia.

DeSipio, Louis. 2001. "Building America, One Person at a Time: Naturalization and Political Behavior of the Naturalized in Contemporary Politics." In *E Pluribus Unum? Contemporary and Historical Perspectives on Immigrant Political Incorporation,* edited by Gary Gerstle and John Mollenkopf. New York: Russell Sage.

DeSipio, Louis. 2002. *Immigrant Organizing, Civic Outcomes: Civic Engagement, Political Activity, National Attachment, and Identity in Latino Immigrant Communities.* Irvine: Center for the Study of Democracy, University of California, Irvine.

DeSipio, Louis, and Rodolfo de la Garza. 2005. "Between Symbolism and Influence: Latinos and the 2000 Elections." In *Muted Voices: Latinos and the*

2000 Elections, edited by Rodolfo de la Garza and Louis DeSipio. Lanham, MD: Rowman and Littlefield.

DeSipio, Louis, Rodolfo de la Garza, and Mark Setzler. 1999. "Awash in the Mainstream: Latinos and the 1996 Elections." In *Awash in the Mainstream: Latino Politics in the 1996 Elections,* edited by Rodolfo de la Garza and Louis DeSipio. Boulder, CO: Westview.

DeSipio, Louis, and Gregory Rocha. 1992. "Latino Influence on National Elections: The Case of 1988." In *From Rhetoric to Reality: Latino Politics and the 1988 Elections,* edited by Rodolfo de la Garza and Louis DeSipio. Boulder, CO: Westview.

Deutsch, Claudia. 1994. "Commercial Property/Flushing's Chinatown; A Chinatown with a Polyglot Accent." *New York Times,* October 2, sec. 9, p. 1.

Dillon, Sam. 2003. "Mexican Consulate in Los Angeles Exudes Power and Energy." *New York Times,* March 14, A-12.

Directory of the Hispanic Community of the County of Los Angeles. 1999–2000. 9th ed. Los Angeles: University of Southern California, Office of Civic and Community Relations.

Dulio, David, and James A. Thurber. 2003. "The Symbolic Relationship between Political Parties and Political Consultants: Partners Past, Present, and Future." In *The State of the Parties: The Changing Role of Contemporary American Parties,* 4th ed., edited by John Green and Rick Farmer. Lanham, MD: Rowman and Littlefield.

Durand, Jorge, Douglas S. Massey, and Emilio A. Parrado. 1999. "The New Era of Mexican Migration to the United States." *Journal of American History* 86:518–36.

Echols, Alice. 1989. *Daring to Be Bad: Radical Feminism in America, 1967–75.* Minneapolis: University of Minnesota Press.

Elder, Laurel Elizabeth. 1999. "Party Behavior: The Response of America's Political Parties to Racial, Religious, and Ethnic Groups." Ph.D. diss., Ohio State University.

Eldersveld, Samuel J. 1956. "Experimental Propaganda Techniques and Voting Behavior." *American Political Science Review* 50:154–65.

Eldersveld, Samuel J., and Hanes Walton Jr., eds. 2000. *Political Parties in American Society.* New York: Bedford/St. Martin's.

Erie, Steven P. 1988. *Rainbow's End.* Berkeley: University of California Press.

Erie, Steven P., and Harold Brackman. 1998. "At Rainbow's End: Empowerment Prospects for Latinos and Asian Pacific Americans in Los Angeles." In *Racial and Ethnic Politics in California,* 2d ed., edited by Bruce E. Cain and Michael B. Preston. Berkeley, CA: Institute for Governmental Studies.

Escobedo, Efrain. 2002. "Parties and Latino Political Incorporation: Style or Substance?" Paper presented at the McNair Scholars Research Institute, University of Southern California, Los Angeles.

Espiritu, Yen Le. 1992. *Asian American Panethnicity.* Philadelphia: Temple University Press.

Espiritu, Yen Le. 2001. "'We Don't Sleep around Like White Girls Do': Family, Culture, and Gender in Filipina American Lives." *Signs* 26:415–41.

Espiritu, Yen Le. 2003. *Home Bound: Filipino American Lives across Cultures, Communities, and Countries.* Berkeley: University of California Press.

Fahim, Hussein M. 1977. "Foreign and Indigenous Anthropology: The Perspective of an Egyptian Anthropologist." *Human Organization* 36:80–86.

Fang, Di, and David Brown. 1999. "Geographic Mobility of the Foreign-Born Chinese in Large Metropolises, 1985–1990." *International Migration Review* 33:137–55.

Fears, Darryl. 2004. "Pollsters Debate Hispanics' Presidential Voting; Discrepancy in Estimates vs. Results Examined." *Washington Post,* November 26, A-4.

Fine, Janice. 2003. "Non-Union, Low-Wage Workers Are Finding a Voice as Immigrant Workers Centers Grow." *Labor Notes,* August. Available at http://www.labornotes.org/archives/2003/08/c.html. Accessed June 18, 2005.

Fletcher, Michael. 2000. "Asian Americans Using Politics as a Megaphone; Growing Population Confronts Bias." *Washington Post,* October 2, A-3.

Fogelson, Robert M. [1967] 1993. *The Fragmented Metropolis: Los Angeles, 1850–1930.* Reprint, Berkeley: University of California Press.

Foner, Nancy. 1997. "What's New about Transnationalism? New York Immigrants Today and at the Turn of the Century." *Diaspora* 6:355–75.

Foner, Nancy. 2000. *From Ellis Island to JFK: New York's Two Great Waves of Immigration.* New Haven: Yale University Press.

Fong, Timothy. 1994. *The First Suburban Chinatown: The Remaking of Monterey Park, California.* Philadelphia: Temple University Press.

Fountain, John. 2000. "The 2000 Campaign: The Hispanic Vote; Candidates Woo Latinos with Ads, but Not Policy." *New York Times,* November 6, A-26.

Fox, Jonathan, and Gaspar Rivera-Salgado. 2004. "Collective Identity and Organizational Strategies between Indigenous and Mestizo Mexican Immigrants." In *Indigenous Mexican Migrants in the United States,* edited by Jonathan Fox and Gaspar Rivera-Salgado. La Jolla: Center for U.S.-Mexican Studies and Center for Comparative Immigration Studies, University of California, San Diego.

Fox, Justin, and Indridi H. Indridason. 2001. "Optimal Campaign Spending in Elections." Paper presented at the annual meeting of the American Political Science Association, San Francisco.

Fraga, Luis R. 1988. "Domination through Democratic Means: Nonpartisan Slating Groups in City Electoral Politics." *Urban Affairs Quarterly* 23:528–55.

Fraga, Luis, and David Leal. 2004. "Playing the Latino Card: Race, Ethnicity, and National Party Politics." *Du Bois Review* 2:297–317.

Fraga, Luis R., and Ricardo Ramirez. 2000. "Evolving Opportunities: Latinos and the 2000 Election." Paper presented at the Conference on Census 2000, Lanier Public Policy Institute, University of Houston.

Fraga, Luis R., and Ricardo Ramirez. 2003. "Latino Political Incorporation in California." In *Latinos and Public Policy in California,* edited by Andrés Jiménez and David López. Los Angeles: Institute for Governmental Studies.

Frankel, Bruce. 1993. "Reality Dashes Refugees' Dreams. Hopes End in 'Work, Work, Work.'" *USA Today,* June 8, 3A.

Frymer, Paul. 1999. *Uneasy Alliances: Race and Party Competition in America.* Princeton: Princeton University Press.

Fuchs, Lawrence H. 1968. Introduction to *American Ethnic Politics,* edited by Lawrence H. Fuchs. New York: Harper and Row.

Fuchs, Lawrence H. 1990. *American Kaleidoscope: Race, Ethnicity, and the Civic Culture.* Hanover: University Press of New England.

Fulton, William. [1997] 2001. *The Reluctant Metropolis: The Politics of Urban Growth in Los Angeles.* Reprint, Baltimore: Johns Hopkins University Press.

Gans, Herbert. 1992. "Comment: Ethnic Invention and Acculturation, A Bumpy Line Approach." *Journal of American Ethnic History* 11:42–52.

Garcia, F. Chris, ed. 1997. *Pursuing Power: Latinos and the Political System.* Notre Dame: University of Notre Dame Press.

Garcia, John A., and Carlos Arce. 1988. "Political Orientations and Behaviors: Trying to Make Sense out of Attitudes and Participation." In *Latinos and the Political System,* edited by F. Chris Garcia. Notre Dame: University of Notre Dame Press.

Georges, Eugenia. 1990. *The Making of a Transnational Community: Migration, Development, and Cultural Change in the Dominican Republic.* New York: Columbia University Press.

Gerber, Alan, and Donald P. Green. 2000. "The Effects of Canvassing, Telephone Calls, and Direct Mail on Voter Turnout: A Field Experiment." *American Political Science Review* 94:653–63.

Gerber, Alan, and Donald P. Green. 2001. "Do Phone Calls Increase Voter Turnout? A Field Experiment." *Public Opinion Quarterly* 65:75–85.

Gerstle, Gary, and John Mollenkopf, eds. 2001. *E Pluribus Unum? Contemporary and Historical Perspectives on Immigrant Political Incorporation.* New York: Russell Sage.

Getlin, Josh. 2003. "Mexicans Finding a Place in a City of Immigrants." *Los Angeles Times,* October 6, A-10.

Geyer, Georgie Anne. 1996. *Americans No More.* New York: Atlantic Monthly Press.

Gibson, Campbell, and Emily Lennon. 1999. "Historical Census Statistics on the Foreign-born Population of the United States: 1850–1990." Population Division Working Paper 29. Available at http://www.census.gov/population/www/documentation/twps0029/twps0029.html#intro. Accessed June 17, 2005.

Glazer, Nathan, and Daniel Patrick Moynihan. 1964. *Beyond the Melting Pot: The Negroes, Puerto Ricans, Jews, Italians, and Irish of New York City.* Cambridge: MIT Press.

Glenn, Evelyn Nakano. 1985. "Racial and Ethnic Women's Labor: The Intersection of Race, Gender, and Class Oppression." *Review of Radical Political Economics* 17:86–108.

Gold, Matea. 1998. "Miracle Workers: A New Priest and a Multiracial Infusion of Newcomers Has Reinvigorated the Once Fading St. Agatha Catholic Church in Mid-City Area." *Los Angeles Times,* July 27, B-1.

Goldman, John. 2003. "2003 Freedom Ride Ends with a New York Rally; Thousands, Including Some Who Traveled on Three Buses from Los Angeles, Demonstrate to Highlight the Plight of Immigrant Workers." *Los Angeles Times,* October 5, A-25.

Gonzalez, Carolina, and Kevin McCoy. 1998. "Mexicans Put New Face on Nueva York; Surging Numbers of Immigrants Are Lured by Jobs, Opportunities." *New York Daily News,* June 21, 6.

Gordon, Milton. 1964. *Assimilation in American Life: The Role of Race, Religion, and National Origins.* New York: Oxford University Press.

Gosnell, Harold. 1927. *Getting out the Vote: An Experiment in the Stimulation of Voting.* Chicago: University of Chicago Press.

Graham, Pamela M. 1997. "Reimagining the Nation and Defining the District: Dominican Migration and Transnational Politics." In *Caribbean Circuits: New Directions in the Study of Caribbean Migration,* edited by Patricia R. Pessar. New York: Center for Migration Studies.

Graham, Pamela. 2001. "Political Incorporation and Re-Incorporation: Simultaneity in the Dominican Migrant Experience." In *Migration, Transnationalization, and Race in a Changing New York,* edited by Héctor R. Cordero-Guzmán, Robert C. Smith, and Ramón Grosfoguel. Philadelphia: Temple University Press.

Grasmuck, Sherri, and Patricia R. Pessar. 1991. *Between Two Islands: Dominican International Migration.* Berkeley: University of California Press.

Greeley, Andrew. 1981. *The Irish Americans.* New York: Harper and Row.

Green, Donald P., and Alan Gerber. 2002. "Reclaiming the Experimental Tradition in Political Science." In *State of the Discipline,* vol. 3, edited by H. Milner and Ira Katznelson. New York: Norton.

Green, John C., and Rick Farmer, eds. 2003. *The State of the Parties: The Changing Role of Contemporary American Parties.* 4th ed. Lanham, MD: Rowman and Littlefield.

Green, John C., and Paul Herrnson. 2002. "Party Development in the Twentieth Century: Laying the Foundations for Responsible Party Government." In *Responsible Partisanship? The Evolution of American Political Parties since 1950,* edited by John C. Green and Paul Herrnson. Lawrence: University Press of Kansas.

Green, Joshua. 2004. "Dumb and Dumber; Why Are Campaign Commercials So Bad?" *Atlantic Monthly* (electronic version), July/August. Available at http://www.theatlantic.com/doc/prem/200407/green. Accessed June 15, 2005.

Greenberg, Stanley, Matt Hogan, Mike Alvarez, and Jonathan Nagler. 2004. *Bush Faltering among Hispanic Voters—And in Key Battleground States.* Democracy Corps Report, July 26. Washington, DC: Democracy Corps.

Greenhouse, Steven. 1998a. "The 1998 Elections: Unions; Republicans Credit Labor for Success by Democrats." *New York Times,* November 6, A-28.

Greenhouse, Steven. 1998b. "In a Switch, Unions Begin Recognizing Republican Allies." *New York Times,* October 25, A-20.

Greenhouse, Steven. 2000a. "Despite Defeat on China Bill, Labor Is on the Rise." *New York Times,* May 30, A-6.

Greenhouse, Steven. 2000b. "Janitors, Long Paid Little, Demand a Larger Slice." *New York Times,* April 28, A-14.

Greenhouse, Steven. 2000c. "Labor Urges Amnesty for Illegal Immigrants." *New York Times,* February 17, A-26.

Greenstone, J. David. 1969. *Labor in American Politics.* New York: Knopf.

Guarnizo, Luis Eduardo, and Michael Peter Smith. 1998. "The Locations of Transnationalism." In *Transnationalism from Below,* edited by Michael Peter Smith and Luis Eduardo Guarnizo. New Brunswick, NJ: Transaction.

Guest, Kenneth J. 2003. *God in Chinatown: Religion and Survival in New York's Evolving Immigrant Community.* New York: New York University Press.

Guglielmo, Thomas A. 2003. *White on Arrival: Italians, Race, Color, and Power in Chicago, 1890–1945.* New York: Oxford University Press.

Gutierrez, Ramon. 1999. "Hispanic Diaspora and Chicano Identity in the United States." *South Atlantic Quarterly* 98:203–15.

Gutmann, Amy. 2003. *Identity in Democracy.* Princeton: Princeton University Press.

Guzman, Betsy. 2001. *Census 2000 Brief: The Hispanic Population 2000.* Washington, DC: U.S. Department of Commerce, Bureau of the Census.

Hajnal, Zoltan, and Mark Baldassare. 2001. *Finding Common Ground: Racial and Ethnic Attitudes in California.* San Francisco: Public Policy Institute of California.

Hajnal, Zoltan, Paul Lewis, and Hugh Louch. 2002. "Municipal Elections in California: Turnout, Timing and Competition." Public Policy Institute of California Report. San Francisco: Public Policy Institute of California.

Hall, Peter Dobkin. 1999. "Vital Signs: Organizational Population Trends and Civic Engagement in New Haven, Connecticut, 1850–1998." In *Civic Engagement in American Democracy,* edited by Theda Skocpol and Morris P. Fiorina. Washington, DC, and New York: Brookings Institution Press and Russell Sage.

Halle, David. 2003. "The New York and Los Angeles Schools." In *New York and Los Angeles: Politics, Society, and Culture: A Comparative View,* edited by David Halle. Chicago: University of Chicago Press.

Hamilton, Nora, and Norma Chinchilla. 2002. *Seeking Community in a Global City.* Philadelphia: Temple University Press.

Handlin, Oscar. 1951. *The Uprooted: The Epic Story of the Great Migrations That Made the American People.* Boston: Little, Brown.

Haney-Lopez, Ian. 1996. *White by Law: The Legal Construction of Race.* New York: New York University Press.

Hardy-Fanta, Carol. 1993. *Latina Politics, Latino Politics: Gender, Culture, and Political Participation in Boston.* Philadelphia: Temple University Press.

Harles, John C. 1993. *Politics in the Lifeboat: Immigrants and the American Democratic Order.* Boulder, CO: Westview.

Harney, James. 1992. "Monterey Park: The Chinatown of Suburban L.A." *USA Today,* May 11, A8.

Harris, Frederick. 1994. "Something Within: Religion as a Mobilizer of African American Political Activism." *Journal of Politics* 56:42–68.

Hatamiya, Leslie T. 1993. *Righting a Wrong: Japanese Americans and the Passage of the Civil Liberties Act of 1988.* Stanford: Stanford University Press.

Hayduk, Ron. 2002. *Non-Citizen Voting: Pipe Dream or Possibility?* Available at http://www.drummajorinstitute.org/plugin/template/dmi/30/1694. Accessed January 24, 2004.

Heimann, Jim. 1998. "The State: Sense of Place: Making over an Ethnic Center." *Los Angeles Times,* December 13, 1.

Hero, Rodney, and Anne G. Campbell. 1996. "Understanding Latino Political Participation: Exploring the Evidence from the Latino National Political Survey." *Hispanic Journal of Behavioral Sciences* 18:129–41.

Hero, Rodney, F. Chris Garcia, John Garcia, and Harry Pachon. 2000. "Latino Participation, Partisanship, and Office Holding." *PS: Political Science and Politics* 33:529–40.

Herszenhorn, David. 1998. "Mexicans Unite to Honor Their Spiritual Mother." *New York Times,* December 13, sec. 1, p. 51.

Higham, John. 1952. "Origins of Immigration Restriction, 1882–1897: A Social Analysis." *Mississippi Valley Historical Review* 39:77–88.

Hockenos, Paul. 2003. *Homeland Calling: Exile Patriotism and the Balkan Wars.* Ithaca: Cornell University Press.

Horsman, Reginald. 1981. *Race and Manifest Destiny: The Origins of American Racial Anglo-Saxonism.* Cambridge: Harvard University Press.

Horton, John. 1995. *The Politics of Diversity: Immigration, Resistance, and Change in Monterey Park, California.* Philadelphia: Temple University Press.

Houghland, James. 1983. "Religion and Politics: The Relationship of Religious Participation to Political Efficacy and Involvement." *Sociology and Social Research* 67:406–20.

Hrebenar, Ronald J., and Ruth K. Scott. 1990. *Interest Group Politics in America.* 2d ed. Englewood Cliffs, NJ: Prentice Hall.

Hsu, Madeline. 2000. *Dreaming of Gold, Dreaming of Home: Transnationalism and Migration between the U.S. and South China, 1882–1943.* Stanford: Stanford University Press.

Hua, Vanessa. 2004. "Asian Media Rip Kerry." *San Francisco Chronicle,* July 22, A-6.

Huckfeldt, Robert, and John Sprague. 1995. *Citizens, Politics, and Social Communication.* New York: Cambridge University Press.

Hum, Tarry, and Michaela Zonta. 2000. "Residential Patterns of Asian Pacific Americans." In *The State of Asian Pacific America: Transforming Race Relations,* edited by Paul M. Ong. Los Angeles: LEAP Asian Pacific American Policy Institute and UCLA Asian American Studies Center.

Huntington, Samuel P. 1968. *Political Order in Changing Societies.* New Haven: Yale University Press.

Huntington, Samuel P. 2004. *Who Are We? The Challenge to America's National Identity.* New York: Simon and Schuster.

Ignatiev, Noel. 1995. *How the Irish Became White*. London: Verso.

Inter-University Program for Latino Research. 2002. *Latino Population Change for Specific Country of Origin by Place (Cities): 1990–2000*. Available at http://www.nd.edu/~iuplr/cic/ethnic_place_htmlfiles/ethnic_place.html. Accessed January 18, 2004.

Itzigsohn, Jose. 2000. "Immigration and the Boundaries of Citizenship: The Institutions of Immigrants' Political Transnationalism." *International Migration Review* 34:1126–55.

Iwabuchi, Koichi. 2002. *Recentering Globalization: Popular Culture and Japanese Transnationalism*. Durham: Duke University Press.

Jackson, Byran O. 1987. "The Effects of Racial Group Consciousness on Political Mobilization in American Cities." *Western Political Quarterly* 40:631–46.

Jacobson, Matthew Frye. 1995. *Special Sorrows: The Diasporic Imagination of Irish, Polish, and Jewish Immigrants in the United States*. Cambridge: Harvard University Press.

Jacobson, Matthew Frye. 1998. *Whiteness of a Different Color*. Cambridge: Harvard University Press.

Jamieson, Amie, Hyon B. Shin, and Jennifer Day. 2002. *Voting and Registration in the Election of November 2000*. Washington, DC: U.S. Department of Commerce, Bureau of the Census.

Jennings, James. 1988. "The Puerto Rican Community: Its Political Background." In *Latinos and the Political System,* edited by F. Chris Garcia. Notre Dame: University of Notre Dame Press.

Johnson, James H., Walter C. Farrell Jr., and Chandra Guinn. 1997. "Immigration Reform and the Browning of America: Tensions, Conflicts, and Community Instability." *International Migration Review* 31:1029–69.

Jones-Correa, Michael. 1998. *Between Two Nations: The Political Predicament of Latinos in New York City*. Ithaca: Cornell University Press.

Jones-Correa, Michael, ed. 2001. *Governing in American Cities*. New York: Russell Sage.

Jones-Correa, Michael, and David Leal. 1996. "Becoming 'Hispanic': Secondary Panethnic Identification among Latin American-Origin Populations in the United States." *Hispanic Journal of Behavioral Sciences* 18:214–54.

Jones-Correa, Michael, and David Leal. 2001. "Political Participation: Does Religion Matter?" *Political Research Quarterly* 54:751–70.

Joppke, Christian, and Ewa Morawska, eds. 2003. *Toward Assimilation and Citizenship: Immigrants in Liberal Nation-States*. New York: Palgrave Macmillan.

Junn, Jane. 1999. "Participation in a Liberal Democracy: The Political Assimilation of Immigrants and Ethnic Minorities in the United States." *American Behavioral Scientist* 42:1417–38.

Kanuha, Valli Kalei. 2000. "'Being' Native versus 'Going Native': Conducting Social Work Research as an Insider." *Social Work* 45:439–49.

Karpathakis, Anna. 1999. "Home Society Politics and Immigrant Political Incorporation: The Case of Greek Immigrants in New York City." *International Migration Review* 33:55–79.

Kasinitz, Philip. 1992. *Caribbean New York: Black Immigrants and the Politics of Race*. Ithaca: Cornell University Press.

Katerberg, William. 1995. "The Irony of Identity: An Essay on Nativism, Liberal Democracy, and Parochial Identities in Canada and the United States." *American Quarterly* 47:493–524.

Katznelson, Ira. 1981. *City Trenches: Urban Politics and the Patterning of Class in the United States*. New York: Pantheon.

Kelley, Robin D. G. 1994. *Race Rebels: Culture, Politics, and the Black Working Class*. New York: Free Press.

Kim, Claire Jean. 1999. "The Racial Triangulation of Asian Americans." *Politics and Society* 27:105–38.

Kim, Claire Jean. 2000. *Bitter Fruit: The Politics of Black-Korean Conflict in New York City*. New Haven: Yale University Press.

Kim, Janet. 2002. "Close Up On: Flushing." *Village Voice*, October 9–15, 155.

Kraut, Alan M. 1982. *The Huddled Masses: The Immigrant in American Society, 1880–1921*. Arlington Heights, IL: Harlan Davidson.

Kwoh, Stewart, and Mindy Hui. 1993. "Empowering Our Communities: Political Policy." In *The State of Asian Pacific America: Policy Issues to the Year 2020*. Los Angeles: LEAP Asian Pacific American Public Policy Institute and UCLA Asian American Studies Center.

Kwong, Peter. 1996. *The New Chinatown*. 2d ed. New York: Hill and Wang.

Kwong, Peter. 1997. *Forbidden Workers: Illegal Chinese Immigrants and American Labor*. New York: New Press.

Kymlicka, Will. 1995. *Multicultural Citizenship*. New York: Oxford University Press.

Ladd, Everett, and Charles Hadley. 1975. *Transformations of the American Party System*. New York: Norton.

Lai, Eric, and Dennis Arguelles, eds. 2003. *The New Face of Asian Pacific America: Numbers, Diversity, and Change in the Twenty-first Century*. San Francisco: Asian Week, UCLA Asian American Studies Center Press.

Lai, James. 2000. "Beyond Voting: The Recruitment of Asian Pacific American Elected Officials and Their Impact on Group Political Mobilization." Ph.D. diss., University of Southern California.

Lambro, Donald. 2002. "GOP Bidding for Union Support." *Washington Times*, May 23, A-19.

Lapinski, John S., Pia Peltola, Greg Shaw, and Alan Yang. 1997. "Immigrants and Immigration." *Public Opinion Quarterly* 61:356–83.

Laslett, John H. M. 1996. "Historical Perspectives: Immigration and the Rise of a Distinctive Urban Region, 1900–1970." In *Ethnic Los Angeles,* edited by Roger Waldinger and Mehdi Bozorgmehr. New York. Russell Sage.

LeDuc, Daniel, and R. H. Melton. 2000. "Delegations Reflect Gains in Grass-Roots Diversity." *Washington Post*, August 3, A-1.

Lee, Robert. 1999. *Orientals: Asian Americans in Popular Culture*. Philadelphia: Temple University Press.

Lee, Taeku. 2000. "Racial Attitudes and the Color Line(s) at the Close of the Twentieth Century." In *The State of Asian Pacific America: Transforming Race*

Relations, edited by Paul M. Ong. Los Angeles: LEAP Asian Pacific American Policy Institute and UCLA Asian American Studies Center.

Lee, Taeku. 2004. "Social Construction, Self-Identification, and the Survey Measurement of 'Race.'" Paper presented at the annual meeting of the American Political Science Association, Chicago.

Leighley, Jan. 2001. *Strength in Numbers? The Political Mobilization of Racial and Ethnic Minorities.* Princeton: Princeton University Press.

Leighley, Jan, and Arnold Vedlitz. 1999. "Race, Ethnicity, and Political Participation: Competing Models and Contrasting Explanations." *Journal of Politics* 61:1092–1114.

Levitt, Peggy. 2001. *The Transnational Villagers.* Berkeley: University of California Press.

Levitt, Peggy. 2002. "Migrant Philanthropy in Latin America: Move over United Way." *ReVista: Harvard Review of Latin America.* Available at http://drclas .fas.harvard.edu/publications/revista/Volunteering/levitt.html. Accessed January 27, 2004.

Li, Wei. 1999. "Building Ethnoburbia: The Emergence and Manifestation of the Chinese Ethnoburb in Los Angeles' San Gabriel Valley." *Journal of Asian American Studies* 2:1–28.

Lie, John. 1995. "From International Migration to Transnational Diaspora." *Contemporary Sociology* 24:303–6.

Lien, Pei-te. 1994. "Ethnicity and Political Participation: A Comparison between Asian and Mexican Americans." *Political Behavior* 16:237–64.

Lien, Pei-te. 1997. *The Political Participation of Asian Americans: Voting Behavior in Southern California.* New York: Garland.

Lien, Pei-te. 2000. "Who Votes in Multiracial America? An Analysis of Voting and Registration by Race and Ethnicity, 1990–96." In *Black and Multiracial Politics in America,* edited by Yvette Alex-Assensoh and Lawrence Hanks. New York: New York University Press.

Lien, Pei-te. 2001. *The Making of Asian America through Political Participation.* Philadelphia: Temple University Press.

Lien, Pei-te. 2004. "Ethnic Homeland of Political Participation: The Case of Chinese Immigrants from Taiwan." Paper presented at the annual meeting of the American Political Science Association, Chicago.

Lien, Pei-te. 2005. "Is Homeland Concern a Deterrent of or a Catalyst for Chinese American Participation in U.S. Politics?" Paper presented at the 2005 annual meeting of the Association for Asian American Studies, Los Angeles.

Lien, Pei-te, M. Margaret Conway, and Janelle Wong. 2003. "The Contours and Sources of Ethnic Identity Choices among Asian Americans." *Social Science Quarterly* 84:461–81.

Lien, Pei-te, M. Margaret Conway, and Janelle Wong. 2004. *The Politics of Asian Americans: Diversity and Community.* New York: Routledge.

Lii, Jane. 1994a. "Neighborhood Report: Chinatown: Latest Wave of Immigrants Is Splitting Chinatown." *New York Times,* June 12, CY6.

Lii, Jane. 1994b. "Neighborhood Report: Lower Manhattan: A New Attraction on Tourist Maps: Chinatown East?" *New York Times,* December 18, CY6.

Lii, Jane. 1996. "Neighborhood Report: Flatbush; Stabbing Stirs Ethnic Dispute." *New York Times,* August 25, sec. 13, p. 9.

Lin, Ann Chih. Forthcoming. "Group Inclusion or Group Rights?: Ethnic Advocacy Groups and the Political Incorporation of Immigrants." In *Framing Equality: Inclusion, Exclusion, and American Political Institutions,* edited by K. Haynie and D. Tichenor.

Lin, Jan. 1998. *Reconstructing Chinatown: Ethnic Enclaves and Global Change.* Minneapolis: University of Minnesota Press.

Lipsitz, George. 1998. *The Possessive Investment in Whiteness: How White People Profit from Identity Politics.* Philadelphia: Temple University Press.

Lollock, Lisa. 2001. *The Foreign-Born Population in the United States: March 2000.* U.S. Census Bureau, Current Population Reports, Series P20–534. Washington, DC: U.S. Government Printing Office.

Lopez, David, and Yen Le Espiritu. 1990. "Panethnicity in the United States: A Theoretical Framework." *Ethnic and Racial Studies* 13:198–224.

Los Angeles Times. 2004. *2004 Presidential Election National Exit Poll.* Available at http://a1022.g.akamai.net/f/1022/8158/5m/images.latimes.com/media/acrobat/2004-11/14935824.pdf. Accessed November 5, 2004.

Louie, Miriam Ching. 1997. "Breaking the Cycle: Women Workers Confront Corporate Greed Locally." In *Dragon Ladies: Asian American Feminists Breathe Fire,* edited by Sonia Shah. Cambridge, MA: South End Press.

Lowe, Lisa. 1996. *Immigrant Acts on Asian American Cultural Politics.* Durham, NC: Duke University Press.

Lowe, Lisa. 1998. "Work, Immigration, Gender: New Subjects of Cultural Politics." *Social Justice* 25:31–42.

Mahler, Sarah J. 1996. "Theoretical and Empirical Contributions toward a Research Agenda for Transnationalism." In *Transnationalism from Below,* edited by Michael Peter Smith and Luis Eduardo Guarnizo. New Brunswick, NJ: Transaction.

Malone, Nolan, Kaari Baluja, Joseph Costanzo, and Cynthia Davis. 2003. *The Foreign Born Population 2000: Census Brief.* C2KBR-34. Washington, DC: U.S. Census Bureau.

Mantsios, Gregory, ed. 1998. *A New Labor Movement for the New Century.* New York: Monthly Review Press.

Marable, Manning. 1984. *Race, Reform and Rebellion: The Second Reconstruction in Black America, 1945–1982.* Jackson: University of Mississippi Press.

Marcelli, Enrico A., and Wayne A. Cornelius. 2005. "Immigrant Voting in Home-Country Elections: Potential Consequences of Extending the Franchise to Expatriate Mexicans." *Mexican Studies/Estudios Mexicanos* 21:431–61.

Marshall, Adriana. 1987. "New Immigrants in New York's Economy." In *New Immigrants in New York,* edited by Nancy Foner. New York: Columbia University Press.

Massey, Douglas, Rafael Alarcon, Jorge Durand, and Humberto Gonzalez. 1987. *Return to Azlan: The Social Process of International Migration in Western Mexico.* Berkeley: University of California Press.

Massey, Douglas, Jorge Durand, and Nolan Malone. 2002. *Beyond Smoke and Mirrors: Mexican Immigration in an Era of Economic Integration.* New York: Russell Sage.

McCoy, Kevin. 1998. "City's Neighborhoods Savor Mexican Flavor." *New York Daily News,* June 21, 1998, 35.

McHugh, Margie. 2000. Paper presented at Immigrant Participation in New York City: A Working Conference, Center for Urban Research, City University of New York Graduate Center.

Medeiros, Jillian. 2004. "The Silenced Issues: A Look at Latinas and the Political Issues of Abortion." Paper presented at the Conference of Ethnic Studies in California, University of California, San Diego.

Milkman, Ruth, ed. 2000. *Organizing Immigrants: The Challenge for Unions in Contemporary California.* Ithaca: Cornell University Press.

Milkman, Ruth, and Kent Wong. 2000. *Voices from the Front Lines: Organizing Immigrant Workers in Los Angeles.* Los Angeles: UCLA, Center for Labor Research and Education.

Miller, Donald, Jon Miller, and Grace Dyrness. 2001. *Immigrant Religion in the City of Angels.* Center for Religion and Civic Culture, University of Southern California.

Mink, Gwendolyn. 1986. *Old Labor and New Immigrants in American Political Development: Union, Party, and State, 1875–1920.* Ithaca: Cornell University Press.

Mogelonsky, Marcia. 1997. "Natural(ized) Americans." *American Demographics* 19:45–49.

Mollenkopf, John. 1992. *A Phoenix in the Ashes: The Rise and Fall of the Koch Coalition in New York City Politics.* Princeton: Princeton University Press.

Mollenkopf, John. 1999. "Urban Political Conflicts and Alliances: New York and Los Angeles Compared." In *Handbook of Immigration: The American Experience,* edited by Charles Hirshman, Philip Kasinitz, and Josh DeWind. New York: Russell Sage.

Mollenkopf, John, with David Olson and Timothy Ross. 2001. "Immigrant Political Participation in New York and Los Angeles." In *Governing in American Cities,* edited by Michael Jones-Correa. New York: Russell Sage.

Mollenkopf, John, Timothy Ross, and David Olson. 1999. "Immigrant Political Participation in New York and Los Angeles." Paper presented at the Project on Negotiating Difference, International Center for Migration, Ethnicity and Citizenship, New School University, New York.

Morawksa, Ewa. 2001. "Immigrants, Transnationalism, and Ethnicization: A Comparison of This Great Wave and the Last." In *E Pluribus Unum? Contemporary and Historical Perspectives on Immigrant Political Incorporation,* edited by Gary Gerstle and John Mollenkopf. New York: Russell Sage.

Moreno, Dario. 1997. "The Cuban Model: Political Empowerment in Miami." In *Pursuing Power: Latinos in the Political System,* edited by F. Chris Garcia. Notre Dame: University of Notre Dame Press.

Morris, Aldon. 1984. *The Origins of the Civil Rights Movement: Black Communities Organizing for Change.* New York: Free Press.

Munch, Richard. 2001. *Nation and Citizenship in the Global Age: From National to Transnational Ties and Identities.* New York: Palgrave.

Muñoz, Carlos. 1989. *Youth, Identity, Power: The Chicano Movement.* New York: Verso.

Musso, Juliet, Chris Weare, Kyu-Nahm Jun, and Alicia Kitsuse. 2004. *Representing Diversity in Community Governance: Neighborhood Councils in Los Angeles.* Neighborhood Participation Project, School of Policy, Planning, and Development, University of Southern California. Available at http://urban.usc.edu/main_doc/downloads/nc_diversity.pdf. Accessed June 20, 2005.

Mustain, Gene. 1997. "A Chinatown Grows in Brooklyn, Too." *New York Daily News,* October 27, 34.

Myer, Julie. 2001. "Age: 2000." *Census 2000 Brief, C2KBR/01–12.* Washington, DC: U.S. Census Bureau.

Myers, Dowell, and John Pitkin. 2001. *Demographic Futures for California.* Los Angeles: Population Dynamics Group, School of Policy, Planning, and Development, University of Southern California.

Myers, Dowell, John Pitkin, and Julie Park. 2005. *California Demographic Futures Projections to 2030, by Immigrant Generations, Nativity, and Time of Arrival in U.S.* Population Dynamics Research Group, School of Policy, Planning, and Development, University of Southern California.

Nakanishi, Don T. 1991. "The Next Swing Vote? Asian Pacific Americans and California Politics." In *Racial and Ethnic Politics in California,* edited by Byran O. Jackson and Michael B. Preston. Berkeley: Institute of Governmental Studies Press, University of California, Berkeley.

Nakanishi, Don T. 1998. "When the Numbers Do Not Add Up: Asian Pacific Americans and California Politics." In *Racial and Ethnic Politics in California,* edited by Michael Preston, Bruce E. Cain, and Sandra Bass. Berkeley: Institute of Governmental Studies Press, University of California.

Nakanishi, Don. 1999a. "Drive-by Victims of DNC Greed." In *1998–1999 National Asian Pacific American Political Almanac,* edited by James Lai. Los Angeles: UCLA Asian American Studies Center.

Nakanishi, Don T. 1999b. "Issue Focus: The Campaign Finance Controversy." In *National Asian Pacific American Political Almanac,* edited by James Lai. Los Angeles: UCLA Asian American Studies Center.

Nakanishi, Don T. 2001. "Beyond Electoral Politics: Renewing a Search for a Paradigm of Asian Pacific American Politics." In *Asian Americans and Politics: Perspectives, Experiences, and Prospects,* edited by Gordon Chang. Stanford: Stanford University Press.

National Association of Latino Elected Officials. 2005. "NALEO Education Fund Analysis of the Vote by Council District." Available at http://www.naleo.org/press_releases/NALEO_Analysis_of_the_Vote.pdf. Accessed June 15, 2005.

Neal, Terry M. 2003. "The Ghost of Prop. 187." *Washington Post.* Available at http://www.washingtonpost.com/ac2/wp-dyn?pagename=article&node

=&contentId=A29830-2003Sep5&notFound=true. Accessed December 5, 2003.

Neuman, Johanna. 2004. "The Republican Convention; GOP to Show a New Face to Minorities; More Delegates Will Be Black and Latino, but Bush's Record May Be a Hindrance." *Los Angeles Times,* August 29, A-26.

New California Media. 2004. "National Survey of Asian and Pacific Islander Likely Voters in the United States." Available at http://www.ncmonline.com/media/pdf/polls/apia_presentation.pdf. Accessed June 20, 2005.

New York City Department of Planning. 2001a. Manhattan Community District 3. Available at http://www.ci.nyc.ny.us/html/dcp/pdf/lucds/mn3profile.pdf. Accessed June 15, 2005.

New York City Department of Planning. 2001b. Community District Profiles. Available at http://www.ci.nyc.ny.us/html/dcp/html/lucds/cdstart.html. Accessed June 15, 2005.

New York Immigration Coalition. n.d. "Background Information." In *Informational Flyer.* New York: New York Immigration Coalition.

New York Immigration Coalition. 2000. "Horror Stories That May Surprise You." *The Newcomer* (spring): 4.

Ngai, Mae M. 1997. "Who Is An American Worker? Asian Immigrants, Race, and the National Boundaries of Class." In *Audacious Democracy: Labor, Intellectuals, and the Social Reconstruction of America,* edited by S. Fraser and J. B. Freeman. Boston: Houghton Mifflin.

Ngai, Mae M. 1999. "The Architecture of Race in American Immigration Law: A Reexamination of the Immigration Act of 1924." *Journal of American History* 86:67–92.

Niebuhr, Gustav. 2000. "Vietnamese Immigrants Swell Catholic Clergy." *New York Times,* April 24, A-17.

Nobles, Melissa. 2000. *Shades of Citizenship: Race and the Census in Modern Politics.* Palo Alto: Stanford University Press.

Nownes, Anthony, and Grant Neeley. 1996. "Toward an Explanation for Public Interest Group Formation and Proliferation: 'Seed Money,' Disturbances, Entrepreneurship, and Patronage." *Policy Studies Journal* 24:74–97.

Oboler, Suzanne. 1995. *Ethnic Labels, Latino Lives: Identity and Politics of (Re)Presentation in the United States.* Minneapolis: University of Minnesota Press.

Okihiro, Gary Y. 2001. *Common Ground: Reimagining American History.* Princeton: Princeton University Press.

Omi, Michael, and Howard Winant. 1994. *Racial Formation in the United States: From the 1960s to the 1990s.* 2d ed. New York: Routledge.

Ong, Paul, and Don T. Nakanishi. 1996. "Becoming Citizens, Becoming Voters: The Naturalization and Political Participation of Asian Pacific Immigrants." In *Reframing the Immigration Debate,* edited by Bill Ong Hing and Ronald Lee. Los Angeles: LEAP Asian Pacific American Public Policy Institute and UCLA Asian American Studies Center.

Orr, John. 1999. *Religion and Multiethnicity in Los Angeles.* Los Angeles: Center for Religion and Civic Culture, University of Southern California.

Ortiz, Vilma. 1996. "The Mexican-Origin Population: Permanent Working Class or Emerging Middle Class?" In *Ethnic Los Angeles,* edited by Roger Waldinger and Mehdi Bozorgmehr. New York: Russell Sage.

Pachon, Harry. 1998. "Latino Politics in the Golden State: Ready for the 21st Century?" In *Racial and Ethnic Politics in California,* edited by Michael B. Preston, Bruce E. Cain, and Sandra Bass. Berkeley: Institute of Governmental Studies Press, University of California.

Padilla, Laura. 1998. "Single-Parent Latinas on the Margin: Seeking a Room with a View, Meals, and Built-in Community." *Wisconsin Women's Law Journal* 13:179–221.

Page, Susan. 2004. "Incumbents Have Never Been So Safe." *USA Today.* Available at http://www.usatoday.com/news/nation/2002–10–29-redistricting-usat-1Acover_x.htm. Accessed November 13, 2004.

Pantoja, Adrian. 2005. "At Home Abroad? The Dominican Diaspora in New York City as a Transnational Political Actor." Paper presented at the annual meeting of the Western Political Science Association, Oakland.

Pantoja, Adrian, Ricardo Ramirez, and Gary Segura. 2001. "Citizens by Choice, Voters by Necessity: Patterns in Political Mobilization in Naturalized Latinos." *Political Research Quarterly* 54:729–50.

Pardo, Mary. 1998. *Mexican American Women Activists: Identity and Resistance in Two Los Angeles Neighborhoods.* Philadelphia: Temple University Press.

Park, Robert. 1925. "The City: Suggestions for the Investigation of Human Behavior in the Urban Environment." In *The City,* edited by Robert E. Park, Ernest Burgess, and Roderick McKenzie. Chicago: University of Chicago Press.

Passell, Jeffrey. 2004. *The Latino and Asian Vote.* Available at http://www.urban.org/UploadedPDF/900723.pdf. Accessed September 11, 2004.

Pateman, Carole. 1970. *Participation and Democratic Theory.* New York: Cambridge University Press.

Patterson, Thomas. 2004. "First-Time Voters Propelled to Polls by Personal Contact: Non-Voters Discouraged by Election Procedures." The Vanishing Voter Project, Shorenstein Center on the Press, Politics, and Public Policy, Harvard University, November 11. Available at http://www.vanishingvoter.org/Releases/release111104_tables.shtml. Accessed June 20, 2005.

Peel, Roy V. 1968 (1935). *The Political Clubs of New York.* New York: Friedman.

Perea, Juan F. 1997. "The Black/White Binary Paradigm of Race: The 'Normal Science' of American Racial Thought." *California Law Review* 85:1242–51.

Perea, Juan F., Richard Delgado, Angela P. Harris, and Stephanie Wildman, eds. 2000. *Race and Races: Cases and Resources for a Diverse America.* St. Paul: West.

Pessar, Patricia R. 1987. "The Dominicans: Women in the Household and the Garment Industry." In *New Immigrants in New York,* edited by Nancy Foner. New York: Columbia University Press.

Pessar, Patricia R., ed. 1997. *Caribbean Circuits: New Directions in the Study of Caribbean Migration*. New York: Center for Migration Studies.

Pew Hispanic Center/Kaiser Family Foundation. 2002. *2002 National Survey of Latinos*. Menlo Park, CA, and Washington, DC: Pew Hispanic Center/Kaiser Family Foundation.

Pinderhughes, Dianne M. 1987. *Race and Ethnicity in Chicago Politics: A Reexamination of Pluralist Theory*. Urbana: University of Illinois Press.

Piven, Francis Fox, and Richard Cloward. 1978. *Poor People's Movements*. New York: Vintage.

Portes, Alejandro. 1996. "Global Villagers: The Rise of Transnational Communities." *American Prospect*, no. 25:74–77.

Portes, Alejandro, and Rubén G. Rumbaut. 1996. *Immigrant America: A Portrait*. Berkeley: University of California Press.

Portes, Alejandro, and Rubén G. Rumbaut. 2001. *Legacies*. New York and Berkeley: Russell Sage and University of California Press.

Putnam, Robert. 2000. *Bowling Alone*. New York: Touchstone.

Rainey, James. 2004. "Election 2004: Balloting Is Boosted by Young and Conservative." *Los Angeles Times*, November 4, A-31.

Ramakrishnan, S. Karthick. 2003. "Race, Political Incorporation, and Civic Voluntarism in the United States." Paper presented at A Nation of Immigrants, Institute for Governmental Studies, University of California, Berkeley.

Ramakrishnan, S. Karthick. 2005. *Democracy in Immigrant America: Changing Demographics and Political Participation*. Stanford: Stanford University Press.

Ramakrishnan, S. Karthick, and Thomas Espenshade. 2001. "Immigrant Incorporation and Political Participation in the United States." *International Migration Review* 35:870–909.

Ramirez, Margaret. 1999. "Huge Throng Hails Virgin of Guadalupe: More Than 50, 000 Attend Service at the Coliseum to See the Icon's Image and Celebrate Her Feast Day." *Los Angeles Times,* December 12, B-1.

Ramirez, Ricardo. Forthcoming. "Giving Voice to Latino Voters: A Field Experiment on the Effectiveness of a National Non-Partisan Mobilization Effort." *Annals of Social and Political Science*.

Ramirez, Ricardo, Alan Gerber, and Donald Green. 2004. *Evaluation of NALEO's 2002 "Voces del Pueblo" Voter Mobilization Campaign*. Los Angeles: National Association of Latino Elected Officials Education Fund.

Ratcliffe, R. G. 2004. "2004 Democratic Convention: Boston: Sleeping Giant." *Houston Chronicle,* July 30, A-3.

Reichley, A. James. 1992. *The Life of the Parties: A History of American Political Parties*. New York: Free Press.

Riley, Michael. 2004. "Hispanics Register on Parties' Radar." *Denver Post*, February 1, 1.

Ríos-Bustamante, Antonio José, and Pedro G. Castillo. 1986. *An Illustrated History of Mexican Los Angeles, 1781–1985*. Los Angeles: University of California Chicano Studies Research Center Publications.

Rivera-Salgado, Gaspar, Rigoberto Rodriguez, and Luis Escala-Rabadan. 2004.

Building Capacity: Insights from the Pilot Program on Immigrant-Led Home-town Associations. Los Angeles: Center for Religion and Civic Culture at the University of Southern California and the Los Angeles Immigrant Funders' Collaborative.

Rodriguez, Cindy. 2001. "Census Bolsters Theory Illegal Immigrants Undercounted." *Boston Globe,* March 20, A-4.

Rogers, Reuel. 2000a. "Between Race and Ethnicity: Afro-Caribbean Immigrants, African Americans, and the Politics of Incorporation." Ph.D. diss., Princeton University.

Rogers, Reuel. 2000b. "Afro-Caribbean Immigrants, African Americans, and the Politics of Group Identity." In *Black and Multiracial Politics in America,* edited by Yvette Alex-Assensoh and Lawrence Hanks. New York: New York University Press.

Romero, Mary. 1992. *Maid in the U.S.A.* New York: Routledge.

Rosenblum, Gerald. 1973. *Immigrant Workers: Their Impact on American Radicalism.* New York: Basic Books.

Rosenstone, Steven J., and John Mark Hansen. 1993. *Mobilization, Participation, and Democracy in America.* New York: Macmillan.

Rossiter, Clinton. 1960. *Parties and Politics in America.* Ithaca: Cornell University Press.

Rouse, Roger. 1992. "Making Sense of Settlement: Class Transformation, Cultural Struggle, and Transnationalism among Mexican Migrants in the United States." In *Towards a Transnational Perspective on Migration: Race, Class, Ethnicity, and Nationalism Reconsidered,* edited by Nina Glick Schiller, Linda Basch, and Cristina Szanton Blanc. New York: New York Academy of Sciences.

Ruiz, Albor. 1999. "A Fresh Look at Chinese Immigration Story." *New York Daily News,* September 9, 3.

Sabagh, Georges, and Mehdi Bozorgmehr. 2003. "From 'Give Me Your Poor' to 'Save Our State': New York and Los Angeles as Immigrant Cities and Regions. In *New York and Los Angeles: Politics, Society, and Culture, A Comparative View,* edited by David Halle. Chicago: University of Chicago Press.

Safa, Helen I. 1988. "Migration and Identity: A Comparison of Puerto Rican and Cuban Migrants in the United States." In *The Hispanic Experience in the United States: Contemporary Issues and Perspectives,* edited by Edna Acosta-Belen and Barbara Sjorstrom. Westport, CT: Praeger.

Saito, Leland. 1998. *Race and Politics: Asian Americans, Latinos, and Whites in a Los Angeles Suburb.* Philadelphia: Temple University Press.

Saito, Leland. 2003. "The Politics of Race and Redistricting in California, 2000–2002." Paper presented at A Nation of Immigrants, Institute for Governmental Studies, University of California, Berkeley.

Saito, Leland, and Edward Park. 2000. "Multiracial Collaborations and Coalitions." In *The State of Asian Pacific America: Transforming Race Relations,* edited by Paul M. Ong. Los Angeles: LEAP Asian Pacific American Policy Institute and UCLA Asian American Studies Center.

Salter, J. T. 1935. *Boss Rule: Portraits in City Politics.* New York: McGraw-Hill.

Sanchez, George J. 1993. *Becoming Mexican American: Ethnicity, Culture, and Identity in Chicano Los Angeles, 1900–1945.* New York: Oxford University Press.

Sanjek, Roger. 1998. *The Future of Us All: Race and Neighborhood Politics in New York City.* Ithaca: Cornell University Press.

Santa Ana, Otto. 2002. *Brown Tide Rising: Metaphors of Latinos in Contemporary American Public Discourse.* Austin: University of Texas Press.

Sawyer, Mark Q., Yesilernis Peña, and Jim Sidanius. 2004. "Cuban Exceptionalism: Group-Based Hierarchy and the Dynamics of Patriotism in Puerto Rico, the Dominican Republic and Cuba." *DuBois Review,* no. 1:93–113.

Schattschneider, E. E. 1942. *Party Government.* New York: Farrar and Rinehart.

Schattschneider, E. E. 1957. "The United States: The Functional Approach to Party Government." In *Modern Political Parties,* edited by Sigmund Neuman. Chicago: University of Chicago Press.

Schier, Steven E. 2002. "From Melting Pot to Centrifuge: Immigrants and American Politics." *Brookings Review* 20:16–19.

Schlesinger, Arthur M. 1993. *The Disuniting of America.* New York: Norton.

Schlozman, Kay Lehman, Sidney Verba, and Henry Brady. 1999. "Civic Participation and the Equality Problem." *Civic Engagement in American Democracy,* edited by Theda Skocpol and Morris P. Fiorina. Washington, DC, and New York: Brookings Institution Press and Russell Sage.

Schmidley, A. Dianne. 2001. *Profile of the Foreign-Born Population in the United States: 2000.* U.S. Census Bureau, Current Population Reports, Series P23–206. Washington, DC: U.S. Government Printing Office.

Schmidt-Camacho, Alicia. 1999. "On the Borders of Solidarity: Race and Gender Contradictions in the 'New Voice' Platform of the AFL-CIO." *Social Justice* 26:79–102.

Schwartz, Emma. 2004. "The Race to the White House; Asian Voters Tilt to Kerry." *Los Angeles Times,* September 15, A-21.

Scott, Allen J. 1996. "The Manufacturing Economy: Ethnic and Gender Divisions of Labor." In *Ethnic Los Angeles,* edited by Roger Waldinger and Mehdi Bozorgmehr. New York: Russell Sage.

Scott, James C. 1985. *Weapons of the Weak.* New Haven: Yale University Press.

Scott, Ruth K., and Ronald Hrebenar. 1984. *Parties in Crisis.* New York: Wiley.

Seelye, Katharine. 1998. "The 1998 Campaign; Turnout; Leery of Backfiring TV Ads, Interest Groups Return to Doorbell, Phone, and Pamphlet." *New York Times,* November 2, A-20.

Seelye, Katharine. 2001. "Poverty Rates Fell in 2000, but Income Was Stagnant." *New York Times,* September 26, A-12.

Segal, Adam. 2004. *Bikini Politics: The 2004 Presidential Campaigns' Hispanic Media Efforts Cover Only the Essential Parts of the Body Politic; A Select Group of Voters in a Few Battleground States.* Baltimore: Hispanic Voter Project, Johns Hopkins University.

Shah, Sonia. 1994. "Presenting the Blue Goddess: Towards a National, Pan-Asian

Feminist Agenda." In *The State of Asian America: Activism and Resistance in the 1990's,* edited by Karin Aguilar-San Juan. Boston: South End Press.

Shah, Sonia. 1997. "Redefining the Home." In *Dragon Ladies: Asian American Feminists Breathe Fire,* edited by Sonia Shah. Boston: South End Press.

Shannon, William. 1963. *The American Irish.* New York: Macmillan.

Sharp, Deborah. 2000. "George Bush at Center of Campaign Buzz." *USA Today.* Available at http://www.usatoday.com/news/opinion/e2099.htm. Accessed December 22, 2003.

Shaw, Daron, Rodolfo de la Garza, and Jongho Lee. 2000. "Examining Latino Turnout in 1996: A Three-State, Validated Survey Approach." *American Journal of Political Science* 44:338–46.

Shea, Daniel. 2003. "Schattschneider's Dismay: Strong Parties and Alienated Voters." In *The State of the Parties: The Changing Role of Contemporary American Parties,* edited by John Green and Rick Farmer. Lanham, MD: Rowman and Littlefield.

Shinagawa, Larry Hajime. 1996. "The Impact of Immigration on the Demography of Asian Pacific Americans." In *Reframing the Immigration Debate,* edited by Bill Ong Hing and Ronald Lee. Los Angeles: LEAP Asian Pacific American Public Policy Institute and UCLA Asian American Studies Center.

Skerry, Peter. 1993. *Mexican Americans: The Ambivalent Minority.* Cambridge: Harvard University Press.

Skerry, Peter. 1997. "E Pluribus Hispanic?" In *Pursuing Power: Latinos and the Political System,* edited by F. Chris Garcia. Notre Dame: Notre Dame University Press.

Skocpol, Theda. 1999a. "Advocates without Members: The Recent Transformation of American Civic Life." In *Civic Engagement in American Democracy,* edited by Theda Skocpol and Morris P. Fiorina. Washington, DC, and New York: Brookings Institution Press and Russell Sage.

Skocpol, Theda. 1999b. "How Americans Became Civic." In *Civic Engagement in American Democracy,* edited by Theda Skocpol and Morris P. Fiorina. Washington, DC, and New York: Brookings Institution Press and Russell Sage.

Smart, Alan, and Josephine Smart. 1998. "Transnational Social Networks and Negotiated Identities in Interactions between Hong Kong and China." In *Transnationalism from Below,* edited by Michael Peter Smith and Luis Guarnizo. New Brunswick, NJ: Transaction.

Smith, Daniel A., and Caroline J. Tolbert. 2001. "The Initiative to Party: Partisanship and Ballot Initiative in California." *Party Politics* 7:739–58.

Smith, Robert C. 1996. "Mexicans in New York: Membership and Incorporation in a New Immigrant Community." In *Latinos in New York: Communities in Transition,* edited by Gabriel Haslip-Viera and Sherrie L. Baver. Notre Dame: University of Notre Dame Press.

Smith, Robert C. 1997. "Transnational Migration, Assimilation, and Political Community." In *The City and the World: New York's Global Future,* edited by Margaret E. Crahan and Alberto Vourvoulias-Bush. New York: Council on Foreign Relations Press.

Smith, Robert C. 1998. "Transnational Localities: Community, Technology, and the Politics of Membership within the Context of Mexico and U.S. Migration." In *Transnationalism from Below,* edited by Michael Peter Smith and Luis Guarnizo. New Brunswick, NJ: Transaction.

Smith, Rogers M. 1997. *Civic Ideals.* New Haven: Yale University Press.

Somashekhar, Sandhya. 2002. "Many Asian Americans Prefer Road Less Traveled in Politics; Forty Percent of Immigrants Taking Independent Route." *Hayward (CA) Daily Review,* November 3, Local-1.

Sonenshein, Raphael. 1993. *Politics in Black and White: Race and Power in Los Angeles.* Princeton: Princeton University Press.

Sonenshein, Raphael. 2003. "Gotham on Our Minds; New York City in the Los Angeles Charter." In *New York and Los Angeles: Politics, Society, and Culture: A Comparative View,* edited by David Halle. Chicago: University of Chicago Press.

Sonenshein, Raphael. 2004. *The City at Stake: Secession, Reform, and the Battle for Los Angeles.* Princeton: Princeton University Press.

Southwest Voter Registration and Education Project. 1997. "UFW March Highlights Strawberry Organizing Drive." *Latino Vote Reporter* (spring): 3.

Southwest Voter Registration and Education Project. 2004. *Latino Vote Expert Disputes Exit Poll.* Available at http://www.svrep.org/press_room/press_clippings/people_week_world_111104.html. Accessed December 23, 2004.

Sowell, Thomas. 1986. *Ethnic America: A History.* New York: Basic Books.

Sterne, Evelyn S. 2001. "Beyond the Boss: Immigration and American Political Culture from 1880 to 1940." In *E. Pluribus Unum? Contemporary and Historical Perspectives on Immigrant Political Incorporation,* edited by Gary Gerstle and John Mollenkopf. New York: Russell Sage.

Stone, Clarence. 1996. "Urban Political Machines: Taking Stock." *PS: Political Science and Politics* 29:446–50.

Stone, Harold A., Don K. Price, and Kathryn H. Stone. 1939. *City Manager Government in Dallas.* Chicago: Public Administration Service.

Strolovitch, Dara. 2002. "Closer to a Pluralist Heaven? Women's, Racial Minority, and Economic Justice Advocacy Groups and the Politics of Representation." Ph.D. diss., Yale University.

Suárez-Orozco, Marcelo M., and Mariela M. Paez, eds. 2002. *Latinos: Remaking America.* Berkeley: University of California Press.

Subervi-Velez, Federico A., and Stacey L. Connaughton. 1999. "Targeting the Latino Vote: The Democratic Party's 1996 Mass Communication Strategy." In *Awash in the Mainstream: Latino Politics in the 1996 Elections,* edited by Rodolfo O. de la Garza and Louis DeSipio. Boulder, CO: Westview.

Sung, Betty Lee. 1967. *Mountain of Gold: The Story of the Chinese in America.* New York: Macmillan.

Takaki, Ronald. 1989. *Strangers from a Different Shore: A History of Asian Americans.* New York: Little, Brown.

Takaki, Ronald. 1993. *A Different Mirror: A History of Multicultural America.* New York: Little, Brown.

Tam, Wendy. 1995. "Asians—A Monolithic Voting Bloc?" *Political Behavior* 17:223–49.

Tate, Katherine. 1991. "Black Political Participation in the 1984 and 1988 Presidential Elections." *American Political Science Review* 85:1159–76.

Tate, Katherine. 1993. *From Protest to Politics: The New Black Voters in American Elections.* Cambridge: Harvard University Press.

Therrien, Melissa, and Roberto Ramirez. 2001. *The Hispanic Population in the United States, March 2000.* Washington, DC: U.S. Census Bureau.

Thomas, Clive S., and Ronald J. Hrebenar. 1999. "Interest Groups in the States." In *Politics in the American States: A Comparative Analysis,* 7th ed., edited by Virginia Gray, Russell L. Hanson, and Herbert Jacob. Washington, DC: CQ Press.

Thomas, William, and Florian Znaniecki. 1984. *The Polish Peasant in Europe and America.* Urbana: University of Illinois Press.

Tobar, Hector. 2000. "Campaign 2000: Latino Votes Pursued in Few, Unusual Places." *Los Angeles Times,* October 30, A-17.

Tocqueville, Alexis de. 1969. *Democracy in America.* Edited by J. P. Mayer. Translated by G. Lawrence. New York: Doubleday.

Tolbert, Caroline J., and Rodney E. Hero. 1996. "Race/Ethnicity and Direct Democracy: An Analysis of California's Illegal Immigration Initiative." *Journal of Politics* 58:806–18.

Torres, Vicki. 1996. "The Great Wall of Chinatown: Merchants Who Cater to Other Southeast Asian Immigrants Now Outnumber Older Businesses." *Los Angeles Times,* March 31, 1.

Trueba, Enrique T. 1999. *Latinos Unidos: From Cultural Diversity to the Politics of Solidarity.* Lanham, MD: Rowman and Littlefield.

Uhlaner, Carole J. 1991. "Perceived Discrimination and Prejudice and the Coalition Prospects of Blacks, Latinos, and Asian Americans." In *Racial and Ethnic Politics in California,* edited by Byran O. Jackson and Michael B. Preston. Berkeley: Institute of Governmental Studies Press, University of California.

Uhlaner, Carole J., Bruce Cain, and D. Roderick Kiewiet. 1989. "Political Participation of Ethnic Minorities in the 1980s." *Political Behavior* 17:195–231.

Uhlaner, Carole J., and F. Chris Garcia. 1998. *Foundations of Latino Party Identification: Learning, Ethnicity, and Demographic Factors among Mexicans, Puerto Ricans, Cubans, and Anglos in the United States.* Irvine: Center for the Study of Democracy, University of California, Irvine.

USA Today. 2004. "Feeling Overlooked, Asian-Americans Raise Political Profile." Available at http://www.usatoday.com/news/politicselections/nation/2004–02–12-asian-americans_x.htm. Accessed September 10, 2004.

U.S. Census Bureau. 2001. *Money Income in the United States: 2000.* Current Population Reports, Series P60–213. Washington, DC: U.S. Government Printing Office.

U.S. Census Bureau. 2002. *A Profile of the Nation's Foreign-Born Population from Asia.* Washington, DC: U.S. Census Bureau.

U.S. Census Bureau. 2004. "U.S. Interim Projections by Age, Sex, Race, and His-panic Origin." Available at http://www.census.gov/ipc/www/usinterimproj/. Accessed June 14, 2005.

U.S. Census Bureau. 2005. *Voting and Registration in the Election of 2004.* Avail-able at http://www.census.gov/population/www/socdemo/voting/cps2004 .html (tab02–3.xls, tab02, tab02–6.xls, tab02–9.xls, tab02–10.xls). Accessed June 14, 2005.

Valdes-Rodriguez, Alisa. 2000. "Conventions Strike up the Band with a Latin Beat." *Los Angeles Times,* August 15, F-3.

Valenzuela, Abel. 1995. "California's Melting Pot Boils Over: The Origins of a Cruel Proposition." *Dollars and Sense,* February–March, 28–31.

Valle, Victor, and Rodolfo D. Torres. 2000. *Latino Metropolis.* Minneapolis: Uni-versity of Minnesota Press.

Verba, Sidney, and Norman H. Nie. 1972. *Participation in America: Political Democracy and Social Equality.* New York: Harper and Row.

Verba, Sidney, Kay Lehman Schlozman, and Henry E. Brady. 1995. *Voice and Equality: Civic Voluntarism in American Politics.* Cambridge: Harvard Univer-sity Press.

Verma, Archana B. 2002. *The Making of Little Punjab in Canada.* Thousand Oaks, CA: Russell Sage.

Wade, Richard D. 1990. "The Withering Away of the Party System." In *Urban Politics New York Style,* edited by Jewel Bellush and Dick Netzer. Armonk, NY: Sharpe.

Wald, Kenneth D., Dennis E. Owen, and Samuel S. Hill Jr. 1988. "Churches as Political Communities." *American Political Science Review* 82:531–48.

Waldinger, Roger, Chris Erickson, Ruth Milkman, Daniel J. B. Mitchell, Abel Valenzuela, Kent Wong, and Maurice Zeitlin. 1997. "Justice for Janitors: Orga-nizing in Difficult Times." *Dissent,* 37–44.

Waldinger, Roger, and Jennifer Lee. 2001. "New Immigrants in Urban America." In *Strangers at the Gates: New Immigrants in Urban America,* edited by Roger Waldinger. Berkeley: University of California Press.

Waldinger, Roger, and Yen-Fen Tseng. 1992. "Divergent Diasporas: The Chinese Communities of New York and Los Angeles Compared." *Revue Européenne des Migrations Internationales* 8:91–115.

Wang, Xinyang. 2001. *Surviving the City: The Chinese Immigrant Experience in New York City, 1890–1970.* Lanham, MD: Rowman and Littlefield.

Warner, Lloyd W., and Leo Srole. 1945. *The Social System of American Ethnic Groups.* New Haven: Yale University Press.

Warren, Dorian. 2003. "A New Labor Movement for a New Century? The Incor-poration and Representation of Marginalized Workers in U.S. Unions." Paper presented at the annual meeting of the American Political Science Association, Philadelphia.

Warren, Mark. 2001. *Dry Bones Rattling: Community Building to Revitalize American Democracy.* Princeton: Princeton University Press.

Washington Post/Kaiser Family Foundation/Harvard University. 2001. *Race and*

Ethnicity in 2001: Attitudes, Perceptions, and Experiences. Available at http://www.kff.org/kaiserpolls/3143-index.cfm. Accessed January 8, 2004.

Waters, Mary C. 2001. *Black Identities: West Indian Immigrant Dreams and American Realities.* Cambridge: Harvard University Press.

Wattenberg, Martin P. 1994. *The Decline of American Political Parties, 1952–1992.* Cambridge: Harvard University Press.

Wattenberg, Martin P. 1996. *The Decline of American Political Parties, 1952–1994.* Cambridge: Harvard University Press.

Wattenberg, Martin P. 2001. *The Rise of Candidate-Centered Politics.* Cambridge: Harvard University Press.

Wei, William. 1993. *The Asian American Movement.* Philadelphia: Temple University Press.

Weinstein, Henry. 2005. "Big Numbers That Finally Add Up; Latinos Had Long Been a Major Part of L.A. but a Minor Force in Politics." *Los Angeles Times,* May 19, B-1.

Weston, Rubin Francis. 1972. *Racism in U.S. Imperialism: The Influence of Racial Assumptions on American Foreign Policy, 1893–1946.* Columbia: University of South Carolina Press.

Westphal, David. 2001. "Immigrants in the United States Are 10. 9 Percent of the Population." *Minneapolis Star Tribune,* January 3, 6A.

Wilson, James Q. 1995. *Political Organizations.* Princeton: Princeton University Press.

Wolfinger, Raymond, and Steven J. Rosenstone. 1980. *Who Votes?* New Haven: Yale University Press.

Wong, Bernard P. 1982. *Chinatown, Economic Adaptation, and the Ethnic Identity of the Chinese.* New York: Holt, Rinehart, and Winston.

Wong, Janelle S. 2000. "The Effects of Age and Political Exposure on the Development of Party Identification among Asian American and Latino Immigrants in the United States." *Political Behavior* 22:341–71.

Wong, Janelle S. 2001. "The New Dynamics of Immigrants' Political Incorporation: A Multi-Method Study of Political Participation and Mobilization among Asian and Latino Immigrants in the United States." Ph.D. diss., Yale University.

Wong, Janelle. 2002. "Shaping the Future: Asian American and Latino/a Immigrant Political Participation Trends in California 1996–2020." Paper presented at the annual meeting of the American Political Science Association, Boston.

Wong, Janelle S. 2004. "Getting out the Vote among Asian Pacific Americans: The Effects of Phone Canvassing." *AAPI Nexus: Asian Americans and Pacific Islanders Policy, Practice, and Community* 2:49–66.

Wong, Janelle S. n.d. "The Role of Length of Residence in Immigrants' Political Participation." Unpublished manuscript.

Wong, Janelle S., Pei-te Lien, and M. Margaret Conway. 2005. "Group-Based Resources and the Political Participation of Asian Americans." *American Politics Research* 33:545–76.

Wong, Kent. 1994. "Building an Asian Pacific Labor Alliance: A New Chapter in

Our History." In *The State of Asian America: Activism and Resistance in the 1990s*, edited by Karin Aguilar San Juan. Boston: South End Press.

Workers' Awaaz. n.d. Brochure about worker rights. New York: Workers' Awaaz.

Wrinkle, Robert D., Jr., Joseph Stewart, J. L. Polinard, Kenneth J. Meier, and John R. Arvizu. 1996. "Ethnicity and Nonelectoral Political Participation." *Hispanic Journal of Behavioral Sciences* 18:142–53.

Wu, Frank H. 2002. *Yellow: Race in America beyond Black and White*. New York: Basic Books.

Zhou, Min. 1992. *Chinatown: The Socioeconomic Potential of an Urban Enclave*. Philadelphia: Temple University Press.

Zhou, Min, and James V. Gatewood. 2000. "Mapping the Terrain: Diversity and the Challenges in the Contemporary Asian American Community." *Asian American Policy Review* 9:2–29.

Zhou, Min, and Rebecca Kim. 2003. "A Tale of Two Metropolises; New Immigrant Chinese Communities in New York and Los Angeles." In *New York and Los Angeles: Politics, Society, and Culture, A Comparative View*, edited by David Halle. Chicago: University of Chicago Press.

Index

Note: Page numbers in italics refer to tables and figures.

269

community organizations (*continued*)
 ethnic identity retention and, 96,
  208
 ethnic voluntary organizations, 12,
  105–12
 financial resources of, 96–97, 159,
  203
 forms and missions of, 98–99, 134,
  159
 hometown associations, 43, 93,
  191, 195
 and immigrant communities,
  200–203
 implications of mobilization by,
  94–96
 incentives and strengths for mobilizing, 90–94
 and issue-specific mobilization, 95,
  120
 labor organizations and workers'
  centers, 99–105
 leaders' expertise in, 92–93, 174,
  201
 and leaders' ties to immigrant communities, 91–92, 174, 201
 limited mobilization by, 9, 159,
  175–76, 198, 202–3
 as mobilizing agents, 10–11, 78, 88,
  139, 204–5
 multiple immigrant identities and,
  119–39, 205, 207
 nonprofit organizations, 89–90
 and nonvoting political participation, 94–95, 112, 117, 142–52
 number of members/people represented in, 90–91, 95, 110
 and relationship with political party
  organizations, 89–90
 and religious institutions, 112–16
 segregation of, 103
 social service organizations,
  105–12
 survey data on, 142–45
 transnational organizations/prac-

tices and, 93–94, 191, 195,
  201–3
 trusted presence of, 207
Constitution (U.S.), Seventeenth
  Amendment, 56–57
Contract with America, 62, 66, 67
Convocation for Working Families,
  102
CPS. *See* Current Population Survey
CSWA. *See* Chinese Staff and Worker's
  Association
Cuban immigrants, 25, 75
 nonvoting political participation
  and, *189, 222*
 representation perceived for various
  organizations and, *143–44*
 survey data on, 142–46, *143–45,
  219–22*
 transnationalism and, 181, *182,* 183,
  184, 186–90, *189,* 195, 236n2
 voter registration of, 145, *145,
  184*
 voting participation of, *184, 221*
Current Population Survey (CPS), 70,
  227n3
 Volunteer Supplement (2002), 160,
  235n3

Davis, Gray, 170–71
day laborers, 97, 106, 107
deconstructionists, 122–23
DeLay, Tom, 232n8
democracy
 ethnic organizing and, 120–23
 future health of in U.S., 49,
  197–212
 immigrant participation and,
  123–28
 nature of, 6–7
 participatory, 197
 role of institutions in, 6–7, 197–99
 role of political parties in, 199–200
Democratic National Committee, 57
 and APIA Voice, 76, 77